Churchill

CHURCHILL
A GRAPHIC BIOGRAPHY

GREENHILL BOOKS

Churchill
This English-language edition first published in 2020 by
Greenhill Books
c/o Pen & Sword Books Ltd,
47 Church Street, Barnsley,
S. Yorkshire, S70 2AS

www.greenhillbooks.com
contact@greenhillbooks.com

Greenhill edition ISBN: 978–1–78438–512–5

Publishing History
First published in French in 2018 as
Ils ont fait l'Histoire: Churchill
by Editions Glénat/Librarie Arthème Fayard

CIP data records for this title are available from the British Library

---

Published in the U.S.A. in 2020 by

Dead Reckoning
291 Wood Road
Annapolis, MD 21402

Dead Reckoning edition ISBN: 978–1–68247–528–7

Dead Reckoning is an imprint of the Naval Institute Press, the book-publishing division of the U.S. Naval Institute, a non-profit organization.

Library of Congress Control Number: 2019951064

28 27 26 25 24 23 22 21 20 9 8 7 6 5 4 3 2 1
First printing

Printed in China by Imago

Text
Vincent Delmas

Translated by
Ivanka Hahnenberger

Historical Consultant
François Kersaudy

Story-Board
Christophe Regnault

Design
Alessio Cammardella

Artwork
Alessia Nocera

Foreword

'Of the writing of biographies of Winston Churchill there shall be no end'

That ought to be a publishers' mantra, as ever since the first one was written in 1905 – when Churchill was thirty years old and only one-third of the way through his life – there have been no fewer than 1,010 biographies written of him. These comprise dozens of excellent, full-scale, cradle-to-grave lives, but also some sub-standard hack biographies churned out during the Second World War and during his Indian Summer premiership of 1951–5. There have been magisterial oversights of the man and his era, but also appalling hagiographies which absurdly attempt to pretend that he could do no wrong.

Yet almost all of these books have adopted the standard practice of telling his life chronologically through the use of words illustrated by as many photos as the publishers' (often limited) budgets could afford. By total contrast, this excellent book uses graphics, and in such a way that both adults and children can appreciate the heroism and splendour of Winston Churchill. Nor does it ignore the many pitfalls of his life and career that all too often he dived into head first and with his eyes open. It is thus a full and wholly fair representation of the most adventurous life in the history of British politics.

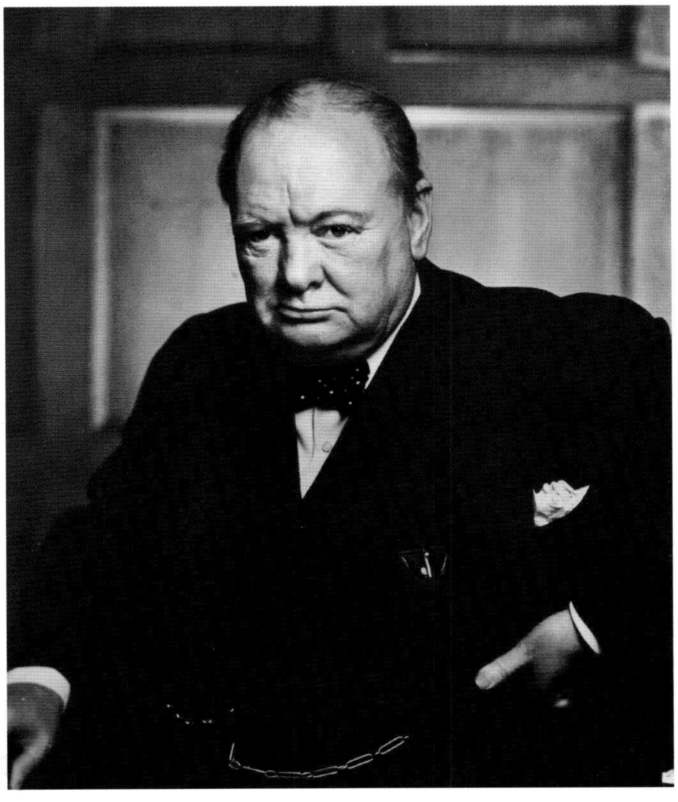

I expected nothing less, for the distinguished Vincent Delmas wrote the script and one of the foremost historians of Churchill and his era, François Kersaudy, was the historical consultant. It was Kersaudy who wrote *De Gaulle and Churchill* (1981) and *Norway, 1940* (1990), which despite being published over a quarter of a century ago are still today the standard texts for both important aspects of the Second World War. Loaded with all the honours that French history has to give, Kersaudy is a giant in his field, and readers can be assured that this book is historically accurate. Having just myself written the 1,010th biography of Churchill, there is not a word I would have changed in the text of this excellent graphical account.

To add to the historical accuracy and fine text of this work, Christophe Regnault, Alessio Cammardella and Alessia Nocera have prepared the illustrations, which in places – especially during the coverage of the Blitz – amount to genuine art, of the kind that Winston Churchill – who painted around 530 pictures in his life – would have approved. The graphics draw the reader into the sheer excitement of a life of pure adventure, as Churchill lived out the destiny that he had prescribed himself as a 16-year-old schoolboy, when he told a fellow pupil, 'I can see vast changes coming over a now peaceful world, great upheavals, terrible struggles; wars such as one cannot imagine. London will be attacked and I shall be in command of the defences of London and I shall save London and England from disaster. In the high position I shall occupy, it will fall to me to save the capital and save the Empire.' Half a century later he did just that, indeed he saved Civilization itself.

How he achieved that is brilliantly illustrated in this superb book, which I hope will bring the Churchill story to an entirely new generation of enthusiasts, who might then go on to join the International Churchill Society to learn more about the Greatest Englishman. Churchill had many flaws and failings – which rightly feature in this book – and he made several important mistakes in his life. Overall, however, his foresight was exemplary, his leadership superb, his heart gigantic, and his courage sublime. All of these qualities – needed today as much as ever before – are evident from this fine work of graphics and of history.

Andrew Roberts

Author of *Churchill: Walking with Destiny*
www.andrew-roberts.net

In Churchill's Footsteps

Helped along by a succession of expressive and impressive illustrations, readers of this book may follow the main turning points in Churchill's eventful life. There remains to fill in the background, in an effort to catch a better glimpse of this elusive and in many ways unique personality. Born half American and a descendant of the great Duke of Marlborough, with four quite remarkable grandparents, a brilliant, ambitious and distant father, an energetic, frivolous and absent mother, a devoted and loving nurse – such are the main ingredients to start with. But the boy's temperament was uniquely his own: unruly, quarrelsome, headstrong and fiercely independent, he developed into a bright but difficult schoolboy, who would work only in the subjects that met his fancy – chiefly English, poetry and history. But even these seemed to wane before his consuming passion: growing up

in the decidedly martial environment of his grandparents' palace of Blenheim, learning from his nurse all about the exploits of his illustrious Marlborough ancestor, receiving from his father's friends and his mother's lovers a sizeable collection of tin soldiers, young Winston developed early on a lifelong interest in all things military. This was to lead him first to the Army class at Harrow, then, aged 19, to the Royal Military College at Sandhurst.

The Lure of War

At Sandhurst, Winston Churchill was to prove an unconventional cadet: rather short with a slight stoop, slimly built, unfit for long marches, hopelessly unpunctual and

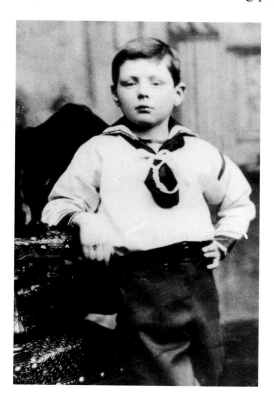

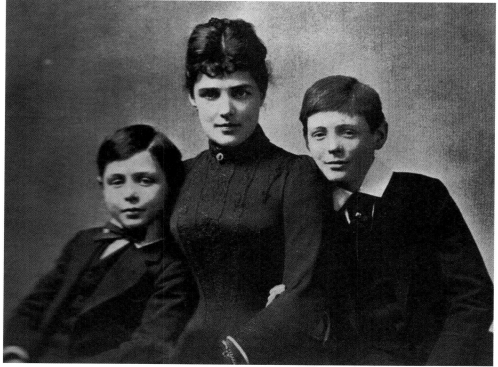

Winston, aged six, and with his mother and younger brother Jack (left) when Jack was about nine and Winston twelve.

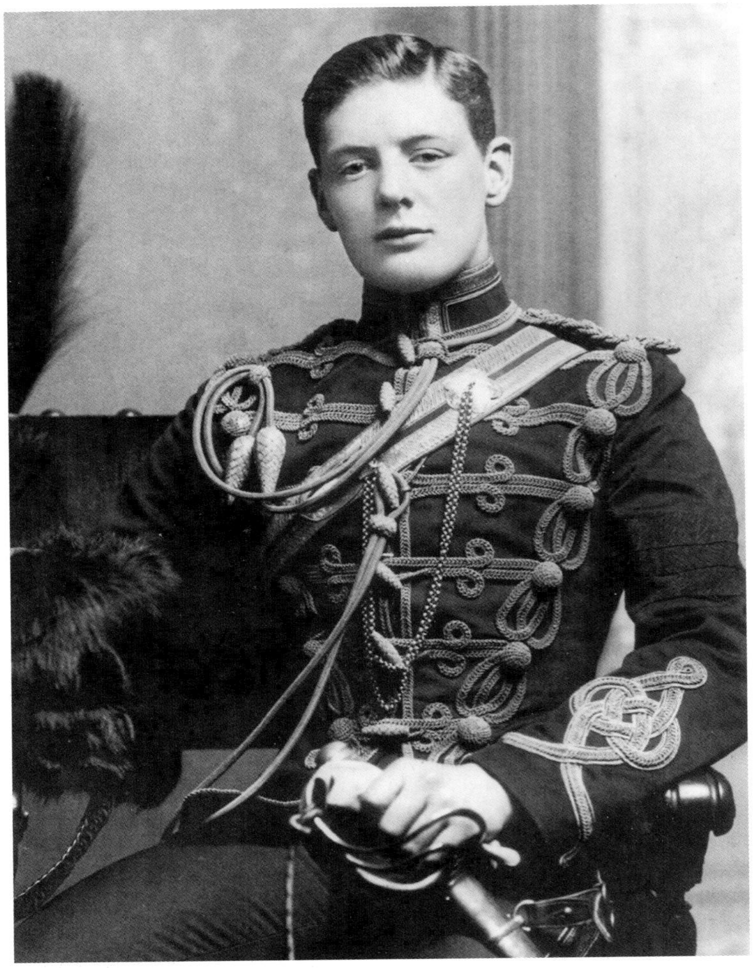
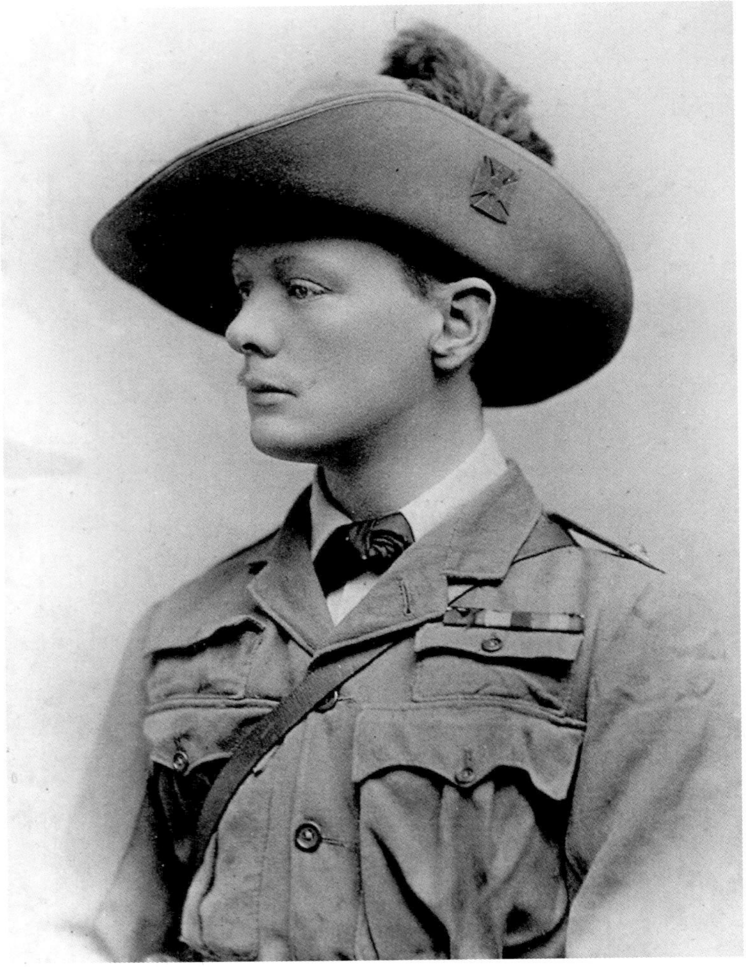
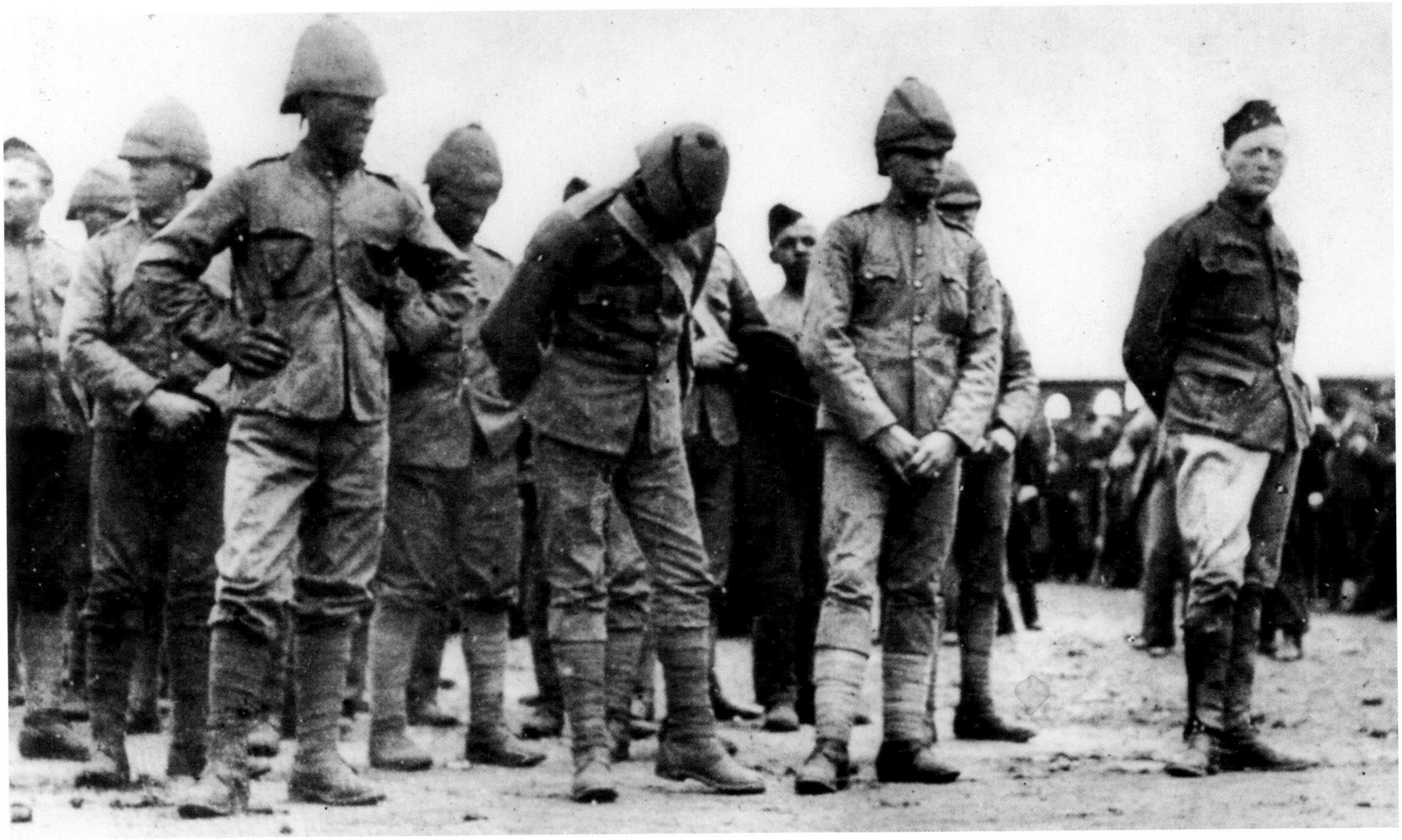

even prone to oppose orders, he was nonetheless a brilliant horseman, practically unbeatable at fencing, swimming and shooting, and his capacious memory enabled him to digest the whole programme of tactics, topography and military law with very little effort. He graduated in December 1894, ranked 20th out of 130 cadets, and four months later, Second Lieutenant Churchill was gazetted to the 4th Queen's Own Hussars. From then on, with or without leave from his regiment, he was to take part in four campaigns in less than five years: Cuba in 1895, the Northwest Frontier in 1896, the Sudan in 1898 and South Africa in 1899. In all these theatres, he drew attention to himself by a bravery verging on foolhardiness, a seemingly innate pugnacity and sense of command, an uncommon luck and a talent for self-advertising – the latter being made easier by the fact that he doubled as a well-paid press correspondent and became the author of five books on his campaigns. From these bloody battlefields he emerged unscathed, with the sense that 'Nothing in life is so exhilarating as to be shot at without result,' but also with the conclusion that journalism and authorship were rather more profitable than a career in the Army – and that, at any rate, he had other ambitions . . .

Into Politics

In his remarkable little book on Churchill, Sebastian Haffner states that young Winston discovered politics at the age of 26. That is erring by only 20 years: from the age of six, Lord Randolph's son assiduously followed his father's career as a Tory MP and Cabinet minister, and dreamed of entering Parliament at his side. That was not to be, since Randolph Churchill died prematurely in 1895, but his son vowed to become an MP because his father had been one, and Prime Minister because his father had been denied that opportunity. On the strength of his reputation as a war hero, he was duly

ABOVE: *Early days as a parliamentarian, and with his new wife Clementine.*

OPPOSITE, CLOCKWISE FROM TOP LEFT: *The young officer in the 4th Hussars; ambitious war correspondent; prisoner of the Boers in South Africa.*

ABOVE LEFT: *As commander of 6th Royal Scots Fusiliers during his front-line service in 1916.*

ABOVE RIGHT: *Wearing a French-style greatcoat and helmet.*

elected to Parliament in October 1900, and for the next six decades, Westminster was to be his second home . . .

The man was not a natural speaker, he had a slight speech impediment and was unable to improvise. Hard work, constant practice and meticulous preparation changed all that, and were soon to make him one of the best orators in Parliament – but not necessarily the most consistent in his views, as later events were to show: in 1904, he crossed the floor of the House and took his seat on the Liberal benches; two decades later, he was to rejoin the Tories, later forming

a one-man opposition within his own party – and eventually becoming its leader . . . But in the meantime, the young man whom Lord Elgin had dubbed 'a curious impulsive creature' had accumulated an unrivalled range of political experience: before 1914, as Under- Secretary of State for the Colonies, President of the Board of Trade, Home Secretary and finally First Lord of the Admiralty from 1911, he sought to know everything about his ministry, then proceeded to reform it from top to bottom – after which it proved almost impossible to prevent him from meddling in his colleagues' affairs as well . . .

In the Line of Fire

In preparing the Navy for war, Winston Churchill was nothing if not successful; he entirely reorganized it, created a naval staff, started changing the propulsion of the fleet from coal to oil, commissioned the mounting of bigger guns than had ever been built, as well as the construction of new types of ships to accommodate them. As a result, the fleet was ready when war broke out in 1914, and so was its First Lord. The next four years were to bring him from the heights of power to the depths of impotence and back again; but whether at the Admiralty, in the trenches of Flanders or at the Ministry of Munitions, Churchill displayed a startling degree of dynamism, courage, inventiveness, organizational talent and oratorical skill that made him something of a national hero – at least for a time.

After the return to peace, Churchill became Secretary of State for War and Air, and from this post, he directed Britain's

On an inspection trip as Secretary of State for Air in the aftermath of World War I.

abortive intervention against the Russian Bolsheviks. After having served three years as Colonial Secretary, he rejoined the Conservative ranks in 1924, and became a somewhat less than successful Chancellor of the Exchequer. After the electoral defeat of 1929, however, he found himself in opposition to his party over government proposals for India, and in 1931 he resigned from the Conservative shadow cabinet. From then until the end of the thirties, Winston Churchill was to be a solitary figure on the British political scene. But the turn of events in Europe soon provided him with a cause to defend that appealed strongly to his vast imagination and intense patriotism: the preservation of the country from the threat of German Nazism . . .

Crying in the Wilderness

Much sooner than most of his compatriots, Churchill realized the danger of Hitler's rise to power. From then on, he was to call ceaselessly on the government to strengthen Britain's defences, to double and redouble the air force, set up a ministry of defence and a ministry of supply, reorganize industry for conversion to war purposes, modernize the fleet, strengthen British alliances on the Continent and support the League of Nations. In countless speeches and articles, he denounced the purges and racial persecutions in Germany, the beginning of German rearmament, the remilitarization of the Rhineland, the annexation of Austria, the invasion of Czechoslovakia and the threat to Poland. With a powerful blend of eloquence, persuasion, irony and sarcasm, he relentlessly took the government to task for the slowness of its rearmament effort, and repeatedly appealed to Parliament and public opinion. But the three successive prime ministers, Ramsay MacDonald, Stanley Baldwin and Neville Chamberlain, managed to weather all attacks by denying past mistakes and present negligence, dismissing Churchill's warnings as alarmist and his speeches as hollow eloquence. As a result, he remained in Parliament a solitary figure whose recurrent diatribes were followed with a mixture of admiration, amusement and indifference by his fellow MPs and by a public opinion that still failed to realize the gravity of the hour. Yet Churchill was convinced that he understood Hitler's ultimate ambitions and, just as in 1914, he had no doubt that he could mobilize and lead the forces of the nation through the impending conflict. It took Hitler's invasion of Poland on 1 September 1939 for the Chamberlain administration to realize the inevitability of conflict and the necessity of bringing back to government the only man who was familiar with war, could manage it, enjoy it, and perhaps go on to win it … On 3 September, Winston Churchill was therefore recalled to the Admiralty.

The Man of Destiny

During the winter and spring of 1940, in the Admiralty as in the government, the First Lord's pugnacity and hyperactivity often worked wonders – and sometimes wreaked havoc – but just as a quarter of a century earlier, he had responsibility without supreme power. That was to change on 10 May 1940, as a result of the Norwegian fiasco and Chamberlain's decision to resign when confronted with an obvious lack of confidence in the House. Churchill's first steps as Prime Minister and Minister of Defence were witnessed by private secretary John Colville, who described them in the following terms: 'Government departments, which under Neville Chamberlain had continued to work at much the same speed as in peacetime, awoke to the realities of war. A sense of urgency was created in the course of a very few days, and respectable civil servants were actually to be seen running along the corridors. No delays were condoned; telephone switchboards quadrupled their efficiency; the chiefs of staff and the joint planning staff were in almost constant session; regular office hours ceased to exist, and weekends disappeared with them.' Quite so. The PM was constantly spurring ministers, officials and generals to greater activity and quicker progress; his directives flowed in all directions, more often than not crowned by the dreaded red labels inscribed 'Action this day'. But Churchill's supreme quality as an organizer was apparent in that he would not only give orders, but also personally supervise their execution; during the summer and autumn of 1940, he could thus be seen inspecting coastal defences, harbour installations, armament and aircraft factories, shipyards, airfields, first-line divisions, Territorial units, warships, command posts, radar stations, hospitals – all these forays being typically followed by such

ABOVE: *Trying his hand as Prime Minister with a Sten submachine gun, a new wartime design.*

RIGHT: *Early trials of newly developed portable radio equipment.*

rousing minutes as: 'Pray let me know how the situation has improved since my visit yesterday.'

In this most perilous time in the history of Great Britain and the world, Churchill's fame stemmed as much from his oratorical talents as from his qualities of leadership. As President Kennedy was later to say: 'He mobilized the English language and sent it into battle.' His immortal public speeches naturally worked wonders to brace and invigorate, but his private rhetoric could be just as efficient – in convincing his colleagues behind closed doors of the necessity of carrying on the fight rather than submitting to a dictated peace; in persuading President Roosevelt to infringe American neutrality by supplying decisive material aid during the Battle of Britain, granting the benefit of Lend-Lease supplies at the beginning of 1941 and even giving

priority to the war against Germany when the United States was attacked by Japan at the end of that same year; and of course it was that very same eloquence that thrice saved the British coalition government from censure votes in the House in 1941 and 1942.

Strategic Enthusiasm

That Churchill was irreplaceable as war leader and as propagandist may easily obscure the fact that he was also a disquieting strategist. Sandhurst in the late 19th century taught its cadets tactics, but not strategy – which Churchill was to deplore occasionally, and his generals frequently during two world wars. In the event, he took early on to

improvising, with his remarkable skills of intuition, tenacity and inventiveness. Unfortunately, this proved insufficient to compensate for some basic gaps and loopholes in his mastery of the art, which resulted in a few serious failings: his eagerness to undertake several operations simultaneously, instead of concentrating on one thing at a time; his permanent temptation – as he put it himself – 'to stick his fingers into every pie before it was cooked'; his neglect of the interdependence of theatres of operations; his inability to adapt his goals to the means available, and last but not least, his incomprehension of the crucial importance of logistics in modern war.

As a result, he was apt to produce such unsound and potentially catastrophic strategic plans as the invasion of

ABOVE: *Visiting the army in Egypt before the Battle of El Alamein, 'the end of the beginning'.*

RIGHT: *Portraits, at different times and in different moods.*

Norway in 1941, the landing in France in 1942, the capture of Rhodes in 1943 or an offensive on the North Adriatic coast in 1944. Fortunately, this effervescent genius was flanked by such less inspired but far more professional strategists as Generals Brooke and Ismay, Air Marshal Portal and Admirals Pound and Cunningham. These brave men had to stand up to him and quash some of his wildest ideas, which was by no means an easy task since it involved braving Churchillian fits of temper, torrents of eloquence and thick clouds of cigar smoke – not to mention sleepiness, as arguments were usually carried on until the early morning hours. It is to their everlasting credit that they did their very best, and to the Prime Minister's own credit that he ended up listening to their advice at certain decisive junctures – thanks to which he was able to avoid some of the grievous mistakes committed by another amateur strategist on the other side of the North Sea, who waged war entirely without the benefit of advisers and contradictors. To a great extent, it was such a fundamental difference that in the end ensured the salvation of Great Britain and the eternal glory of Winston Churchill.

François Kersaudy

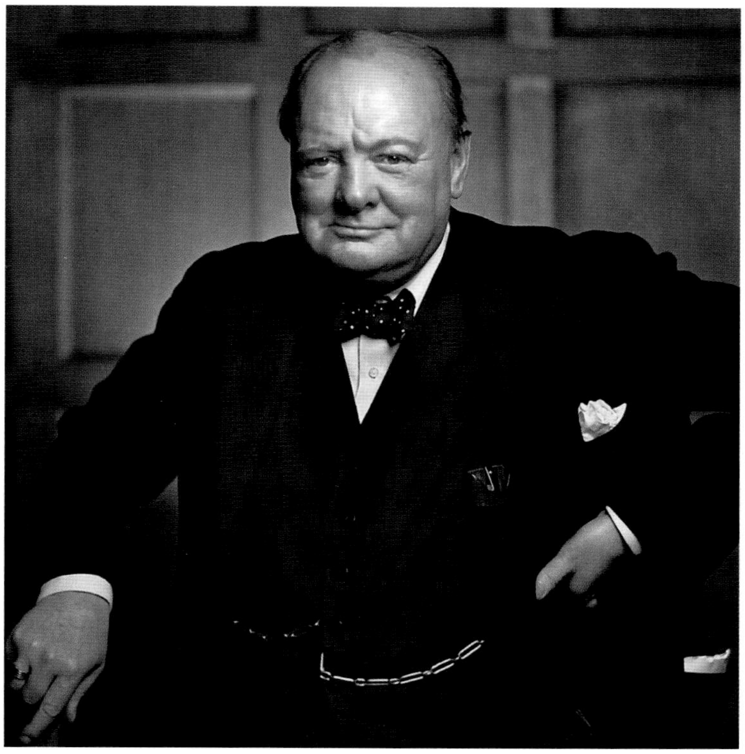
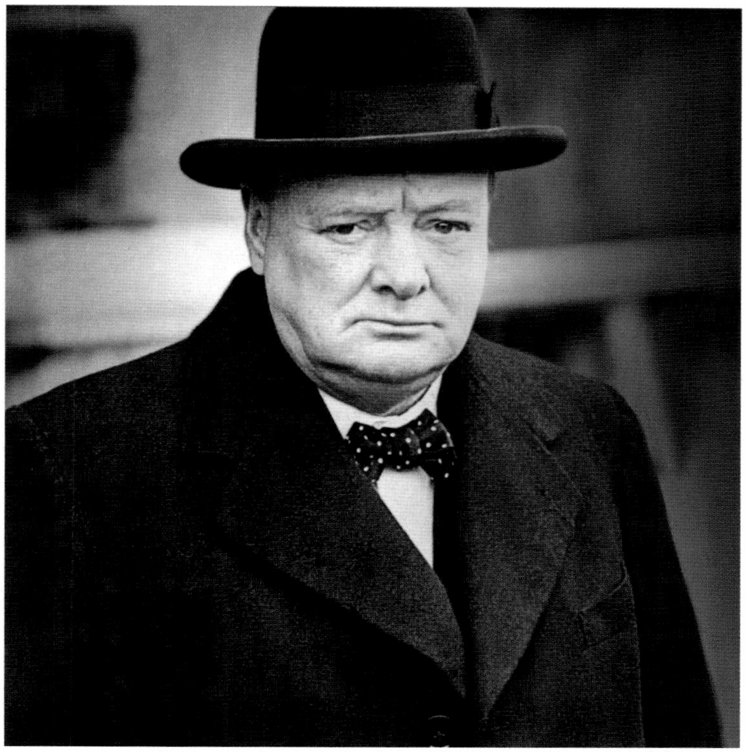
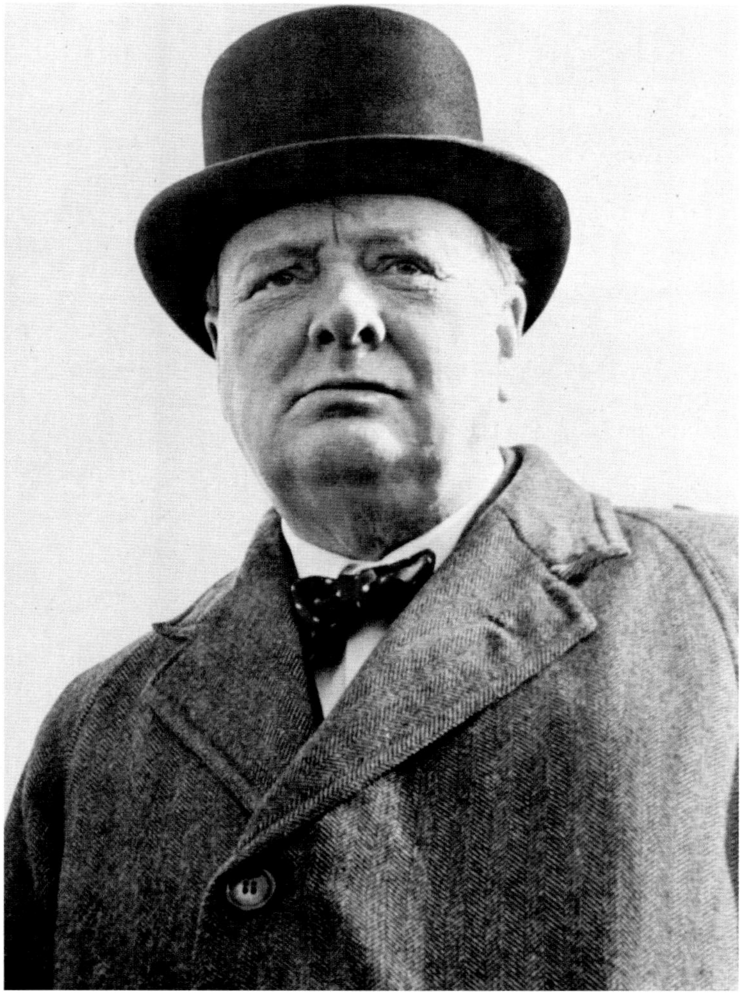
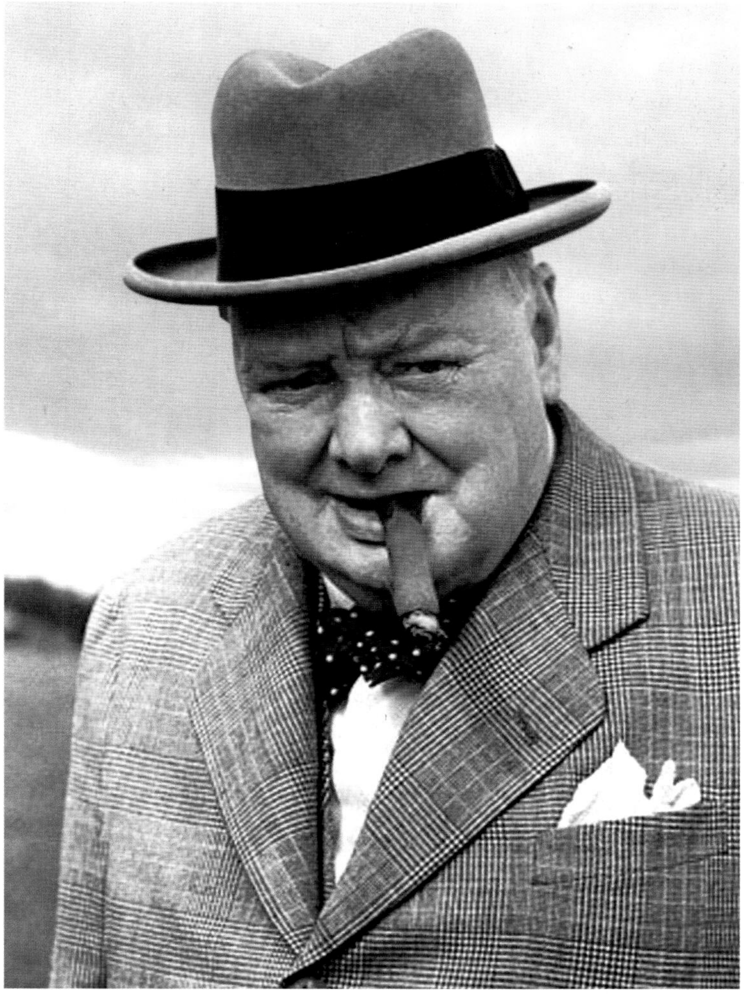

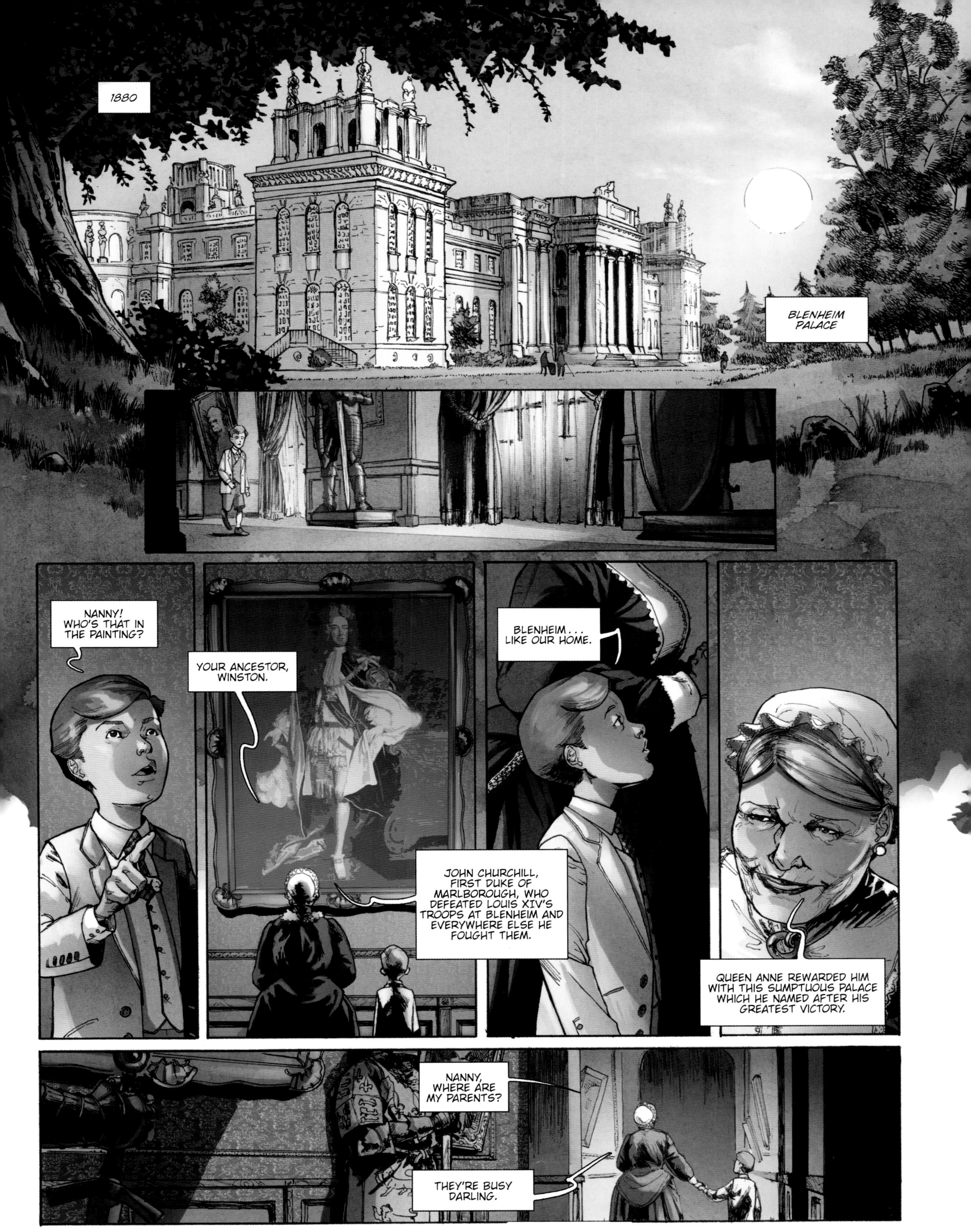

1880
BLENHEIM PALACE
NANNY! WHO'S THAT IN THE PAINTING?
YOUR ANCESTOR, WINSTON.
JOHN CHURCHILL, FIRST DUKE OF MARLBOROUGH, WHO DEFEATED LOUIS XIV'S TROOPS AT BLENHEIM AND EVERYWHERE ELSE HE FOUGHT THEM.
BLENHEIM . . . LIKE OUR HOME.
QUEEN ANNE REWARDED HIM WITH THIS SUMPTUOUS PALACE WHICH HE NAMED AFTER HIS GREATEST VICTORY.
NANNY, WHERE ARE MY PARENTS?
THEY'RE BUSY DARLING.

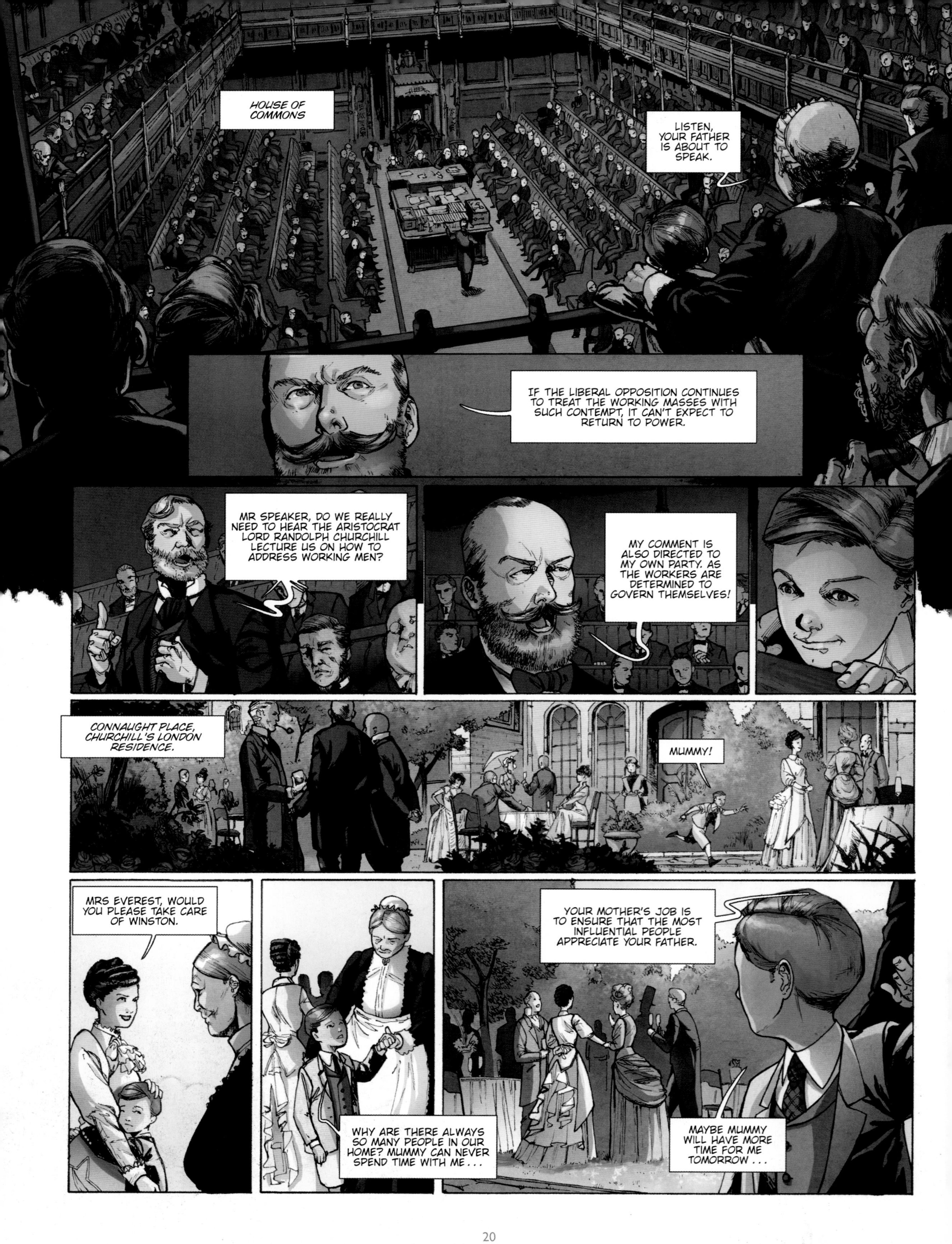
HOUSE OF COMMONS
LISTEN, YOUR FATHER IS ABOUT TO SPEAK.
IF THE LIBERAL OPPOSITION CONTINUES TO TREAT THE WORKING MASSES WITH SUCH CONTEMPT, IT CAN'T EXPECT TO RETURN TO POWER.
MR SPEAKER, DO WE REALLY NEED TO HEAR THE ARISTOCRAT LORD RANDOLPH CHURCHILL LECTURE US ON HOW TO ADDRESS WORKING MEN?
MY COMMENT IS ALSO DIRECTED TO MY OWN PARTY. AS THE WORKERS ARE DETERMINED TO GOVERN THEMSELVES!
CONNAUGHT PLACE, CHURCHILL'S LONDON RESIDENCE.
MUMMY!
MRS EVEREST, WOULD YOU PLEASE TAKE CARE OF WINSTON.
WHY ARE THERE ALWAYS SO MANY PEOPLE IN OUR HOME? MUMMY CAN NEVER SPEND TIME WITH ME . . .
YOUR MOTHER'S JOB IS TO ENSURE THAT THE MOST INFLUENTIAL PEOPLE APPRECIATE YOUR FATHER.
MAYBE MUMMY WILL HAVE MORE TIME FOR ME TOMORROW . . .

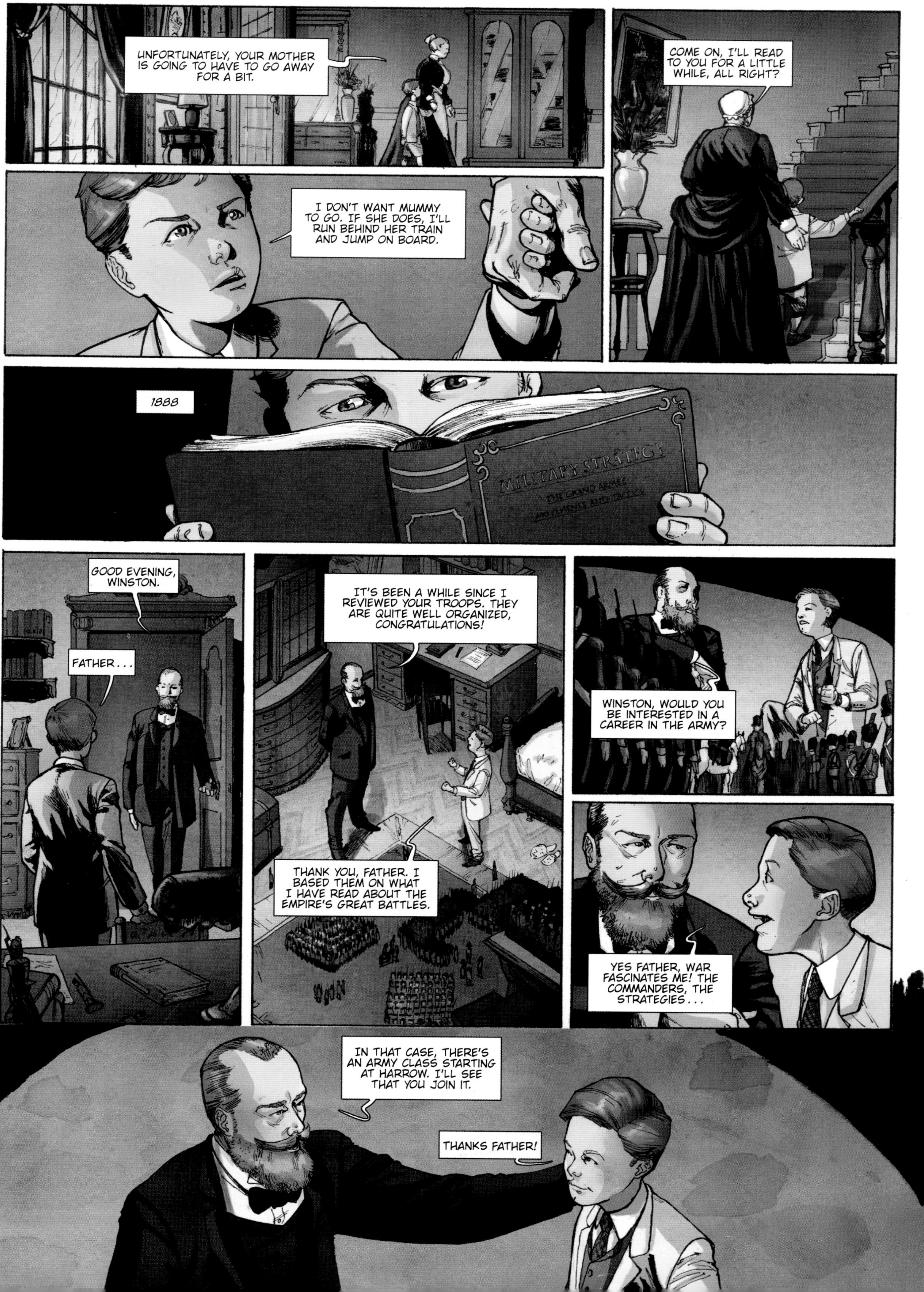
UNFORTUNATELY, YOUR MOTHER IS GOING TO HAVE TO GO AWAY FOR A BIT.
COME ON, I'LL READ TO YOU FOR A LITTLE WHILE, ALL RIGHT?
I DON'T WANT MUMMY TO GO. IF SHE DOES, I'LL RUN BEHIND HER TRAIN AND JUMP ON BOARD.
1888
MILITARY STRATEGY
GOOD EVENING, WINSTON.
FATHER...
IT'S BEEN A WHILE SINCE I REVIEWED YOUR TROOPS. THEY ARE QUITE WELL ORGANIZED, CONGRATULATIONS!
THANK YOU, FATHER. I BASED THEM ON WHAT I HAVE READ ABOUT THE EMPIRE'S GREAT BATTLES.
WINSTON, WOULD YOU BE INTERESTED IN A CAREER IN THE ARMY?
YES FATHER, WAR FASCINATES ME! THE COMMANDERS, THE STRATEGIES...
IN THAT CASE, THERE'S AN ARMY CLASS STARTING AT HARROW. I'LL SEE THAT YOU JOIN IT.
THANKS FATHER!

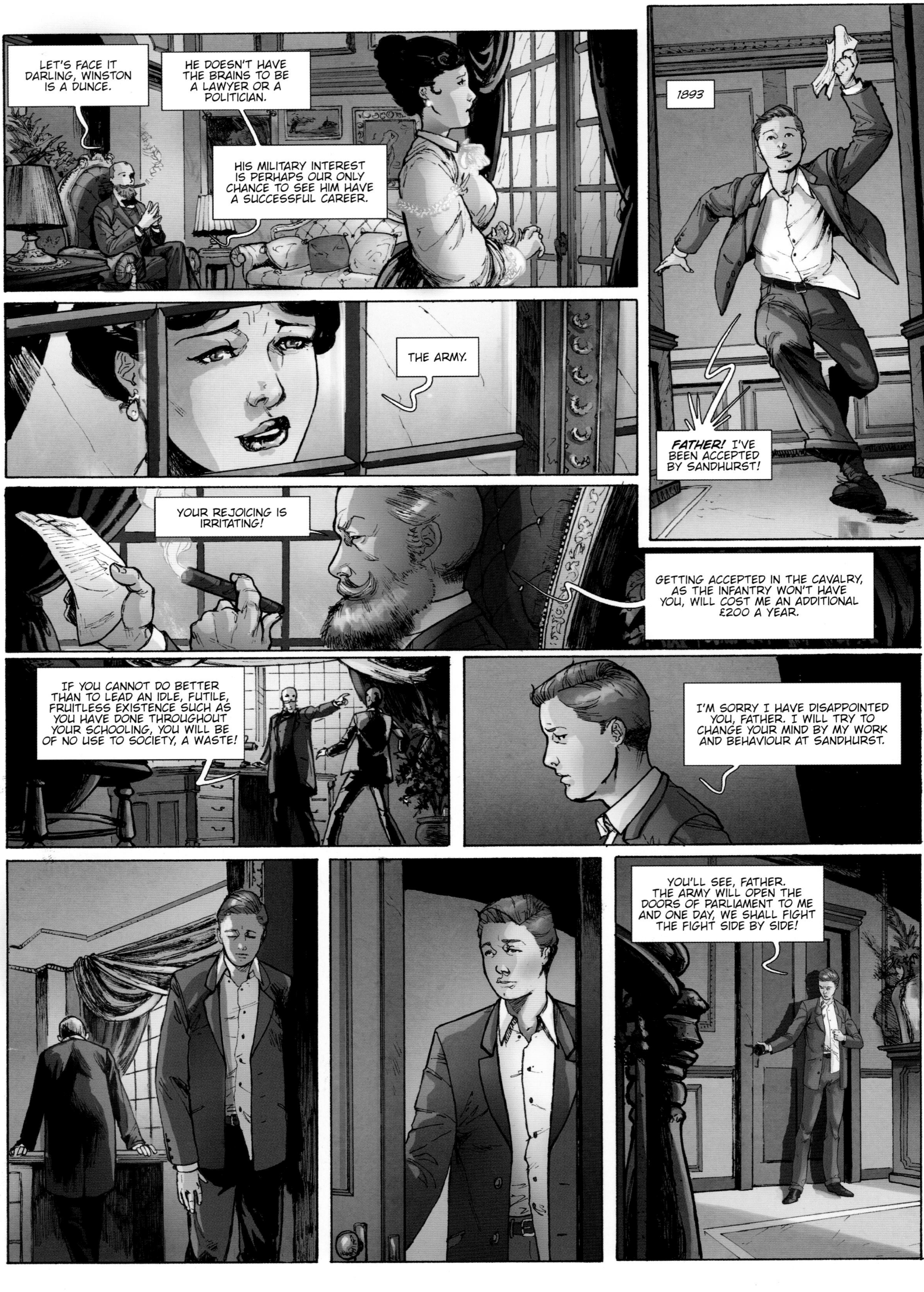
LET'S FACE IT DARLING, WINSTON IS A DUNCE.
HE DOESN'T HAVE THE BRAINS TO BE A LAWYER OR A POLITICIAN.
HIS MILITARY INTEREST IS PERHAPS OUR ONLY CHANCE TO SEE HIM HAVE A SUCCESSFUL CAREER.
THE ARMY.
1893
FATHER! I'VE BEEN ACCEPTED BY SANDHURST!
YOUR REJOICING IS IRRITATING!
GETTING ACCEPTED IN THE CAVALRY, AS THE INFANTRY WON'T HAVE YOU, WILL COST ME AN ADDITIONAL £200 A YEAR.
IF YOU CANNOT DO BETTER THAN TO LEAD AN IDLE, FUTILE, FRUITLESS EXISTENCE SUCH AS YOU HAVE DONE THROUGHOUT YOUR SCHOOLING, YOU WILL BE OF NO USE TO SOCIETY, A WASTE!
I'M SORRY I HAVE DISAPPOINTED YOU, FATHER. I WILL TRY TO CHANGE YOUR MIND BY MY WORK AND BEHAVIOUR AT SANDHURST.
YOU'LL SEE, FATHER. THE ARMY WILL OPEN THE DOORS OF PARLIAMENT TO ME AND ONE DAY, WE SHALL FIGHT THE FIGHT SIDE BY SIDE!

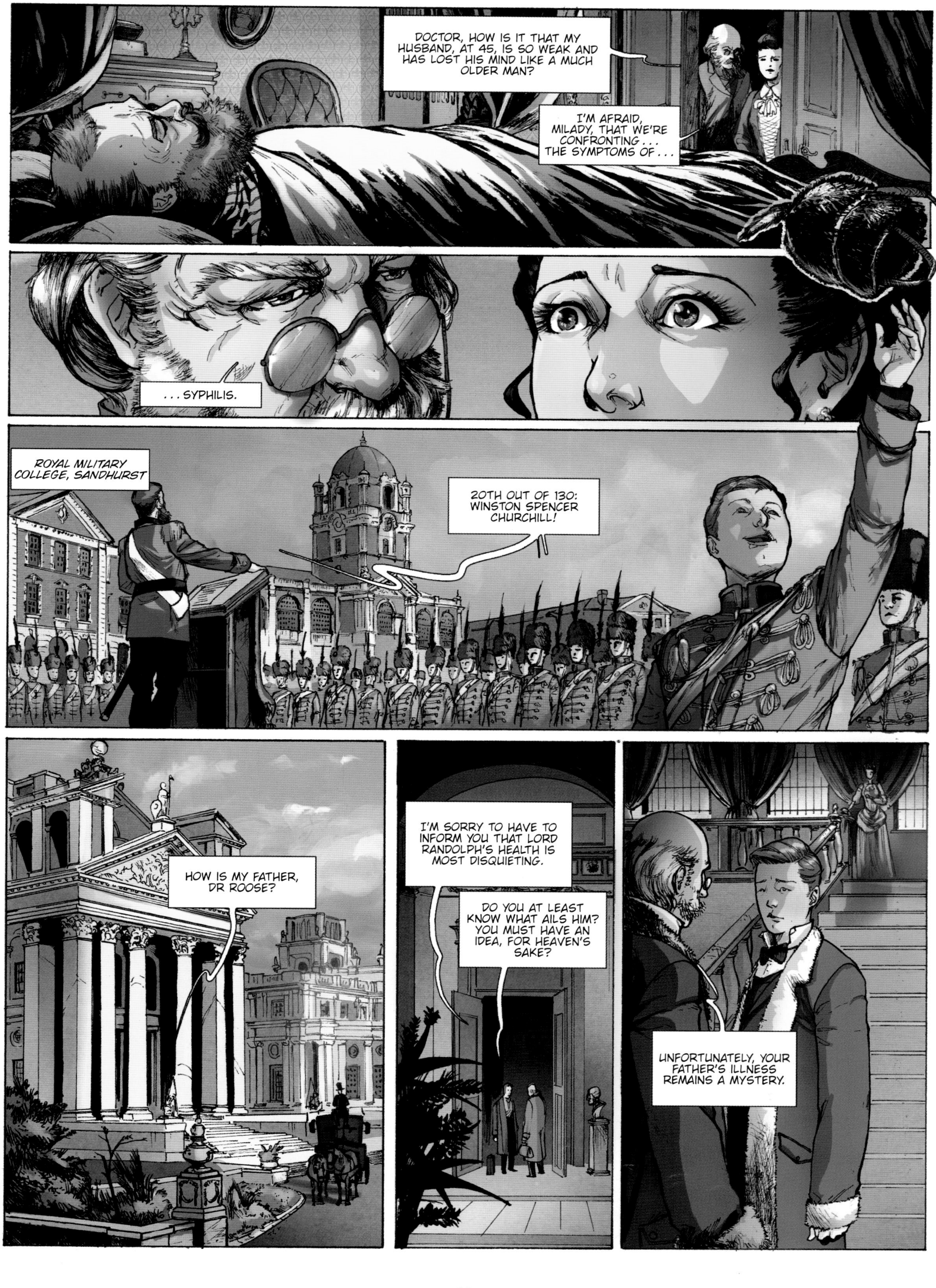
DOCTOR, HOW IS IT THAT MY HUSBAND, AT 45, IS SO WEAK AND HAS LOST HIS MIND LIKE A MUCH OLDER MAN?
I'M AFRAID, MILADY, THAT WE'RE CONFRONTING . . . THE SYMPTOMS OF . . .
. . . SYPHILIS.
ROYAL MILITARY COLLEGE, SANDHURST
20TH OUT OF 130: WINSTON SPENCER CHURCHILL!
HOW IS MY FATHER, DR ROOSE?
I'M SORRY TO HAVE TO INFORM YOU THAT LORD RANDOLPH'S HEALTH IS MOST DISQUIETING.
DO YOU AT LEAST KNOW WHAT AILS HIM? YOU MUST HAVE AN IDEA, FOR HEAVEN'S SAKE?
UNFORTUNATELY, YOUR FATHER'S ILLNESS REMAINS A MYSTERY.

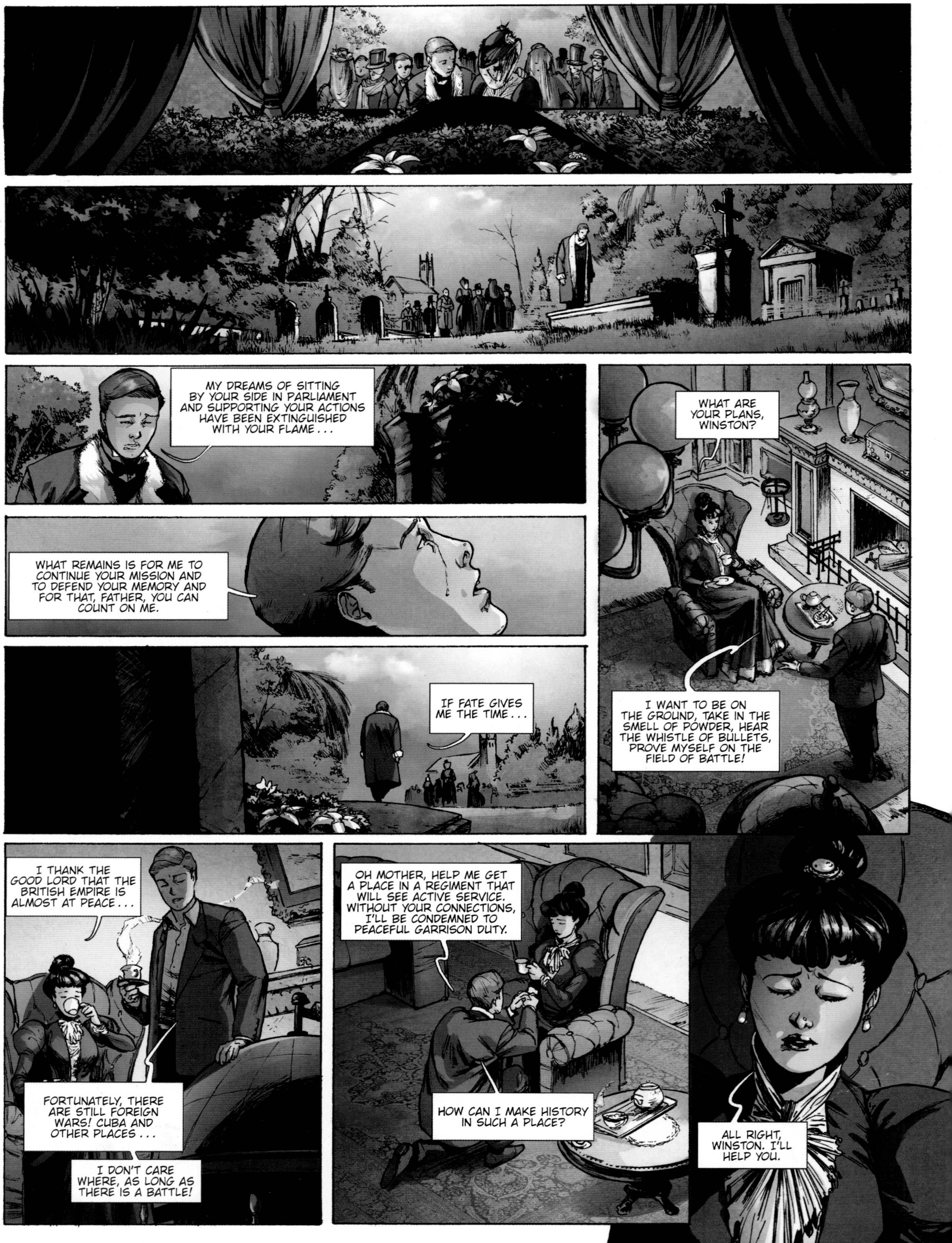
MY DREAMS OF SITTING BY YOUR SIDE IN PARLIAMENT AND SUPPORTING YOUR ACTIONS HAVE BEEN EXTINGUISHED WITH YOUR FLAME . . .
WHAT REMAINS IS FOR ME TO CONTINUE YOUR MISSION AND TO DEFEND YOUR MEMORY AND FOR THAT, FATHER, YOU CAN COUNT ON ME.
IF FATE GIVES ME THE TIME . . .
WHAT ARE YOUR PLANS, WINSTON?
I WANT TO BE ON THE GROUND, TAKE IN THE SMELL OF POWDER, HEAR THE WHISTLE OF BULLETS, PROVE MYSELF ON THE FIELD OF BATTLE!
I THANK THE GOOD LORD THAT THE BRITISH EMPIRE IS ALMOST AT PEACE . . .
FORTUNATELY, THERE ARE STILL FOREIGN WARS! CUBA AND OTHER PLACES . . .
I DON'T CARE WHERE, AS LONG AS THERE IS A BATTLE!
OH MOTHER, HELP ME GET A PLACE IN A REGIMENT THAT WILL SEE ACTIVE SERVICE. WITHOUT YOUR CONNECTIONS, I'LL BE CONDEMNED TO PEACEFUL GARRISON DUTY.
HOW CAN I MAKE HISTORY IN SUCH A PLACE?
ALL RIGHT, WINSTON. I'LL HELP YOU.

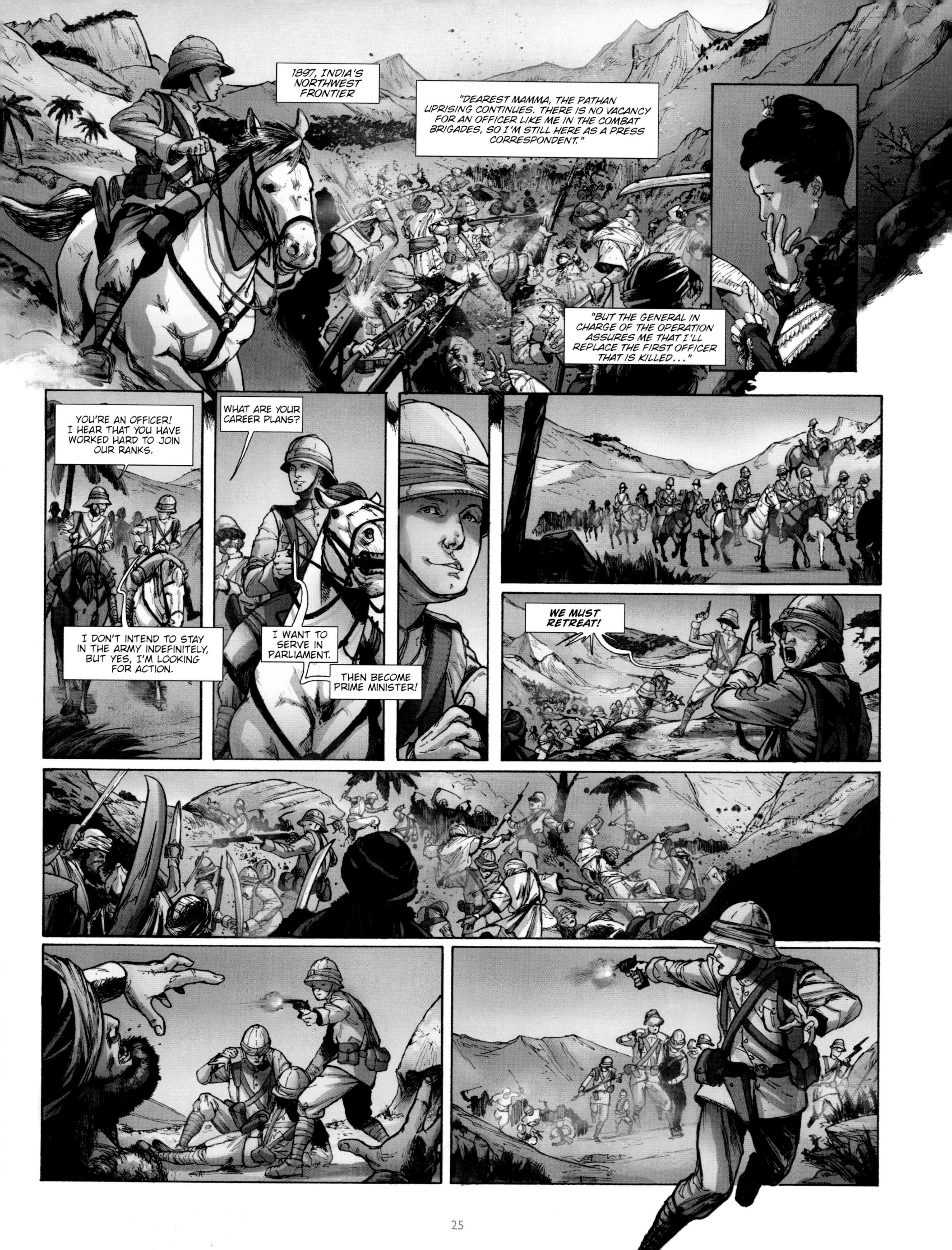

1897, INDIA'S NORTHWEST FRONTIER
"DEAREST MAMMA, THE PATHAN UPRISING CONTINUES. THERE IS NO VACANCY FOR AN OFFICER LIKE ME IN THE COMBAT BRIGADES, SO I'M STILL HERE AS A PRESS CORRESPONDENT."
"BUT THE GENERAL IN CHARGE OF THE OPERATION ASSURES ME THAT I'LL REPLACE THE FIRST OFFICER THAT IS KILLED..."
YOU'RE AN OFFICER! I HEAR THAT YOU HAVE WORKED HARD TO JOIN OUR RANKS.
I DON'T INTEND TO STAY IN THE ARMY INDEFINITELY, BUT YES, I'M LOOKING FOR ACTION.
WHAT ARE YOUR CAREER PLANS?
I WANT TO SERVE IN PARLIAMENT.
THEN BECOME PRIME MINISTER!
WE MUST RETREAT!

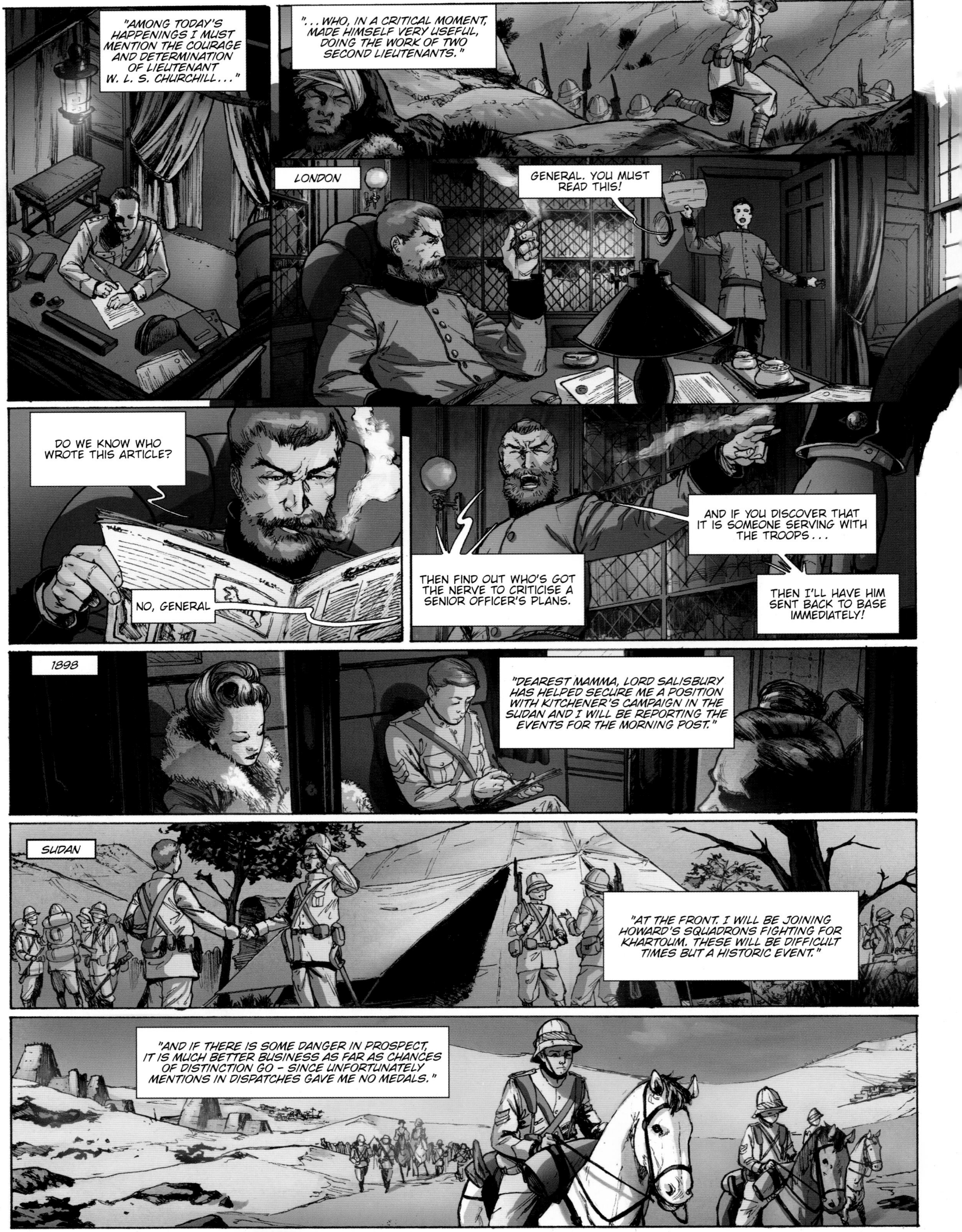
"AMONG TODAY'S HAPPENINGS I MUST MENTION THE COURAGE AND DETERMINATION OF LIEUTENANT W. L. S. CHURCHILL . . ."
". . . WHO, IN A CRITICAL MOMENT, MADE HIMSELF VERY USEFUL, DOING THE WORK OF TWO SECOND LIEUTENANTS."
LONDON
GENERAL. YOU MUST READ THIS!
DO WE KNOW WHO WROTE THIS ARTICLE?
NO, GENERAL
THEN FIND OUT WHO'S GOT THE NERVE TO CRITICISE A SENIOR OFFICER'S PLANS.
AND IF YOU DISCOVER THAT IT IS SOMEONE SERVING WITH THE TROOPS . . .
THEN I'LL HAVE HIM SENT BACK TO BASE IMMEDIATELY!
1898
"DEAREST MAMMA, LORD SALISBURY HAS HELPED SECURE ME A POSITION WITH KITCHENER'S CAMPAIGN IN THE SUDAN AND I WILL BE REPORTING THE EVENTS FOR THE MORNING POST."
SUDAN
"AT THE FRONT. I WILL BE JOINING HOWARD'S SQUADRONS FIGHTING FOR KHARTOUM. THESE WILL BE DIFFICULT TIMES BUT A HISTORIC EVENT."
"AND IF THERE IS SOME DANGER IN PROSPECT, IT IS MUCH BETTER BUSINESS AS FAR AS CHANCES OF DISTINCTION GO - SINCE UNFORTUNATELY MENTIONS IN DISPATCHES GAVE ME NO MEDALS."

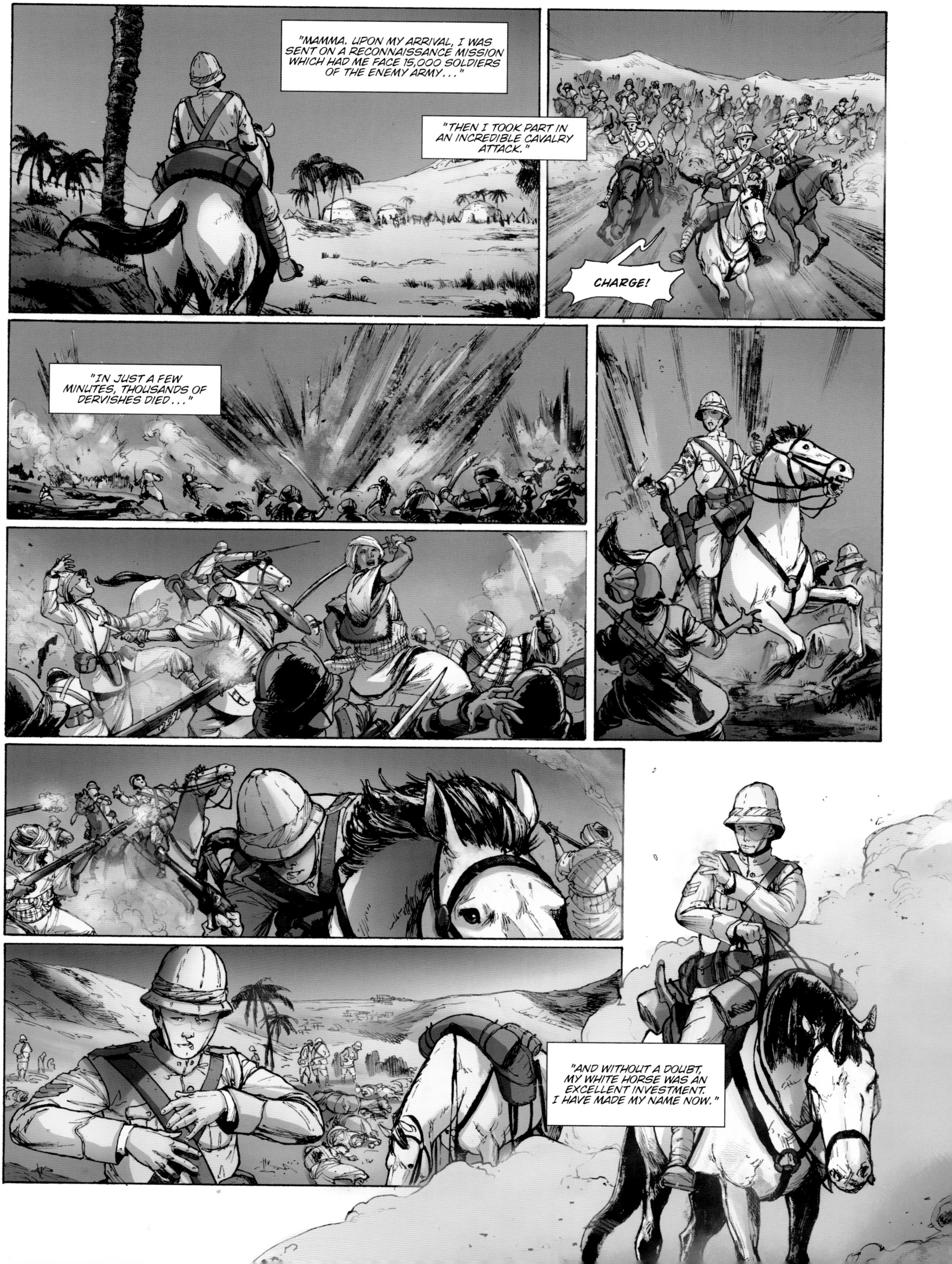
"MAMMA. UPON MY ARRIVAL, I WAS SENT ON A RECONNAISSANCE MISSION WHICH HAD ME FACE 15,000 SOLDIERS OF THE ENEMY ARMY . . ."
"THEN I TOOK PART IN AN INCREDIBLE CAVALRY ATTACK."
CHARGE!
"IN JUST A FEW MINUTES, THOUSANDS OF DERVISHES DIED . . ."
"AND WITHOUT A DOUBT, MY WHITE HORSE WAS AN EXCELLENT INVESTMENT. I HAVE MADE MY NAME NOW."

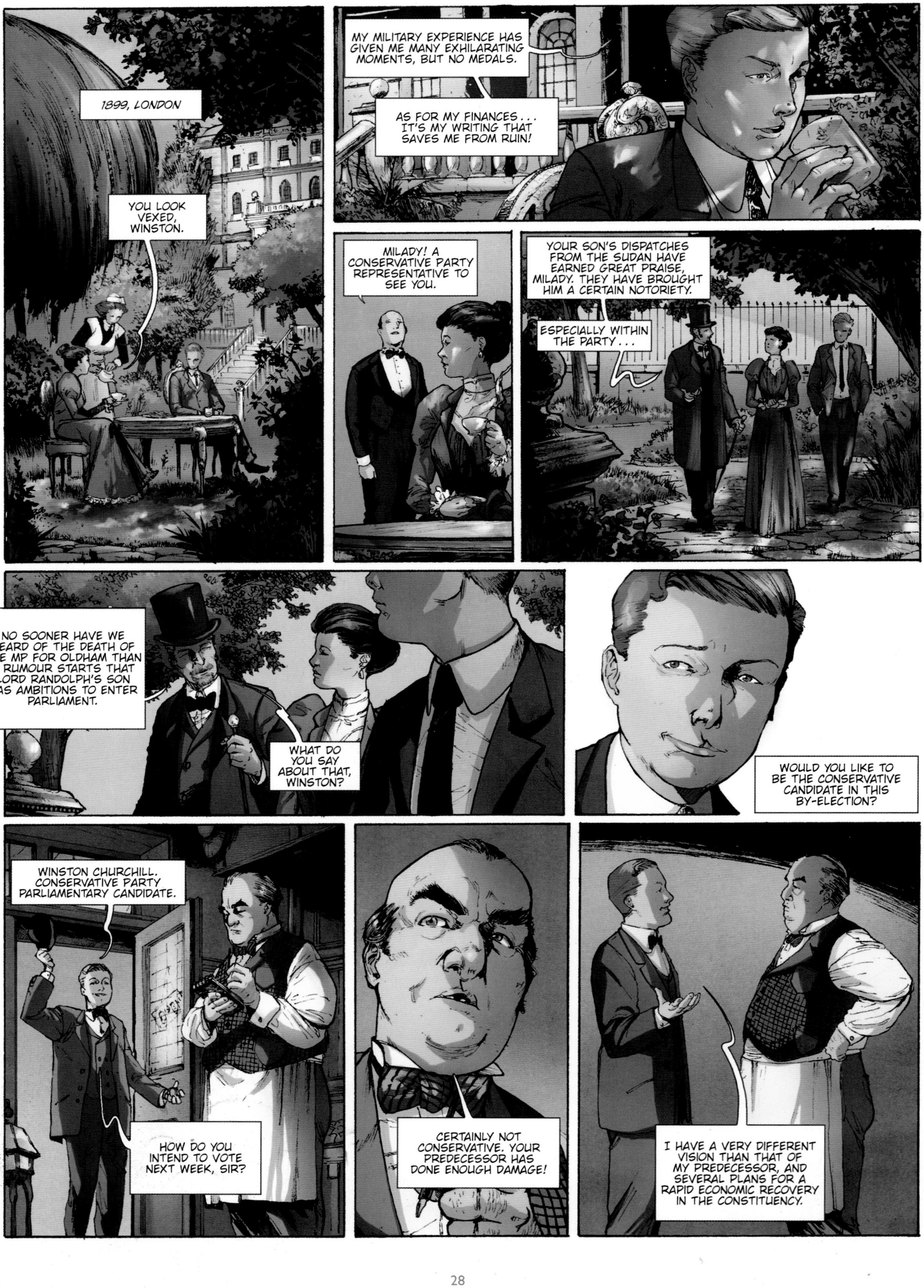
1899, LONDON
YOU LOOK VEXED, WINSTON.
MY MILITARY EXPERIENCE HAS GIVEN ME MANY EXHILARATING MOMENTS, BUT NO MEDALS.
AS FOR MY FINANCES . . . IT'S MY WRITING THAT SAVES ME FROM RUIN!
MILADY! A CONSERVATIVE PARTY REPRESENTATIVE TO SEE YOU.
YOUR SON'S DISPATCHES FROM THE SUDAN HAVE EARNED GREAT PRAISE, MILADY. THEY HAVE BROUGHT HIM A CERTAIN NOTORIETY.
ESPECIALLY WITHIN THE PARTY . . .
NO SOONER HAVE WE HEARD OF THE DEATH OF THE MP FOR OLDHAM THAN A RUMOUR STARTS THAT LORD RANDOLPH'S SON HAS AMBITIONS TO ENTER PARLIAMENT.
WHAT DO YOU SAY ABOUT THAT, WINSTON?
WOULD YOU LIKE TO BE THE CONSERVATIVE CANDIDATE IN THIS BY-ELECTION?
WINSTON CHURCHILL. CONSERVATIVE PARTY PARLIAMENTARY CANDIDATE.
HOW DO YOU INTEND TO VOTE NEXT WEEK, SIR?
CERTAINLY NOT CONSERVATIVE. YOUR PREDECESSOR HAS DONE ENOUGH DAMAGE!
I HAVE A VERY DIFFERENT VISION THAN THAT OF MY PREDECESSOR, AND SEVERAL PLANS FOR A RAPID ECONOMIC RECOVERY IN THE CONSTITUENCY.

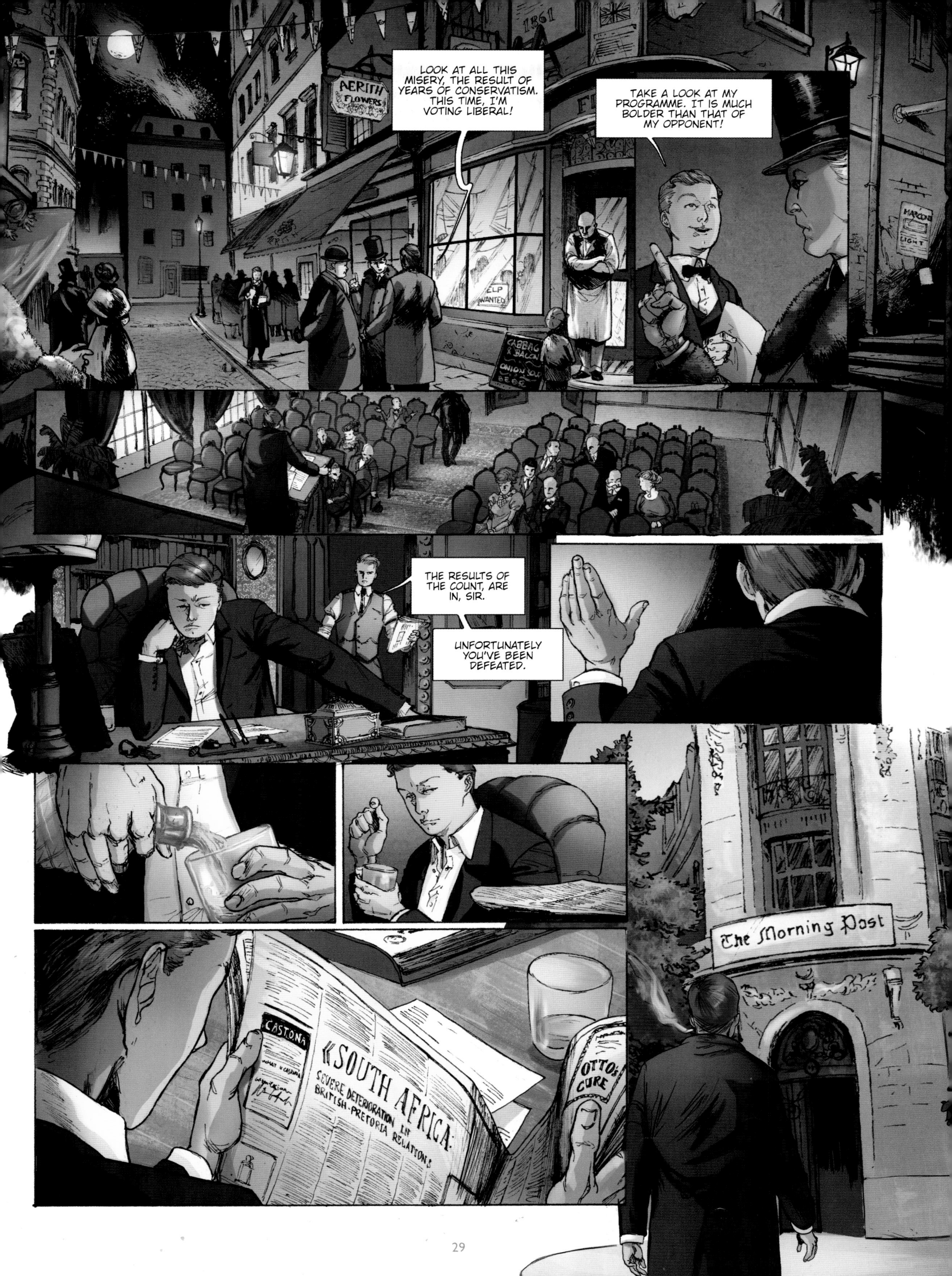
AERITH FLOWERS
LOOK AT ALL THIS MISERY, THE RESULT OF YEARS OF CONSERVATISM. THIS TIME, I'M VOTING LIBERAL!
TAKE A LOOK AT MY PROGRAMME. IT IS MUCH BOLDER THAN THAT OF MY OPPONENT!
THE RESULTS OF THE COUNT, ARE IN, SIR.
UNFORTUNATELY YOU'VE BEEN DEFEATED.
SOUTH AFRICA:
SEVERE DETERIORATION IN BRITISH-PRETORIA RELATIONS
OTTO'S CURE
The Morning Post

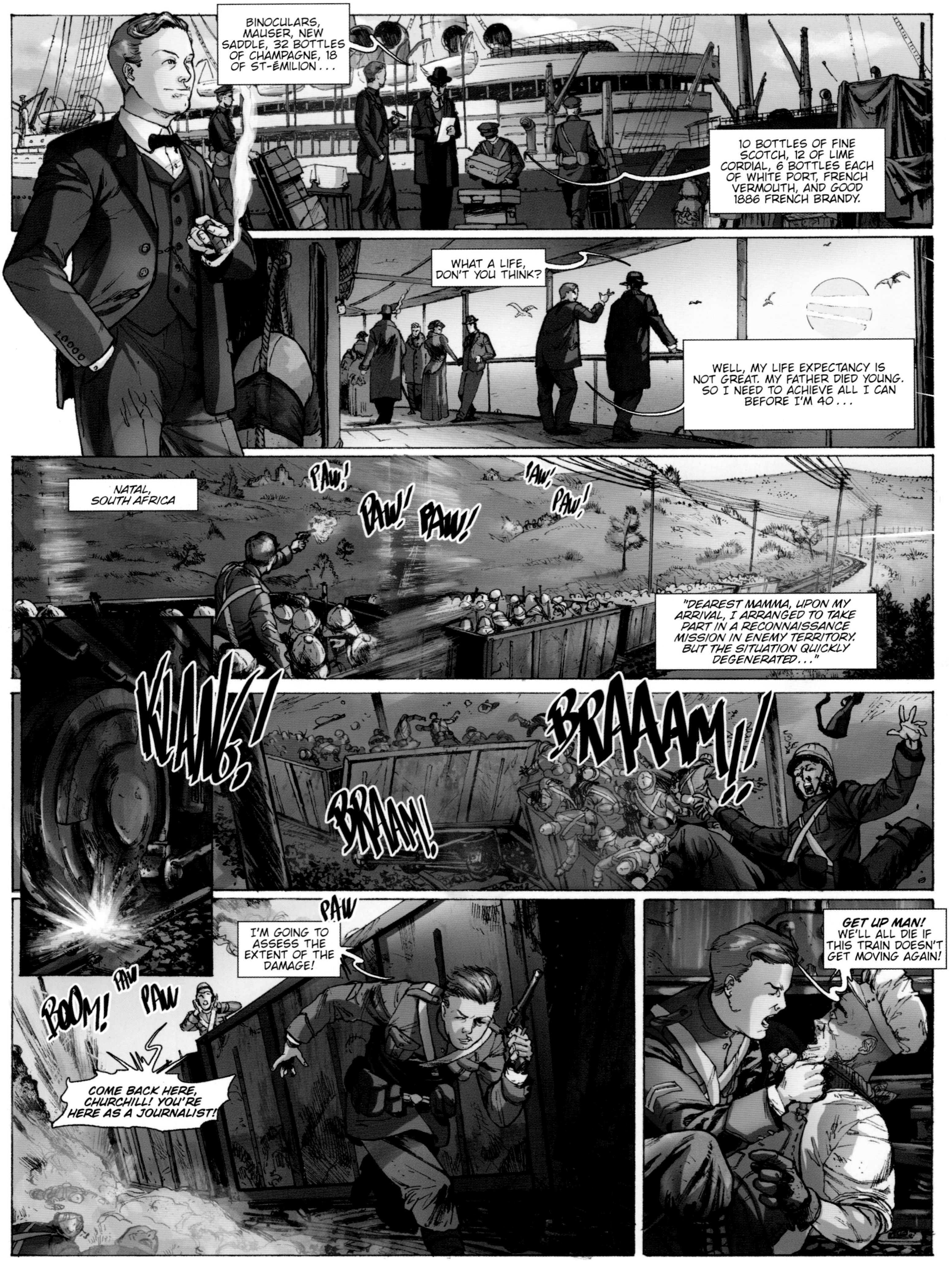
BINOCULARS, MAUSER, NEW SADDLE, 32 BOTTLES OF CHAMPAGNE, 18 OF ST-ÉMILION . . .
10 BOTTLES OF FINE SCOTCH, 12 OF LIME CORDIAL, 6 BOTTLES EACH OF WHITE PORT, FRENCH VERMOUTH, AND GOOD 1886 FRENCH BRANDY.
WHAT A LIFE, DON'T YOU THINK?
WELL, MY LIFE EXPECTANCY IS NOT GREAT. MY FATHER DIED YOUNG. SO I NEED TO ACHIEVE ALL I CAN BEFORE I'M 40 . . .
NATAL, SOUTH AFRICA
PAW!
PAW!
PAW!
PAW!
PAW!
"DEAREST MAMMA, UPON MY ARRIVAL, I ARRANGED TO TAKE PART IN A RECONNAISSANCE MISSION IN ENEMY TERRITORY. BUT THE SITUATION QUICKLY DEGENERATED . . ."
KLANG!
BRAAAM!!
BRAAM!
PAW
I'M GOING TO ASSESS THE EXTENT OF THE DAMAGE!
BOOM!
PAW
PAW
COME BACK HERE, CHURCHILL! YOU'RE HERE AS A JOURNALIST!
GET UP MAN! WE'LL ALL DIE IF THIS TRAIN DOESN'T GET MOVING AGAIN!

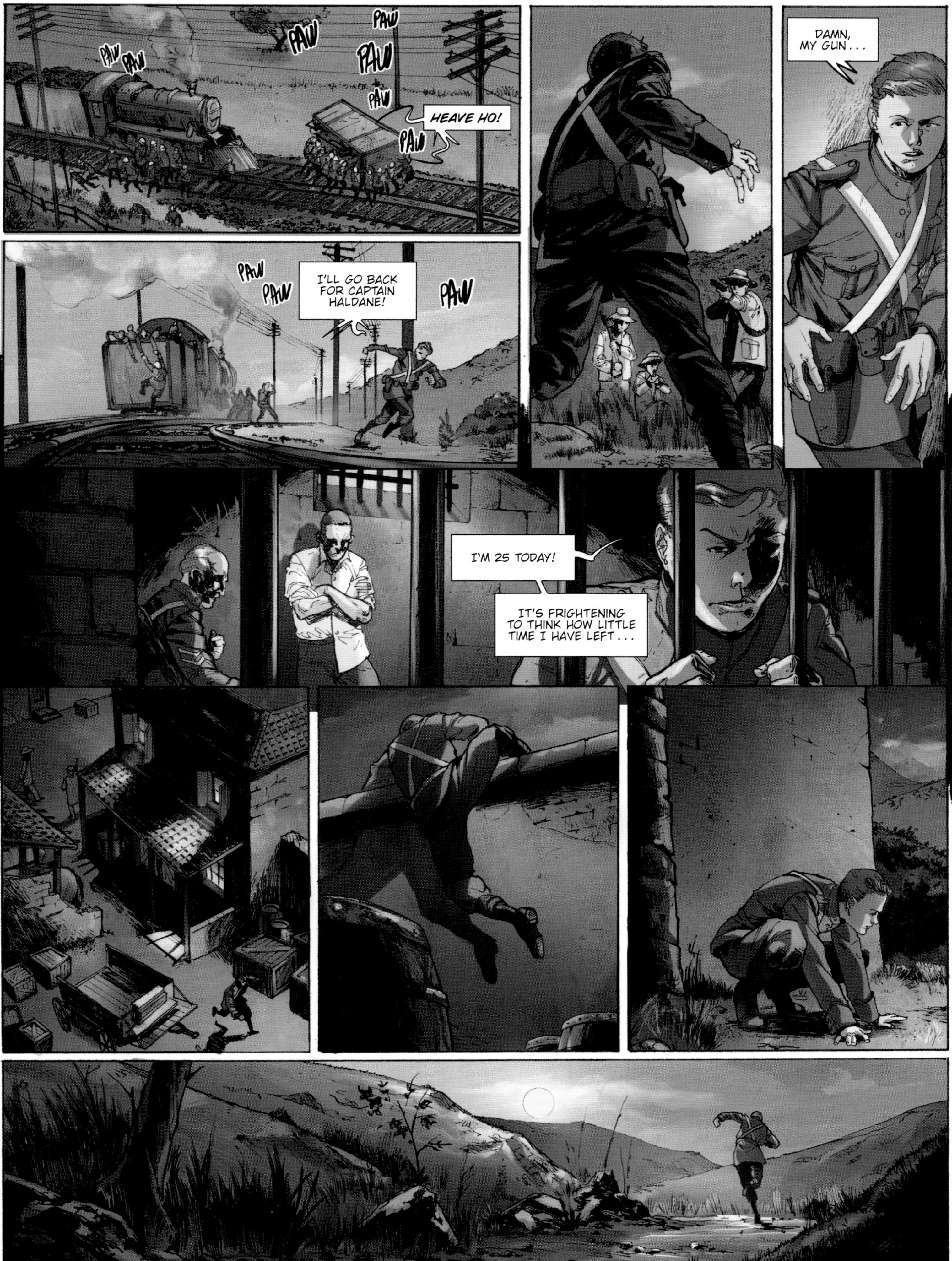
PAW
PAW
PAW
PAW
PAW
PAW
PAW
HEAVE HO!
PAW
DAMN, MY GUN . . .
PAW
PAW
I'LL GO BACK FOR CAPTAIN HALDANE!
PAW
I'M 25 TODAY!
IT'S FRIGHTENING TO THINK HOW LITTLE TIME I HAVE LEFT . . .

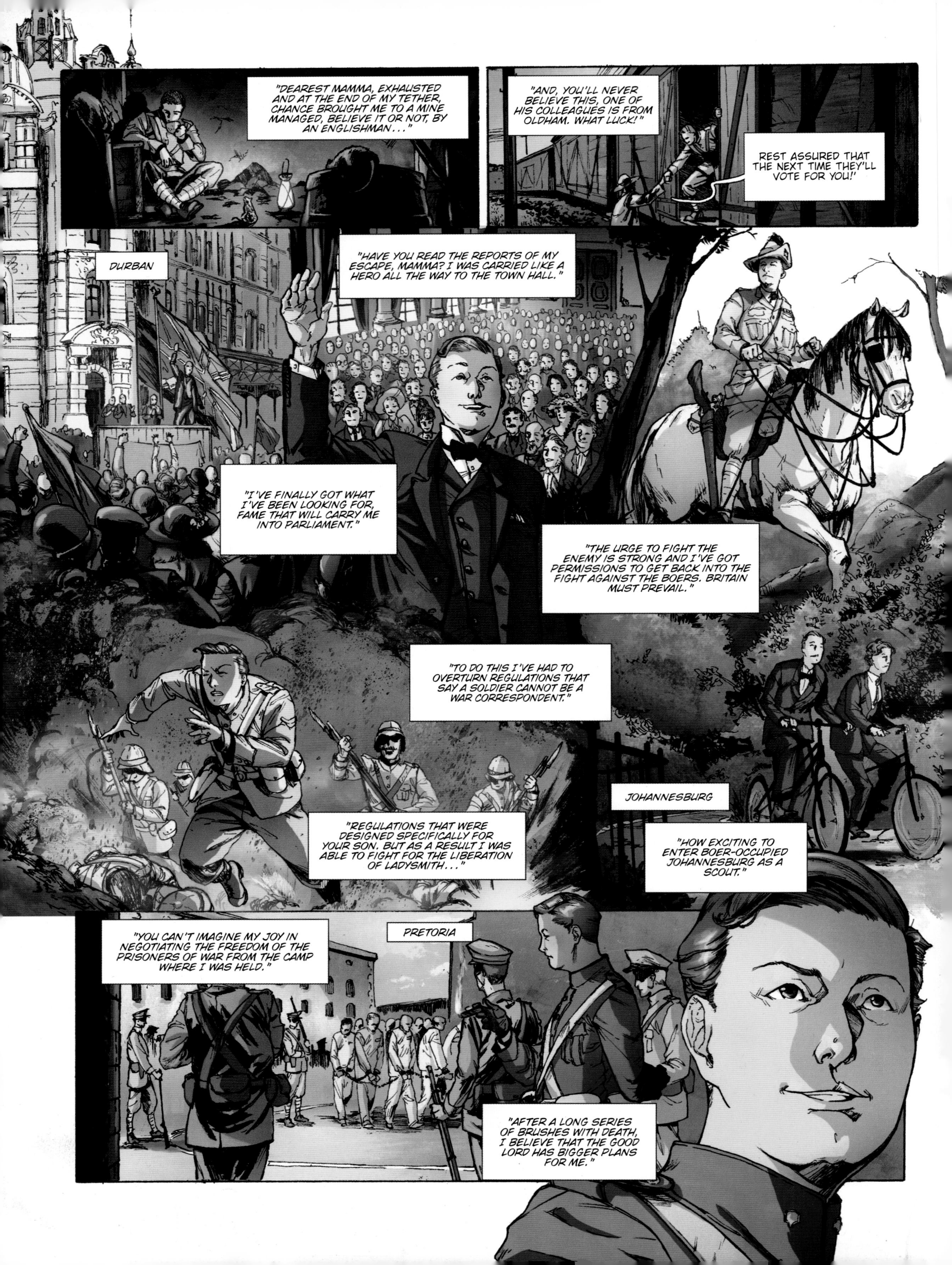

"DEAREST MAMMA, EXHAUSTED AND AT THE END OF MY TETHER, CHANCE BROUGHT ME TO A MINE MANAGED, BELIEVE IT OR NOT, BY AN ENGLISHMAN..."
"AND, YOU'LL NEVER BELIEVE THIS, ONE OF HIS COLLEAGUES IS FROM OLDHAM. WHAT LUCK!"
REST ASSURED THAT THE NEXT TIME THEY'LL VOTE FOR YOU!'
DURBAN
"HAVE YOU READ THE REPORTS OF MY ESCAPE, MAMMA? I WAS CARRIED LIKE A HERO ALL THE WAY TO THE TOWN HALL."
"I'VE FINALLY GOT WHAT I'VE BEEN LOOKING FOR, FAME THAT WILL CARRY ME INTO PARLIAMENT."
"THE URGE TO FIGHT THE ENEMY IS STRONG AND I'VE GOT PERMISSIONS TO GET BACK INTO THE FIGHT AGAINST THE BOERS. BRITAIN MUST PREVAIL."
"TO DO THIS I'VE HAD TO OVERTURN REGULATIONS THAT SAY A SOLDIER CANNOT BE A WAR CORRESPONDENT."
"REGULATIONS THAT WERE DESIGNED SPECIFICALLY FOR YOUR SON. BUT AS A RESULT I WAS ABLE TO FIGHT FOR THE LIBERATION OF LADYSMITH..."
JOHANNESBURG
"HOW EXCITING TO ENTER BOER-OCCUPIED JOHANNESBURG AS A SCOUT."
PRETORIA
"YOU CAN'T IMAGINE MY JOY IN NEGOTIATING THE FREEDOM OF THE PRISONERS OF WAR FROM THE CAMP WHERE I WAS HELD."
"AFTER A LONG SERIES OF BRUSHES WITH DEATH, I BELIEVE THAT THE GOOD LORD HAS BIGGER PLANS FOR ME."

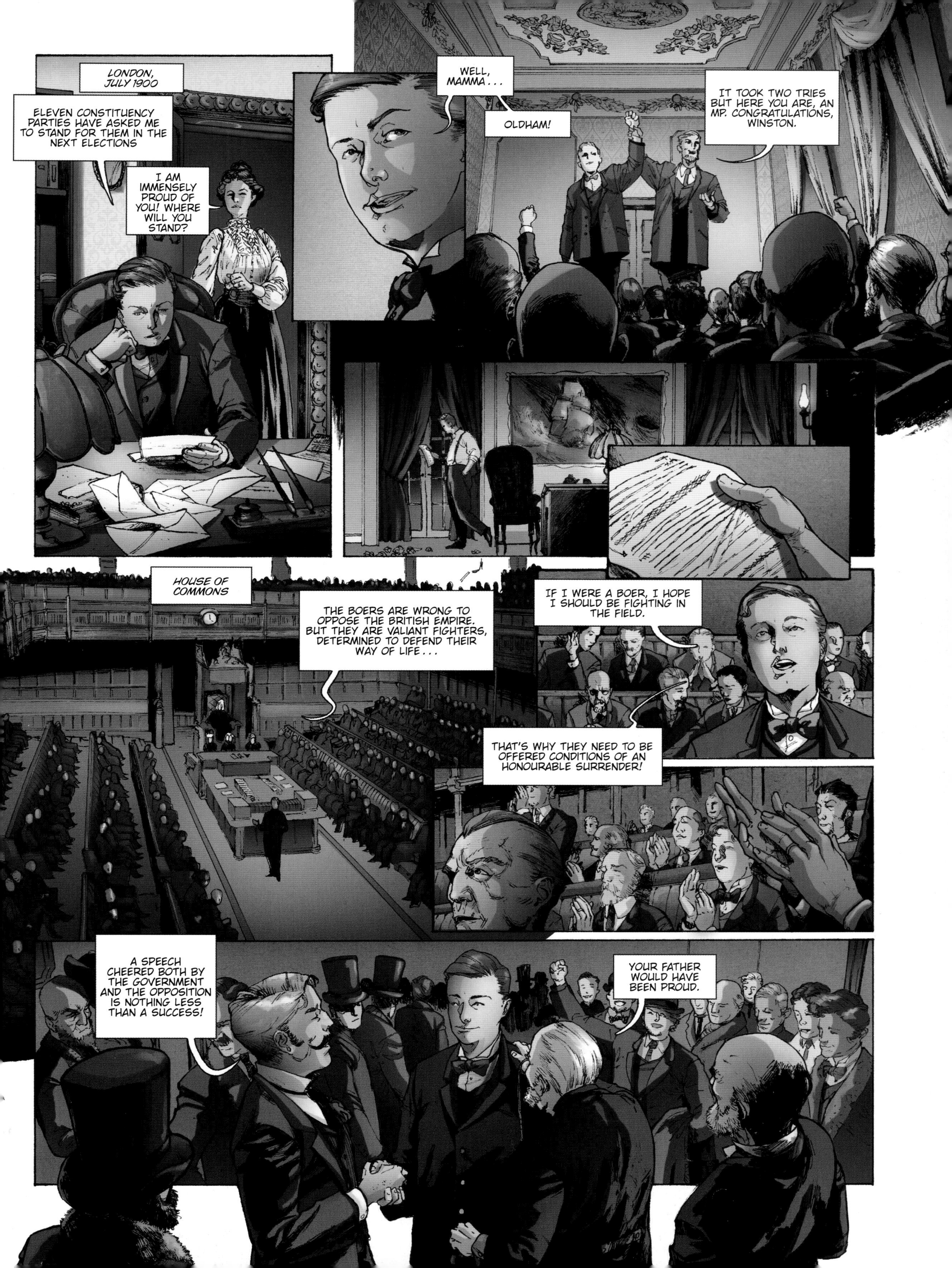
LONDON, JULY 1900
ELEVEN CONSTITUENCY PARTIES HAVE ASKED ME TO STAND FOR THEM IN THE NEXT ELECTIONS
I AM IMMENSELY PROUD OF YOU! WHERE WILL YOU STAND?
WELL, MAMMA . . .
OLDHAM!
IT TOOK TWO TRIES BUT HERE YOU ARE, AN MP. CONGRATULATIONS, WINSTON.
HOUSE OF COMMONS
THE BOERS ARE WRONG TO OPPOSE THE BRITISH EMPIRE. BUT THEY ARE VALIANT FIGHTERS, DETERMINED TO DEFEND THEIR WAY OF LIFE . . .
IF I WERE A BOER, I HOPE I SHOULD BE FIGHTING IN THE FIELD.
THAT'S WHY THEY NEED TO BE OFFERED CONDITIONS OF AN HONOURABLE SURRENDER!
A SPEECH CHEERED BOTH BY THE GOVERNMENT AND THE OPPOSITION IS NOTHING LESS THAN A SUCCESS!
YOUR FATHER WOULD HAVE BEEN PROUD.

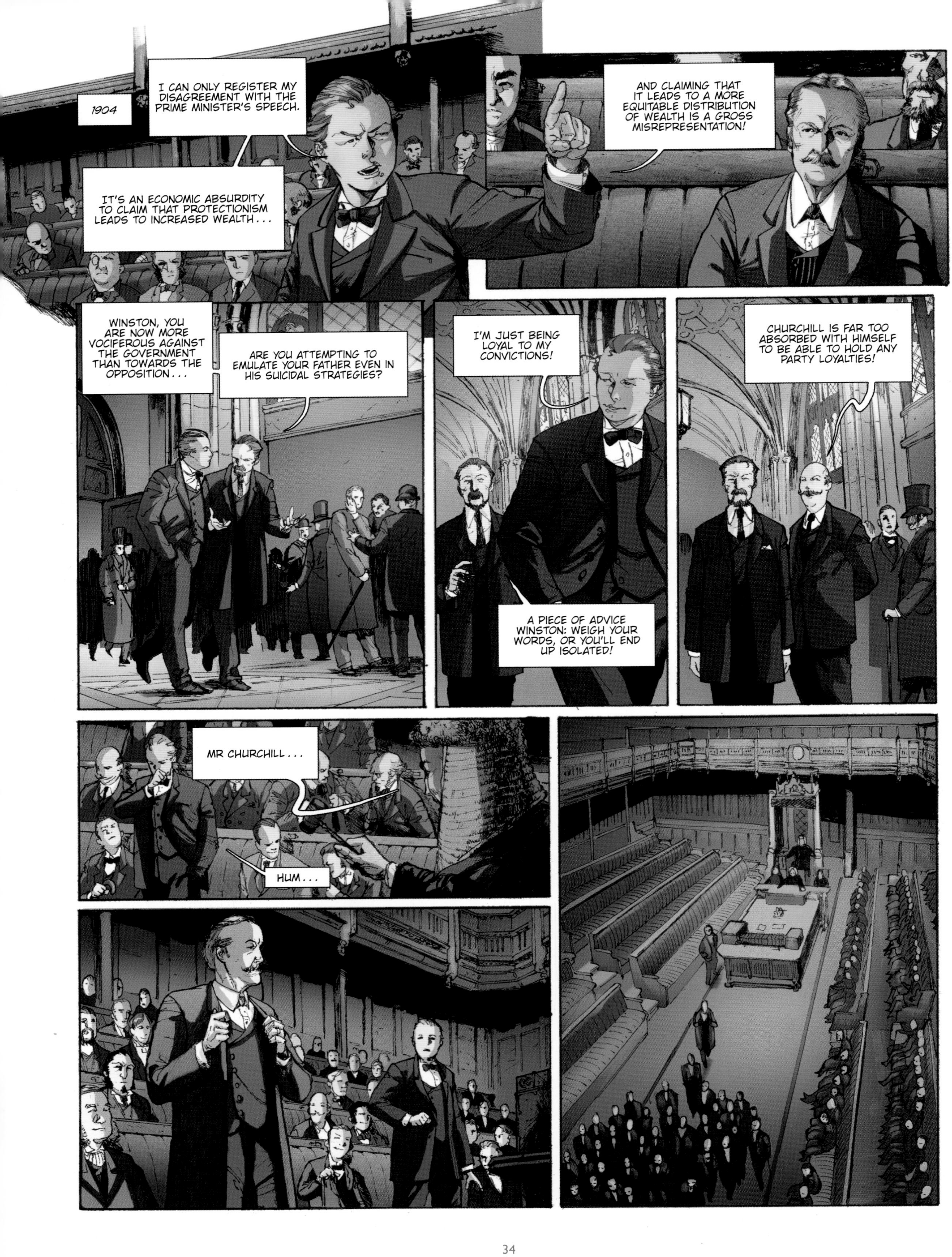
1904
I CAN ONLY REGISTER MY DISAGREEMENT WITH THE PRIME MINISTER'S SPEECH.
IT'S AN ECONOMIC ABSURDITY TO CLAIM THAT PROTECTIONISM LEADS TO INCREASED WEALTH . . .
AND CLAIMING THAT IT LEADS TO A MORE EQUITABLE DISTRIBUTION OF WEALTH IS A GROSS MISREPRESENTATION!
WINSTON, YOU ARE NOW MORE VOCIFEROUS AGAINST THE GOVERNMENT THAN TOWARDS THE OPPOSITION . . .
ARE YOU ATTEMPTING TO EMULATE YOUR FATHER EVEN IN HIS SUICIDAL STRATEGIES?
I'M JUST BEING LOYAL TO MY CONVICTIONS!
A PIECE OF ADVICE WINSTON: WEIGH YOUR WORDS, OR YOU'LL END UP ISOLATED!
CHURCHILL IS FAR TOO ABSORBED WITH HIMSELF TO BE ABLE TO HOLD ANY PARTY LOYALTIES!
MR CHURCHILL . . .
HUM . . .

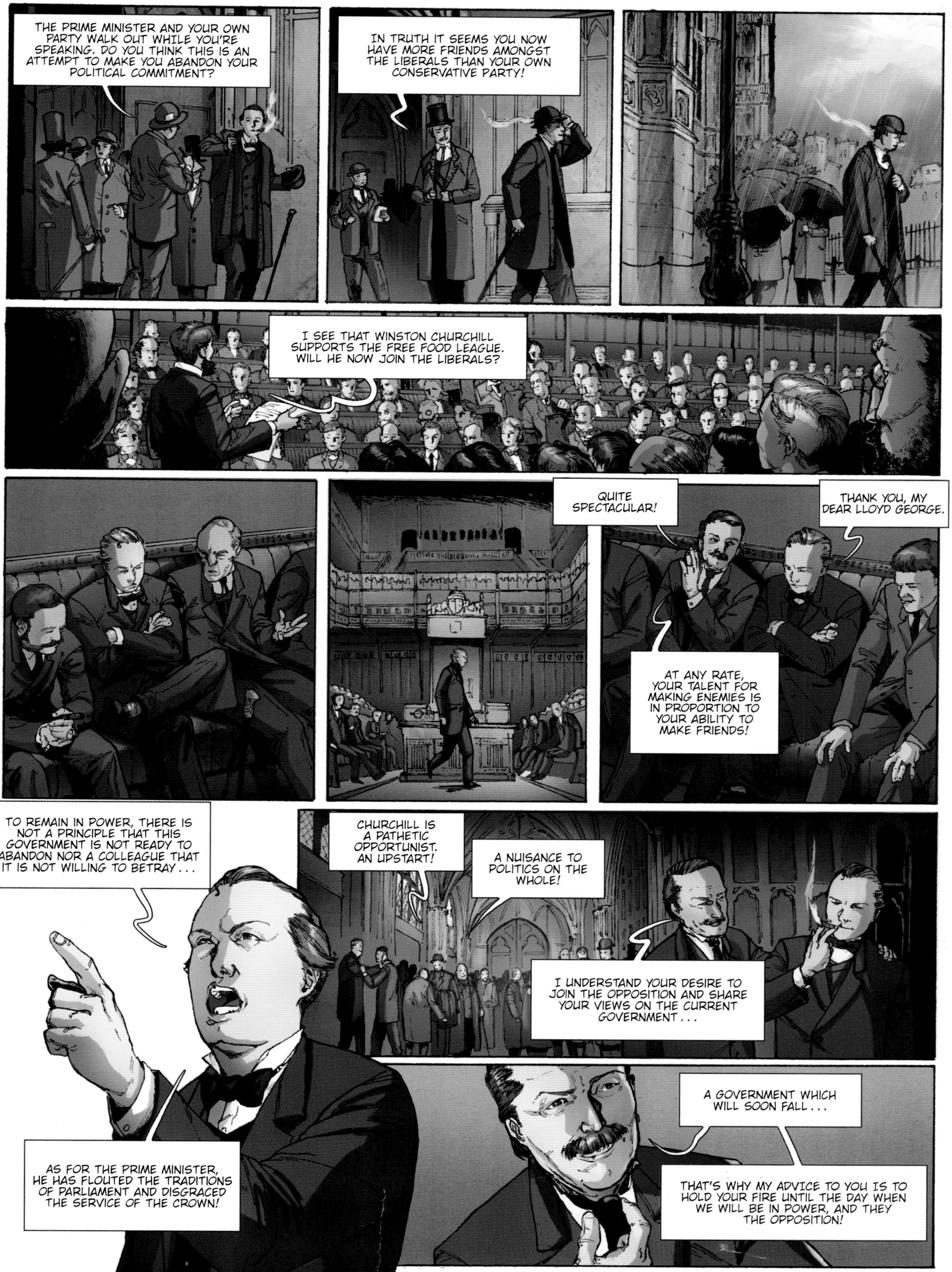
THE PRIME MINISTER AND YOUR OWN PARTY WALK OUT WHILE YOU'RE SPEAKING. DO YOU THINK THIS IS AN ATTEMPT TO MAKE YOU ABANDON YOUR POLITICAL COMMITMENT?
IN TRUTH IT SEEMS YOU NOW HAVE MORE FRIENDS AMONGST THE LIBERALS THAN YOUR OWN CONSERVATIVE PARTY!
I SEE THAT WINSTON CHURCHILL SUPPORTS THE FREE FOOD LEAGUE. WILL HE NOW JOIN THE LIBERALS?
QUITE SPECTACULAR!
THANK YOU, MY DEAR LLOYD GEORGE.
AT ANY RATE, YOUR TALENT FOR MAKING ENEMIES IS IN PROPORTION TO YOUR ABILITY TO MAKE FRIENDS!
TO REMAIN IN POWER, THERE IS NOT A PRINCIPLE THAT THIS GOVERNMENT IS NOT READY TO ABANDON NOR A COLLEAGUE THAT IT IS NOT WILLING TO BETRAY . . .
AS FOR THE PRIME MINISTER, HE HAS FLOUTED THE TRADITIONS OF PARLIAMENT AND DISGRACED THE SERVICE OF THE CROWN!
CHURCHILL IS A PATHETIC OPPORTUNIST. AN UPSTART!
A NUISANCE TO POLITICS ON THE WHOLE!
I UNDERSTAND YOUR DESIRE TO JOIN THE OPPOSITION AND SHARE YOUR VIEWS ON THE CURRENT GOVERNMENT . . .
A GOVERNMENT WHICH WILL SOON FALL . . .
THAT'S WHY MY ADVICE TO YOU IS TO HOLD YOUR FIRE UNTIL THE DAY WHEN WE WILL BE IN POWER, AND THEY THE OPPOSITION!

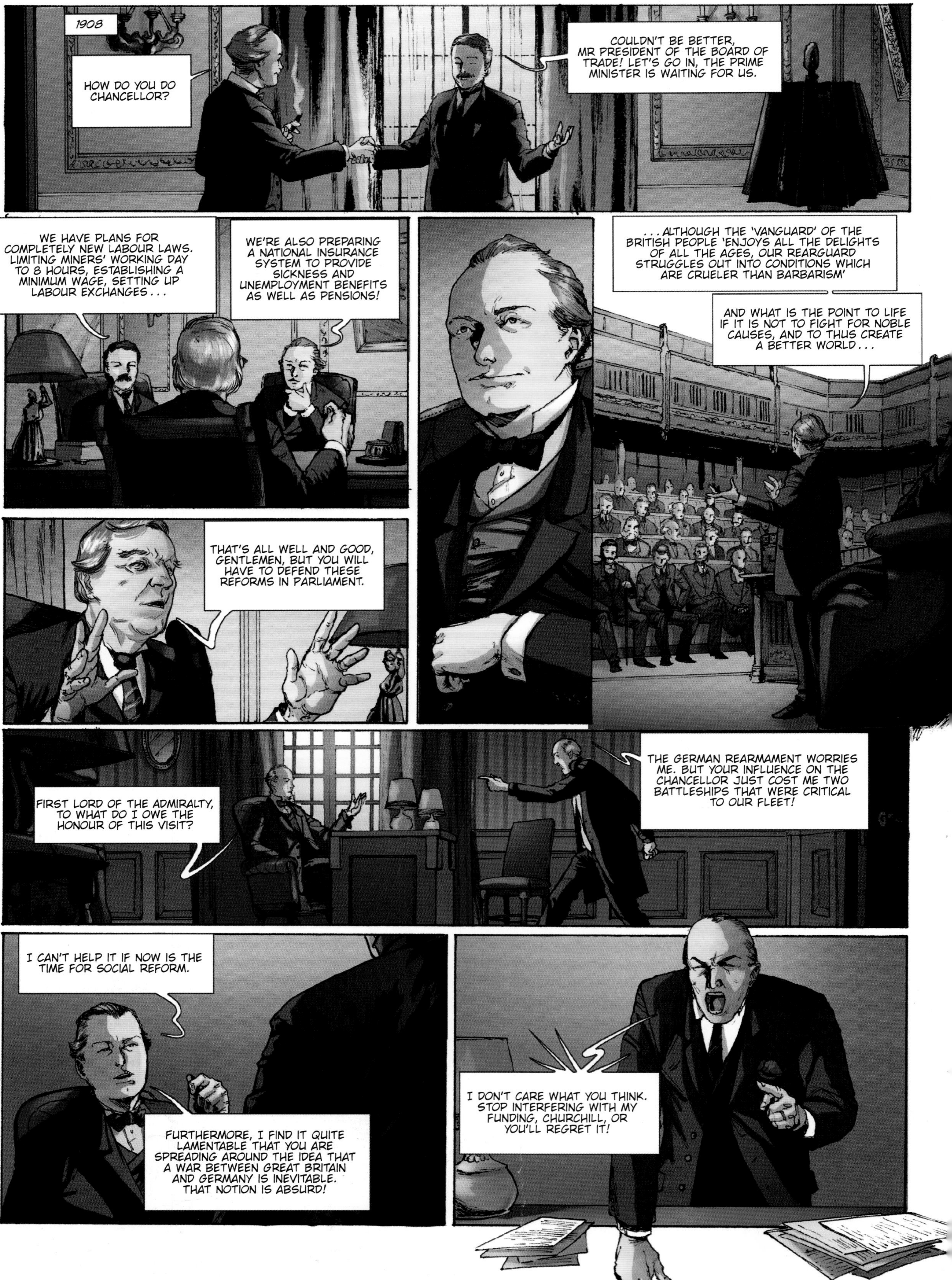
1908
HOW DO YOU DO CHANCELLOR?
COULDN'T BE BETTER, MR PRESIDENT OF THE BOARD OF TRADE! LET'S GO IN, THE PRIME MINISTER IS WAITING FOR US.
WE HAVE PLANS FOR COMPLETELY NEW LABOUR LAWS. LIMITING MINERS' WORKING DAY TO 8 HOURS, ESTABLISHING A MINIMUM WAGE, SETTING UP LABOUR EXCHANGES . . .
WE'RE ALSO PREPARING A NATIONAL INSURANCE SYSTEM TO PROVIDE SICKNESS AND UNEMPLOYMENT BENEFITS AS WELL AS PENSIONS!
THAT'S ALL WELL AND GOOD, GENTLEMEN, BUT YOU WILL HAVE TO DEFEND THESE REFORMS IN PARLIAMENT.
. . . ALTHOUGH THE 'VANGUARD' OF THE BRITISH PEOPLE 'ENJOYS ALL THE DELIGHTS OF ALL THE AGES, OUR REARGUARD STRUGGLES OUT INTO CONDITIONS WHICH ARE CRUELER THAN BARBARISM'
AND WHAT IS THE POINT TO LIFE IF IT IS NOT TO FIGHT FOR NOBLE CAUSES, AND TO THUS CREATE A BETTER WORLD . . .
FIRST LORD OF THE ADMIRALTY, TO WHAT DO I OWE THE HONOUR OF THIS VISIT?
THE GERMAN REARMAMENT WORRIES ME. BUT YOUR INFLUENCE ON THE CHANCELLOR JUST COST ME TWO BATTLESHIPS THAT WERE CRITICAL TO OUR FLEET!
I CAN'T HELP IT IF NOW IS THE TIME FOR SOCIAL REFORM.
FURTHERMORE, I FIND IT QUITE LAMENTABLE THAT YOU ARE SPREADING AROUND THE IDEA THAT A WAR BETWEEN GREAT BRITAIN AND GERMANY IS INEVITABLE. THAT NOTION IS ABSURD!
I DON'T CARE WHAT YOU THINK. STOP INTERFERING WITH MY FUNDING, CHURCHILL, OR YOU'LL REGRET IT!

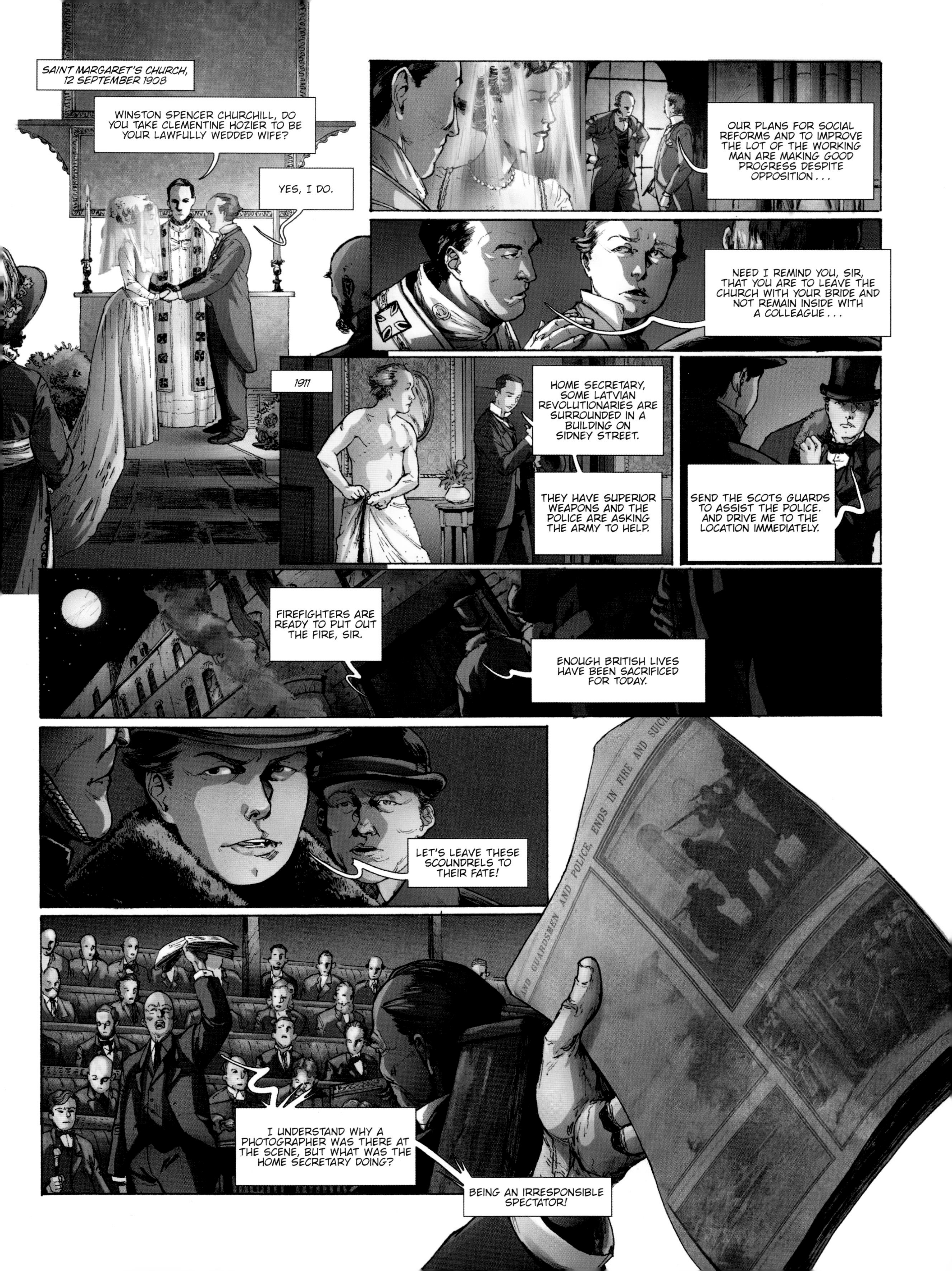

SAINT MARGARET'S CHURCH, 12 SEPTEMBER 1908
WINSTON SPENCER CHURCHILL, DO YOU TAKE CLEMENTINE HOZIER TO BE YOUR LAWFULLY WEDDED WIFE?
YES, I DO.
OUR PLANS FOR SOCIAL REFORMS AND TO IMPROVE THE LOT OF THE WORKING MAN ARE MAKING GOOD PROGRESS DESPITE OPPOSITION . . .
NEED I REMIND YOU, SIR, THAT YOU ARE TO LEAVE THE CHURCH WITH YOUR BRIDE AND NOT REMAIN INSIDE WITH A COLLEAGUE . . .
1911
HOME SECRETARY, SOME LATVIAN REVOLUTIONARIES ARE SURROUNDED IN A BUILDING ON SIDNEY STREET.
THEY HAVE SUPERIOR WEAPONS AND THE POLICE ARE ASKING THE ARMY TO HELP.
SEND THE SCOTS GUARDS TO ASSIST THE POLICE. AND DRIVE ME TO THE LOCATION IMMEDIATELY.
FIREFIGHTERS ARE READY TO PUT OUT THE FIRE, SIR.
ENOUGH BRITISH LIVES HAVE BEEN SACRIFICED FOR TODAY.
LET'S LEAVE THESE SCOUNDRELS TO THEIR FATE!
GUARDSMEN AND POLICE, ENDS IN FIRE AND
I UNDERSTAND WHY A PHOTOGRAPHER WAS THERE AT THE SCENE, BUT WHAT WAS THE HOME SECRETARY DOING?
BEING AN IRRESPONSIBLE SPECTATOR!

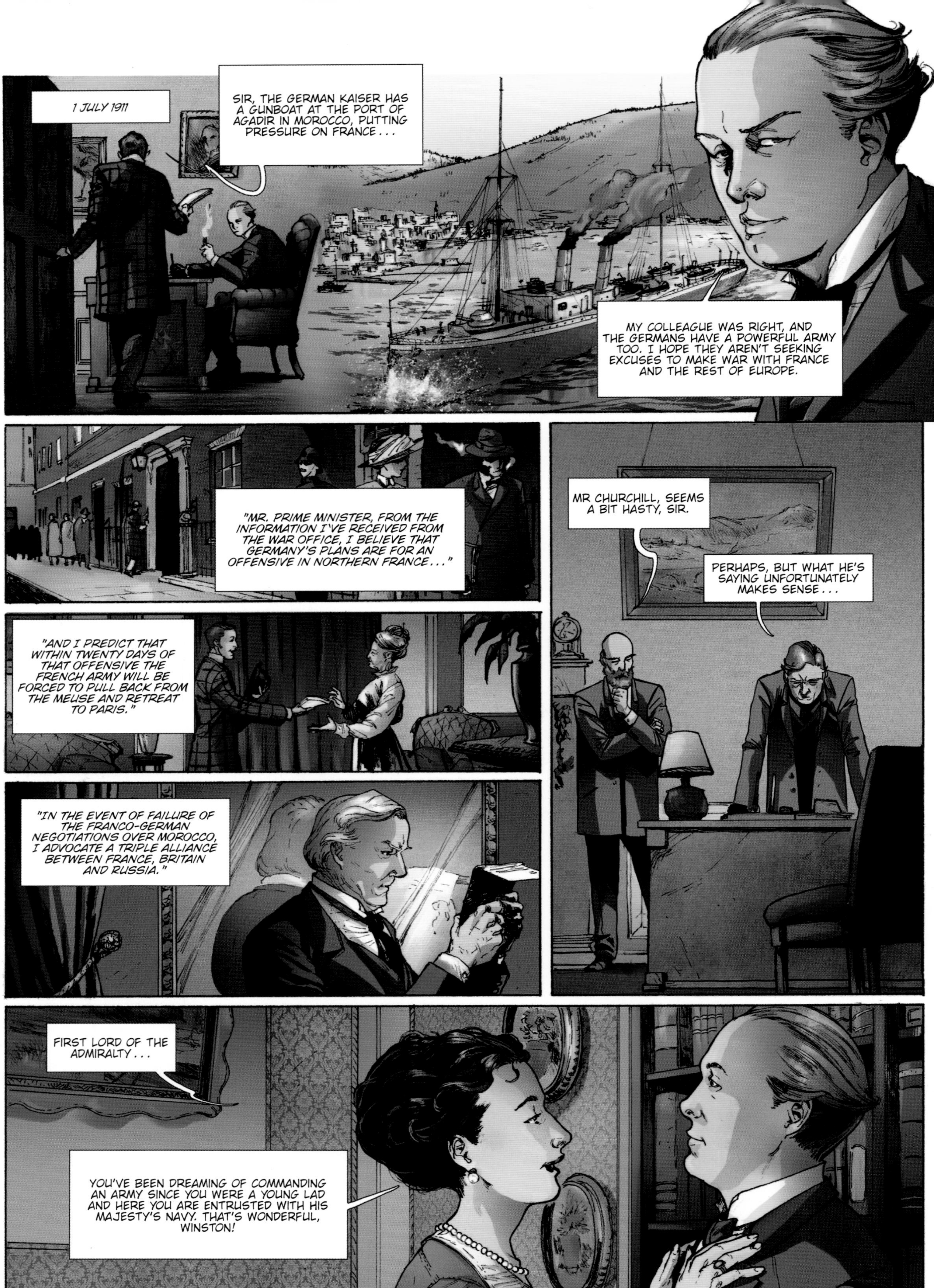
1 JULY 1911
SIR, THE GERMAN KAISER HAS A GUNBOAT AT THE PORT OF AGADIR IN MOROCCO, PUTTING PRESSURE ON FRANCE . . .
MY COLLEAGUE WAS RIGHT, AND THE GERMANS HAVE A POWERFUL ARMY TOO. I HOPE THEY AREN'T SEEKING EXCUSES TO MAKE WAR WITH FRANCE AND THE REST OF EUROPE.
"MR. PRIME MINISTER, FROM THE INFORMATION I'VE RECEIVED FROM THE WAR OFFICE, I BELIEVE THAT GERMANY'S PLANS ARE FOR AN OFFENSIVE IN NORTHERN FRANCE . . ."
"AND I PREDICT THAT WITHIN TWENTY DAYS OF THAT OFFENSIVE THE FRENCH ARMY WILL BE FORCED TO PULL BACK FROM THE MEUSE AND RETREAT TO PARIS."
"IN THE EVENT OF FAILURE OF THE FRANCO-GERMAN NEGOTIATIONS OVER MOROCCO, I ADVOCATE A TRIPLE ALLIANCE BETWEEN FRANCE, BRITAIN AND RUSSIA."
MR CHURCHILL, SEEMS A BIT HASTY, SIR.
PERHAPS, BUT WHAT HE'S SAYING UNFORTUNATELY MAKES SENSE . . .
FIRST LORD OF THE ADMIRALTY . . .
YOU'VE BEEN DREAMING OF COMMANDING AN ARMY SINCE YOU WERE A YOUNG LAD AND HERE YOU ARE ENTRUSTED WITH HIS MAJESTY'S NAVY. THAT'S WONDERFUL, WINSTON!

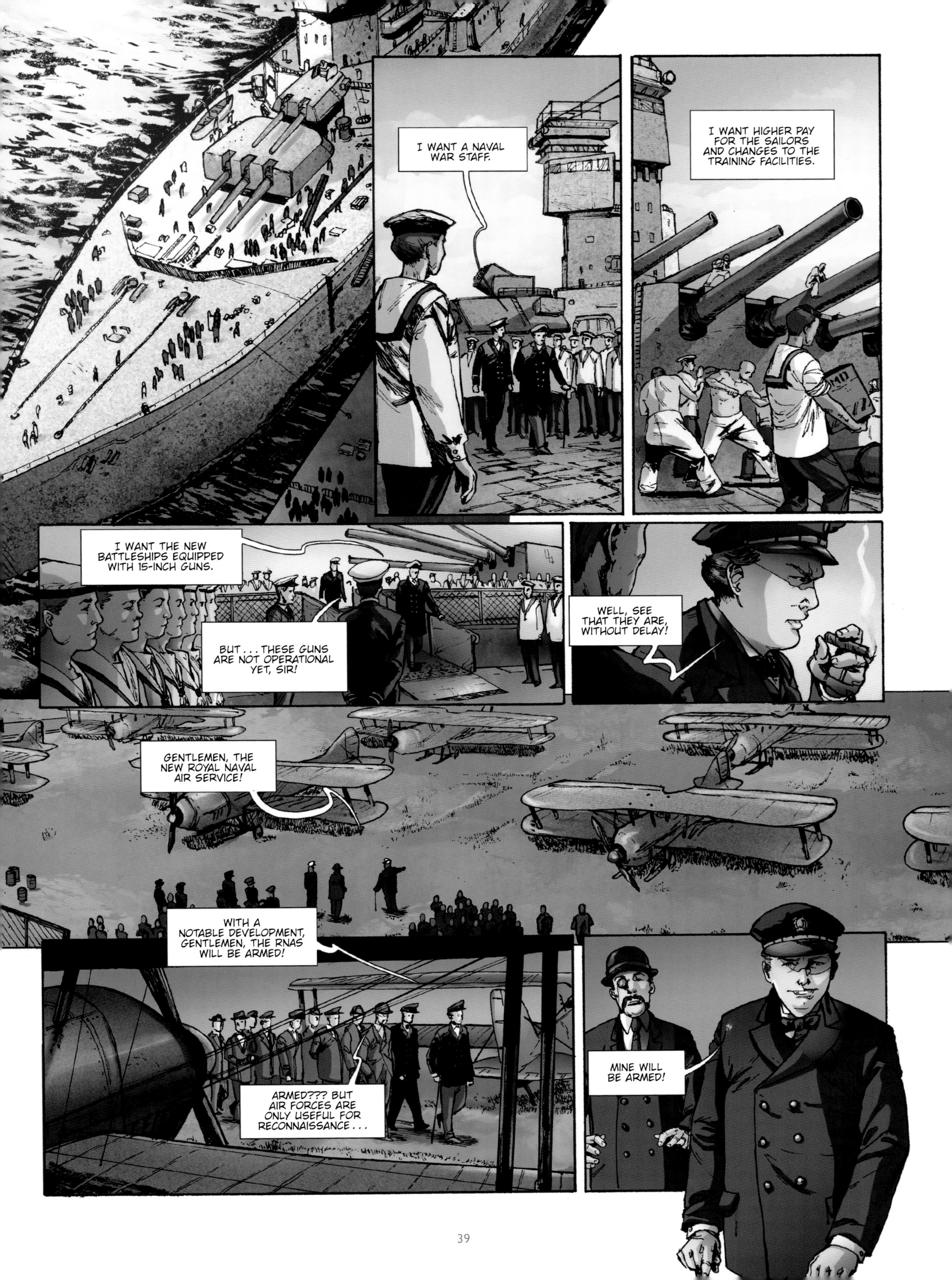
I WANT A NAVAL WAR STAFF.
I WANT HIGHER PAY FOR THE SAILORS AND CHANGES TO THE TRAINING FACILITIES.
I WANT THE NEW BATTLESHIPS EQUIPPED WITH 15-INCH GUNS.
BUT . . . THESE GUNS ARE NOT OPERATIONAL YET, SIR!
WELL, SEE THAT THEY ARE, WITHOUT DELAY!
GENTLEMEN, THE NEW ROYAL NAVAL AIR SERVICE!
WITH A NOTABLE DEVELOPMENT, GENTLEMEN, THE RNAS WILL BE ARMED!
ARMED??? BUT AIR FORCES ARE ONLY USEFUL FOR RECONNAISSANCE . . .
MINE WILL BE ARMED!

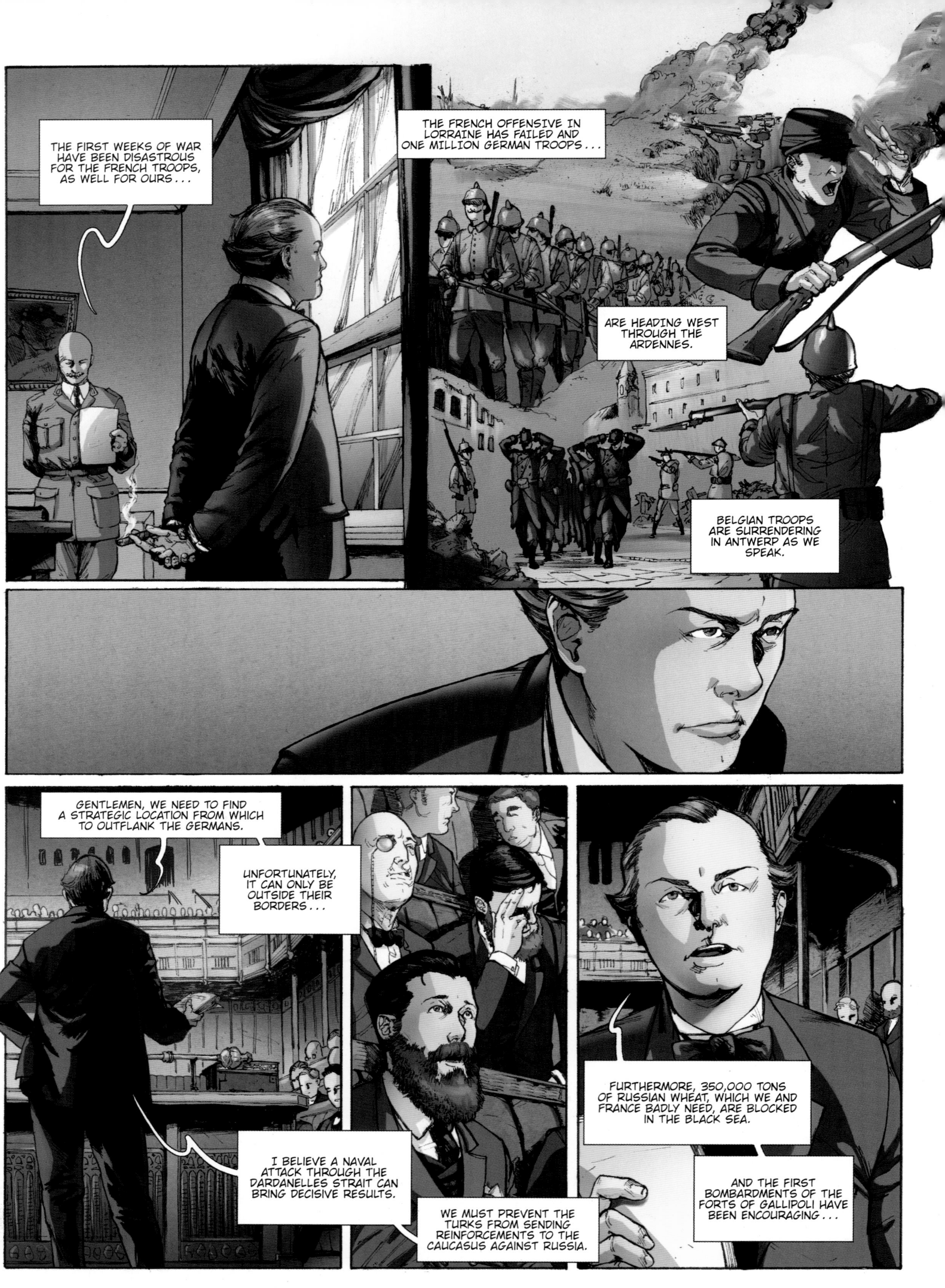

THE FIRST WEEKS OF WAR HAVE BEEN DISASTROUS FOR THE FRENCH TROOPS, AS WELL FOR OURS . . .
THE FRENCH OFFENSIVE IN LORRAINE HAS FAILED AND ONE MILLION GERMAN TROOPS . . .
ARE HEADING WEST THROUGH THE ARDENNES.
BELGIAN TROOPS ARE SURRENDERING IN ANTWERP AS WE SPEAK.
GENTLEMEN, WE NEED TO FIND A STRATEGIC LOCATION FROM WHICH TO OUTFLANK THE GERMANS.
UNFORTUNATELY, IT CAN ONLY BE OUTSIDE THEIR BORDERS . . .
I BELIEVE A NAVAL ATTACK THROUGH THE DARDANELLES STRAIT CAN BRING DECISIVE RESULTS.
WE MUST PREVENT THE TURKS FROM SENDING REINFORCEMENTS TO THE CAUCASUS AGAINST RUSSIA.
FURTHERMORE, 350,000 TONS OF RUSSIAN WHEAT, WHICH WE AND FRANCE BADLY NEED, ARE BLOCKED IN THE BLACK SEA.
AND THE FIRST BOMBARDMENTS OF THE FORTS OF GALLIPOLI HAVE BEEN ENCOURAGING . . .

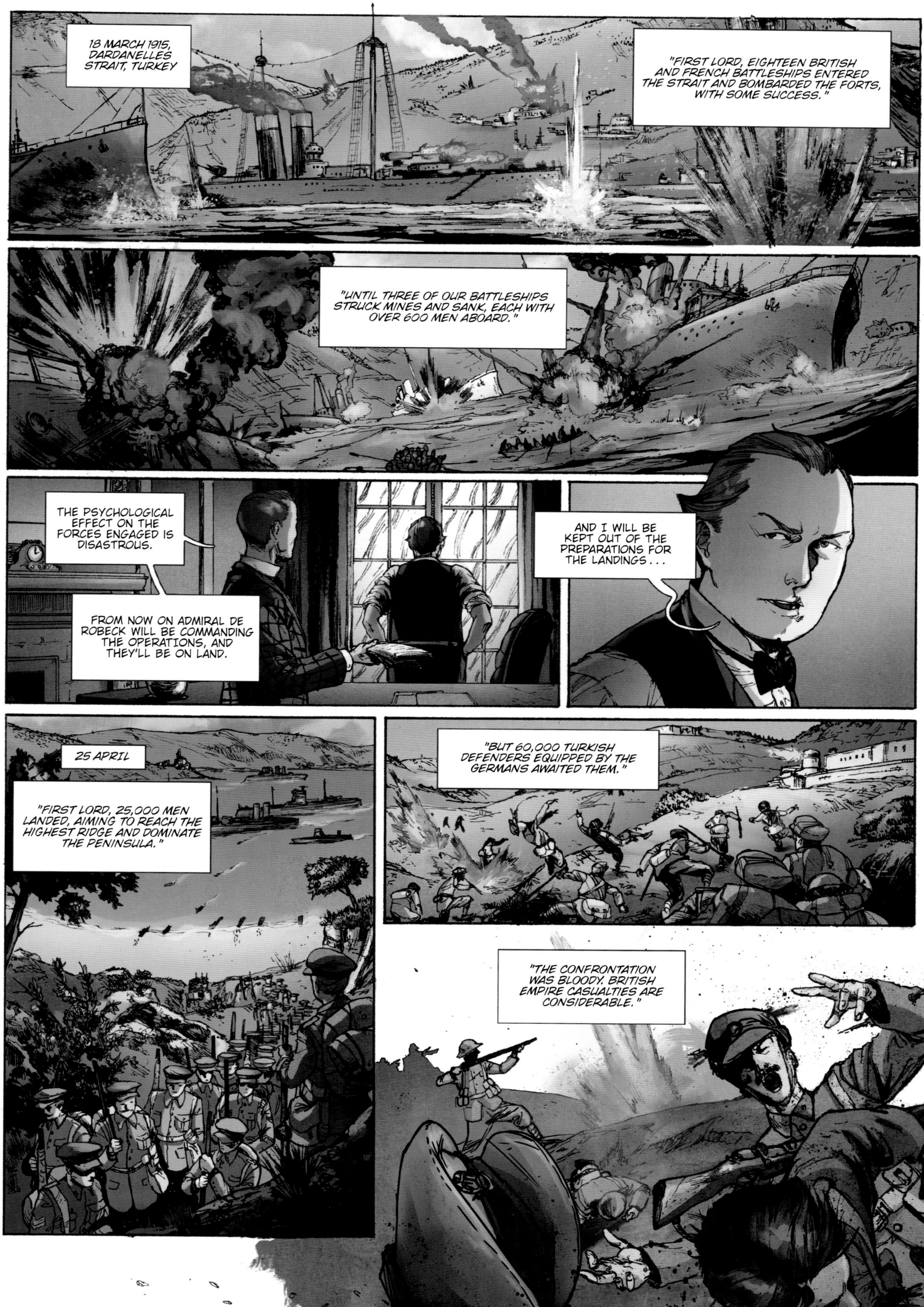
18 MARCH 1915, DARDANELLES STRAIT, TURKEY
"FIRST LORD, EIGHTEEN BRITISH AND FRENCH BATTLESHIPS ENTERED THE STRAIT AND BOMBARDED THE FORTS, WITH SOME SUCCESS."
"UNTIL THREE OF OUR BATTLESHIPS STRUCK MINES AND SANK, EACH WITH OVER 600 MEN ABOARD."
THE PSYCHOLOGICAL EFFECT ON THE FORCES ENGAGED IS DISASTROUS.
FROM NOW ON ADMIRAL DE ROBECK WILL BE COMMANDING THE OPERATIONS, AND THEY'LL BE ON LAND.
AND I WILL BE KEPT OUT OF THE PREPARATIONS FOR THE LANDINGS . . .
25 APRIL
"FIRST LORD, 25,000 MEN LANDED, AIMING TO REACH THE HIGHEST RIDGE AND DOMINATE THE PENINSULA."
"BUT 60,000 TURKISH DEFENDERS EQUIPPED BY THE GERMANS AWAITED THEM."
"THE CONFRONTATION WAS BLOODY. BRITISH EMPIRE CASUALTIES ARE CONSIDERABLE."

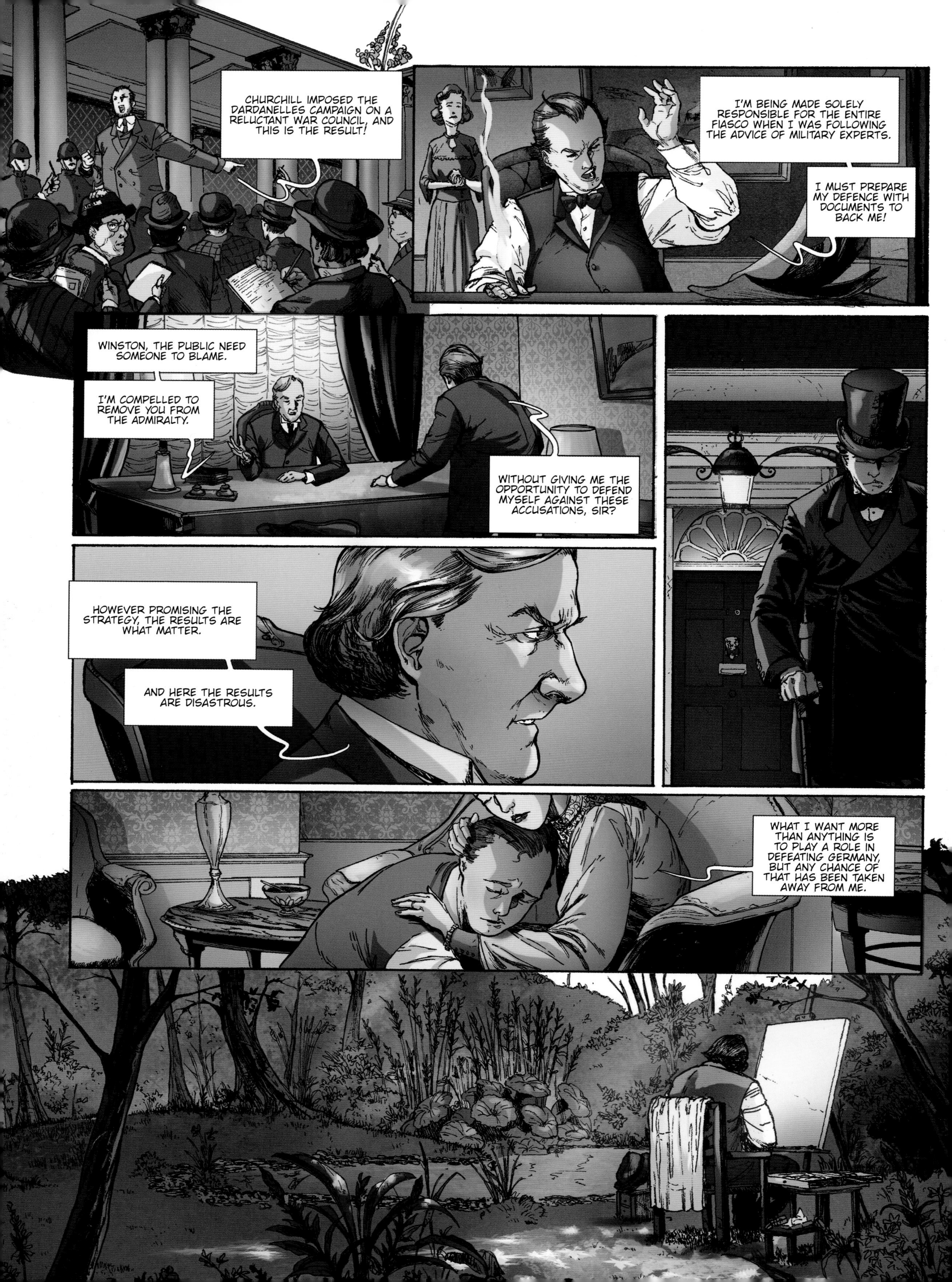
CHURCHILL IMPOSED THE DARDANELLES CAMPAIGN ON A RELUCTANT WAR COUNCIL, AND THIS IS THE RESULT!
I'M BEING MADE SOLELY RESPONSIBLE FOR THE ENTIRE FIASCO WHEN I WAS FOLLOWING THE ADVICE OF MILITARY EXPERTS.
I MUST PREPARE MY DEFENCE WITH DOCUMENTS TO BACK ME!
WINSTON, THE PUBLIC NEED SOMEONE TO BLAME.
I'M COMPELLED TO REMOVE YOU FROM THE ADMIRALTY.
WITHOUT GIVING ME THE OPPORTUNITY TO DEFEND MYSELF AGAINST THESE ACCUSATIONS, SIR?
HOWEVER PROMISING THE STRATEGY, THE RESULTS ARE WHAT MATTER.
AND HERE THE RESULTS ARE DISASTROUS.
WHAT I WANT MORE THAN ANYTHING IS TO PLAY A ROLE IN DEFEATING GERMANY, BUT ANY CHANCE OF THAT HAS BEEN TAKEN AWAY FROM ME.

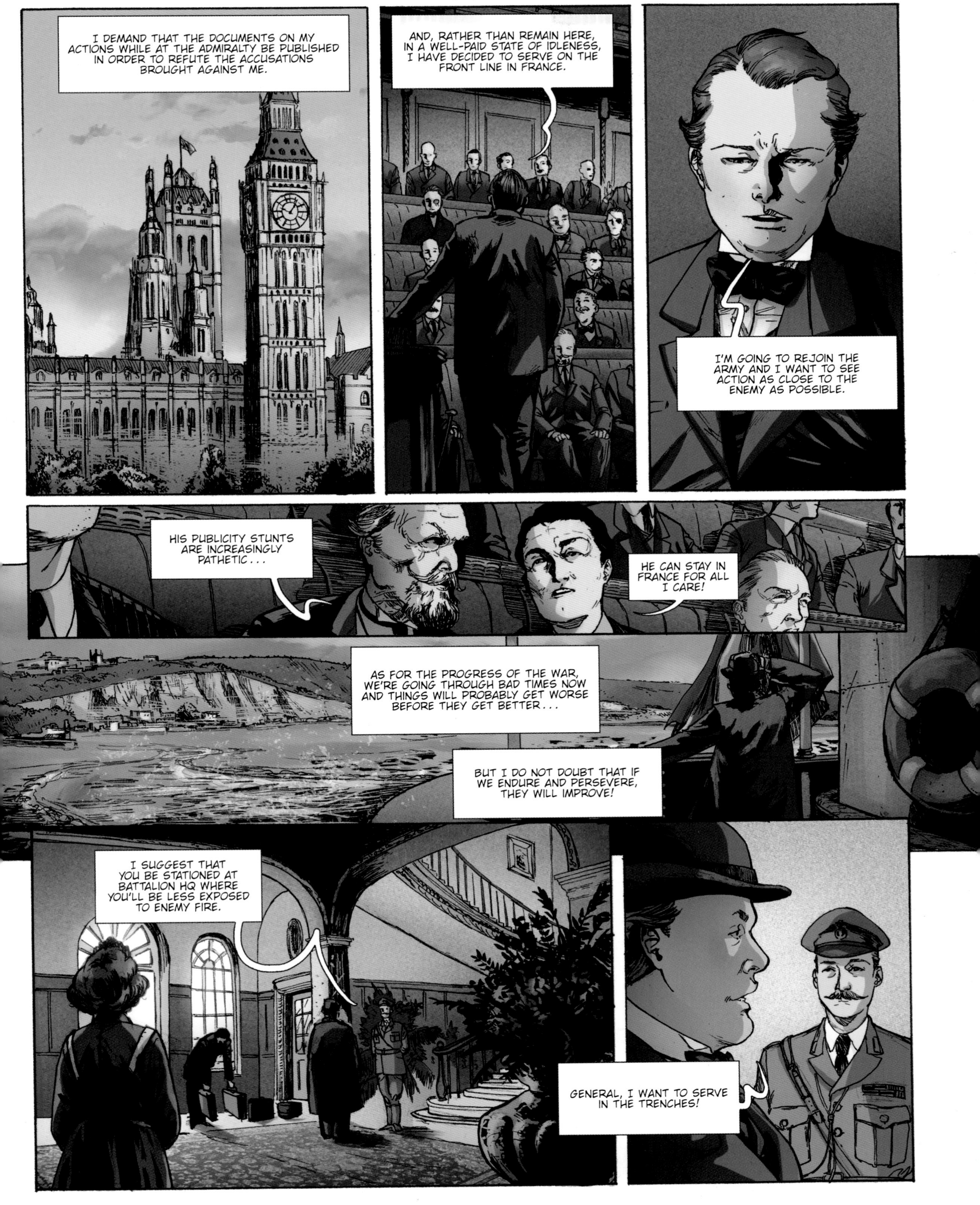
I DEMAND THAT THE DOCUMENTS ON MY ACTIONS WHILE AT THE ADMIRALTY BE PUBLISHED IN ORDER TO REFUTE THE ACCUSATIONS BROUGHT AGAINST ME.
AND, RATHER THAN REMAIN HERE, IN A WELL-PAID STATE OF IDLENESS, I HAVE DECIDED TO SERVE ON THE FRONT LINE IN FRANCE.
I'M GOING TO REJOIN THE ARMY AND I WANT TO SEE ACTION AS CLOSE TO THE ENEMY AS POSSIBLE.
HIS PUBLICITY STUNTS ARE INCREASINGLY PATHETIC . . .
HE CAN STAY IN FRANCE FOR ALL I CARE!
AS FOR THE PROGRESS OF THE WAR, WE'RE GOING THROUGH BAD TIMES NOW AND THINGS WILL PROBABLY GET WORSE BEFORE THEY GET BETTER . . .
BUT I DO NOT DOUBT THAT IF WE ENDURE AND PERSEVERE, THEY WILL IMPROVE!
I SUGGEST THAT YOU BE STATIONED AT BATTALION HQ WHERE YOU'LL BE LESS EXPOSED TO ENEMY FIRE.
GENERAL, I WANT TO SERVE IN THE TRENCHES!

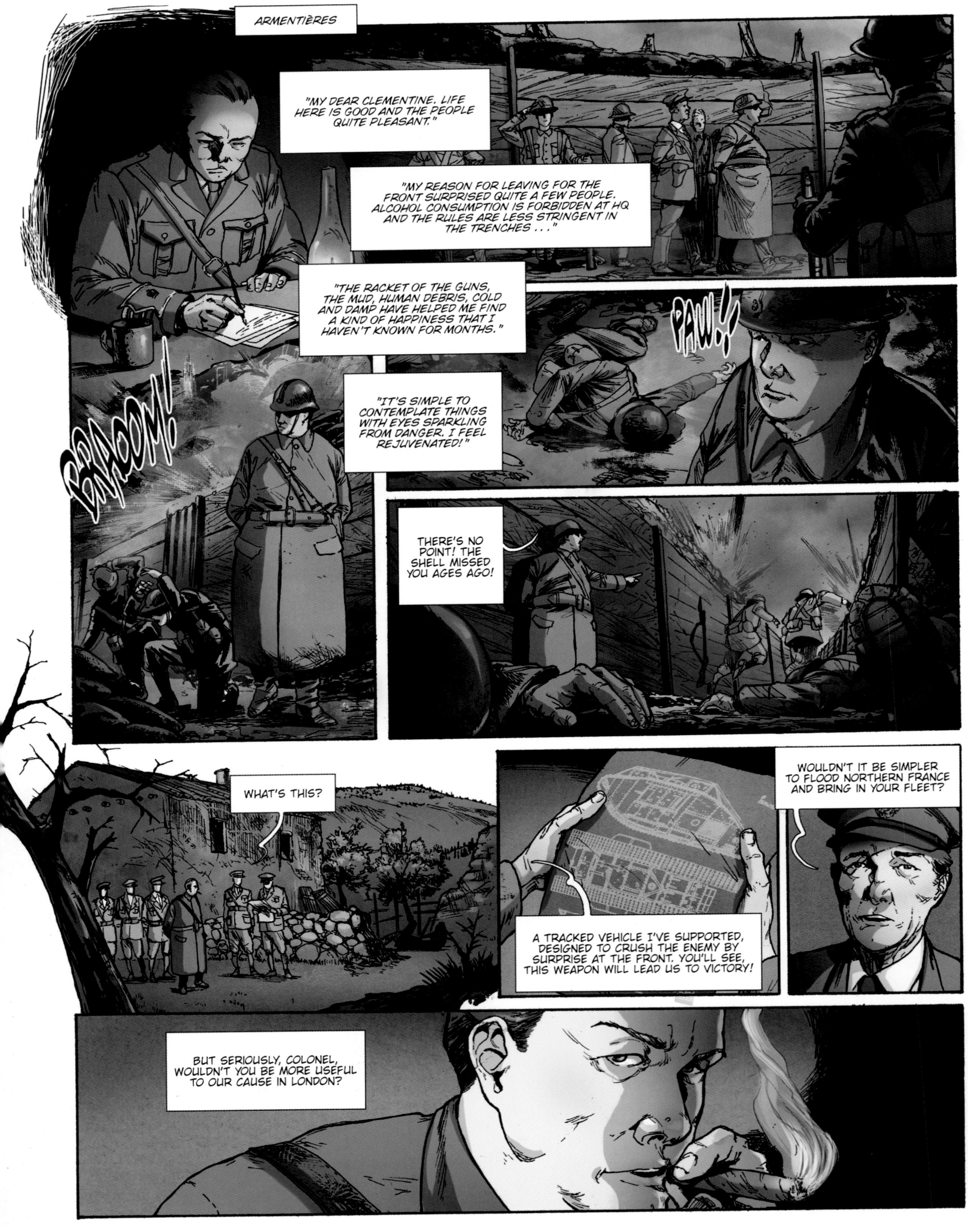
ARMENTIÈRES
"MY DEAR CLEMENTINE. LIFE HERE IS GOOD AND THE PEOPLE QUITE PLEASANT."
"MY REASON FOR LEAVING FOR THE FRONT SURPRISED QUITE A FEW PEOPLE. ALCOHOL CONSUMPTION IS FORBIDDEN AT HQ AND THE RULES ARE LESS STRINGENT IN THE TRENCHES . . ."
"THE RACKET OF THE GUNS, THE MUD, HUMAN DEBRIS, COLD AND DAMP HAVE HELPED ME FIND A KIND OF HAPPINESS THAT I HAVEN'T KNOWN FOR MONTHS."
PAW!
"IT'S SIMPLE TO CONTEMPLATE THINGS WITH EYES SPARKLING FROM DANGER. I FEEL REJUVENATED!"
BRAOOM!
THERE'S NO POINT! THE SHELL MISSED YOU AGES AGO!
WHAT'S THIS?
A TRACKED VEHICLE I'VE SUPPORTED, DESIGNED TO CRUSH THE ENEMY BY SURPRISE AT THE FRONT. YOU'LL SEE, THIS WEAPON WILL LEAD US TO VICTORY!
WOULDN'T IT BE SIMPLER TO FLOOD NORTHERN FRANCE AND BRING IN YOUR FLEET?
BUT SERIOUSLY, COLONEL, WOULDN'T YOU BE MORE USEFUL TO OUR CAUSE IN LONDON?

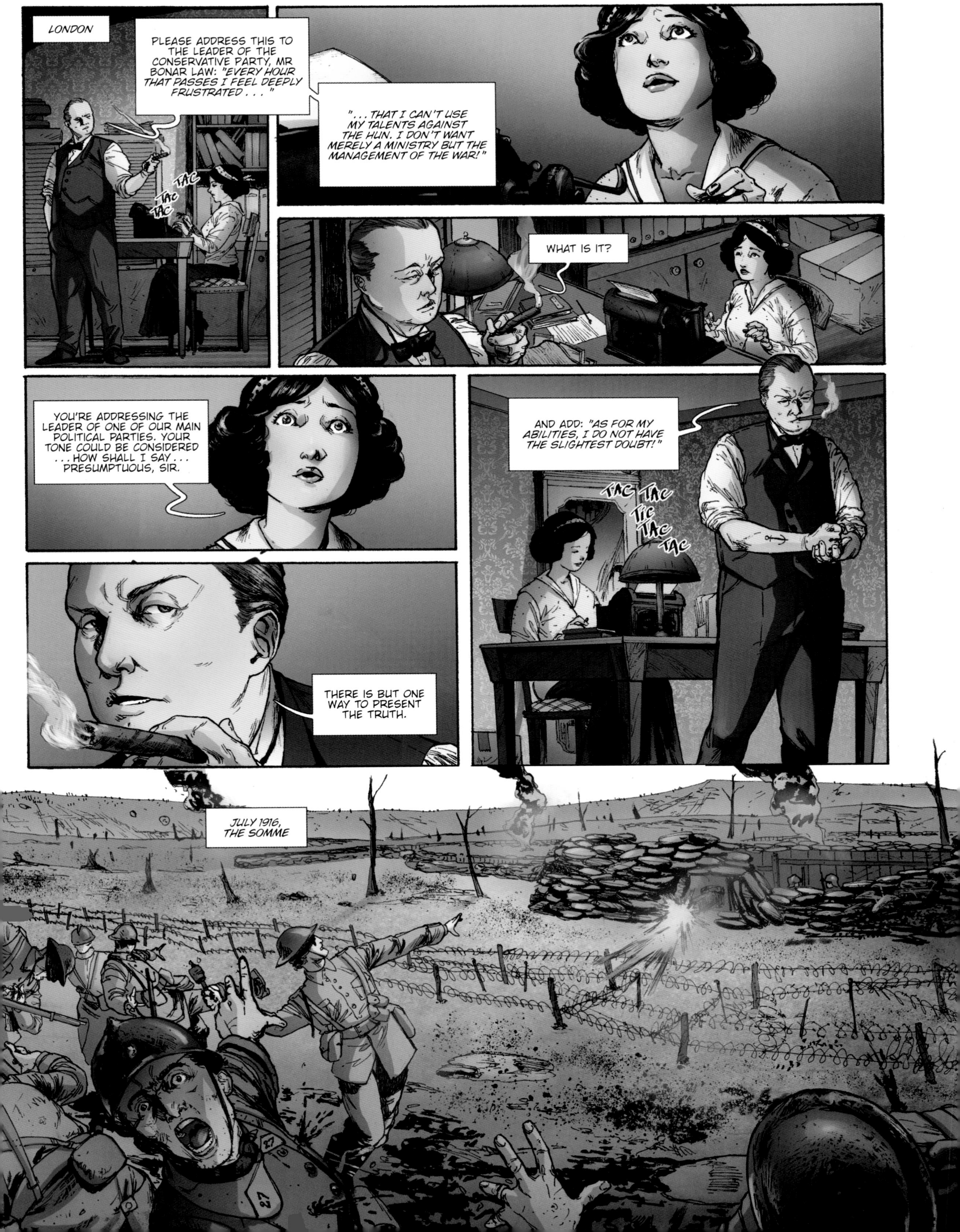
LONDON
PLEASE ADDRESS THIS TO THE LEADER OF THE CONSERVATIVE PARTY, MR BONAR LAW: "EVERY HOUR THAT PASSES I FEEL DEEPLY FRUSTRATED . . . "
TAC
TAC
TAC
" . . . THAT I CAN'T USE MY TALENTS AGAINST THE HUN. I DON'T WANT MERELY A MINISTRY BUT THE MANAGEMENT OF THE WAR!"
WHAT IS IT?
YOU'RE ADDRESSING THE LEADER OF ONE OF OUR MAIN POLITICAL PARTIES. YOUR TONE COULD BE CONSIDERED . . . HOW SHALL I SAY . . . PRESUMPTUOUS, SIR.
AND ADD: "AS FOR MY ABILITIES, I DO NOT HAVE THE SLIGHTEST DOUBT!"
TAC TAC
TIC
TAC
TAC
THERE IS BUT ONE WAY TO PRESENT THE TRUTH.
JULY 1916, THE SOMME

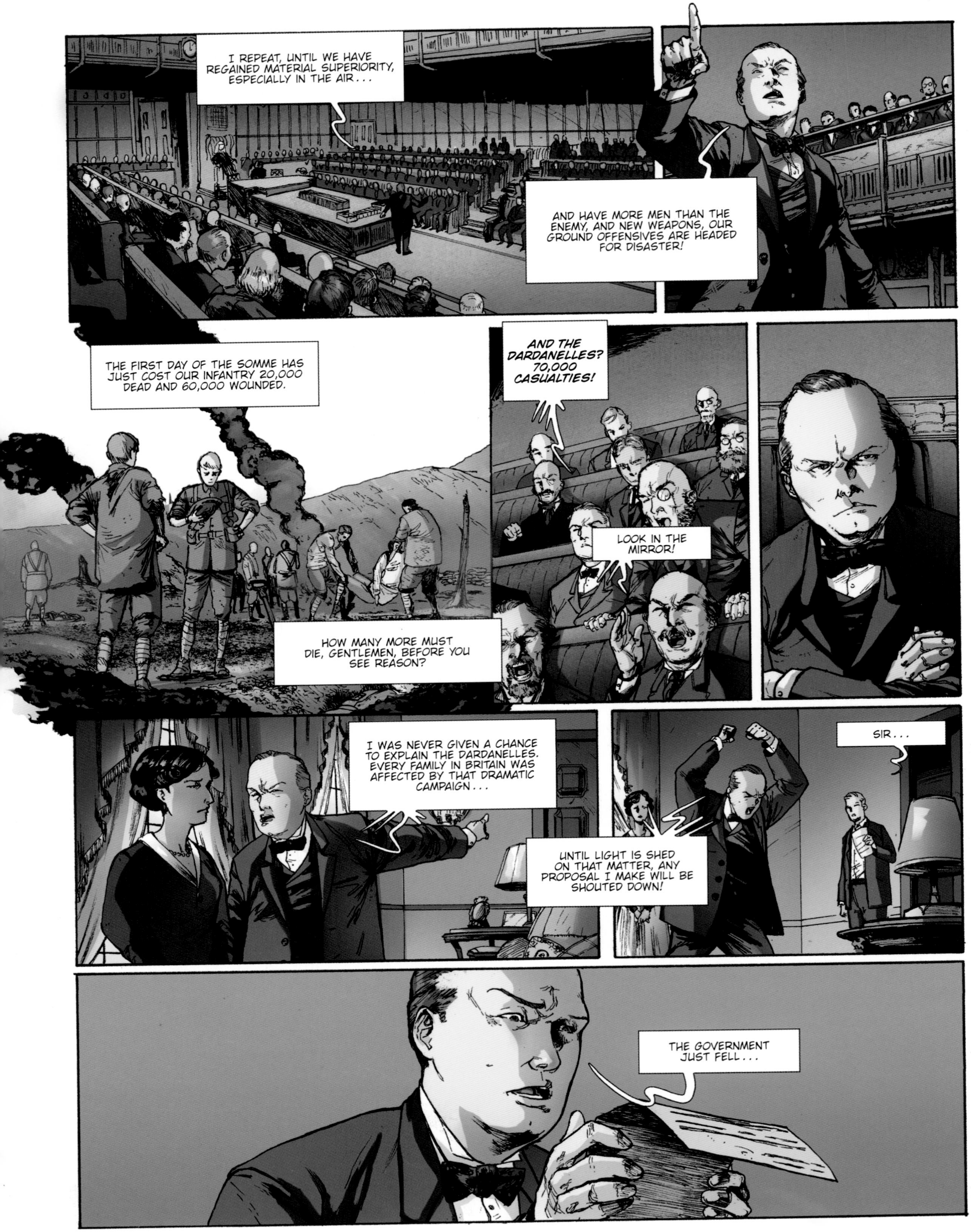

I REPEAT, UNTIL WE HAVE REGAINED MATERIAL SUPERIORITY, ESPECIALLY IN THE AIR . . .
AND HAVE MORE MEN THAN THE ENEMY, AND NEW WEAPONS, OUR GROUND OFFENSIVES ARE HEADED FOR DISASTER!
THE FIRST DAY OF THE SOMME HAS JUST COST OUR INFANTRY 20,000 DEAD AND 60,000 WOUNDED.
HOW MANY MORE MUST DIE, GENTLEMEN, BEFORE YOU SEE REASON?
AND THE DARDANELLES? 70,000 CASUALTIES!
LOOK IN THE MIRROR!
I WAS NEVER GIVEN A CHANCE TO EXPLAIN THE DARDANELLES. EVERY FAMILY IN BRITAIN WAS AFFECTED BY THAT DRAMATIC CAMPAIGN . . .
UNTIL LIGHT IS SHED ON THAT MATTER, ANY PROPOSAL I MAKE WILL BE SHOUTED DOWN!
SIR . . .
THE GOVERNMENT JUST FELL . . .

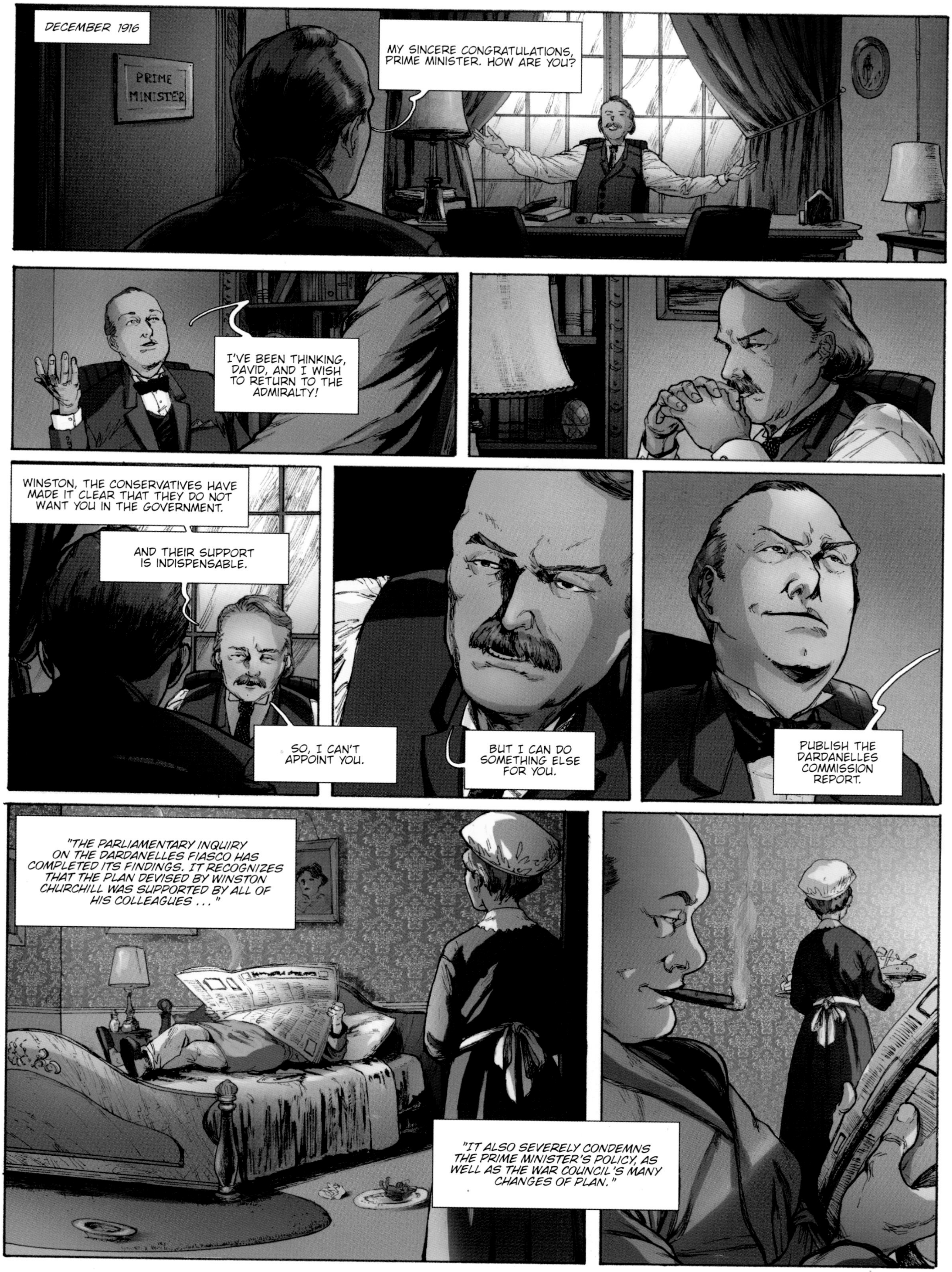
DECEMBER 1916
PRIME MINISTER
MY SINCERE CONGRATULATIONS, PRIME MINISTER. HOW ARE YOU?
I'VE BEEN THINKING, DAVID, AND I WISH TO RETURN TO THE ADMIRALTY!
WINSTON, THE CONSERVATIVES HAVE MADE IT CLEAR THAT THEY DO NOT WANT YOU IN THE GOVERNMENT.
AND THEIR SUPPORT IS INDISPENSABLE.
SO, I CAN'T APPOINT YOU.
BUT I CAN DO SOMETHING ELSE FOR YOU.
PUBLISH THE DARDANELLES COMMISSION REPORT.
"THE PARLIAMENTARY INQUIRY ON THE DARDANELLES FIASCO HAS COMPLETED ITS FINDINGS. IT RECOGNIZES THAT THE PLAN DEVISED BY WINSTON CHURCHILL WAS SUPPORTED BY ALL OF HIS COLLEAGUES . . ."
"IT ALSO SEVERELY CONDEMNS THE PRIME MINISTER'S POLICY, AS WELL AS THE WAR COUNCIL'S MANY CHANGES OF PLAN."

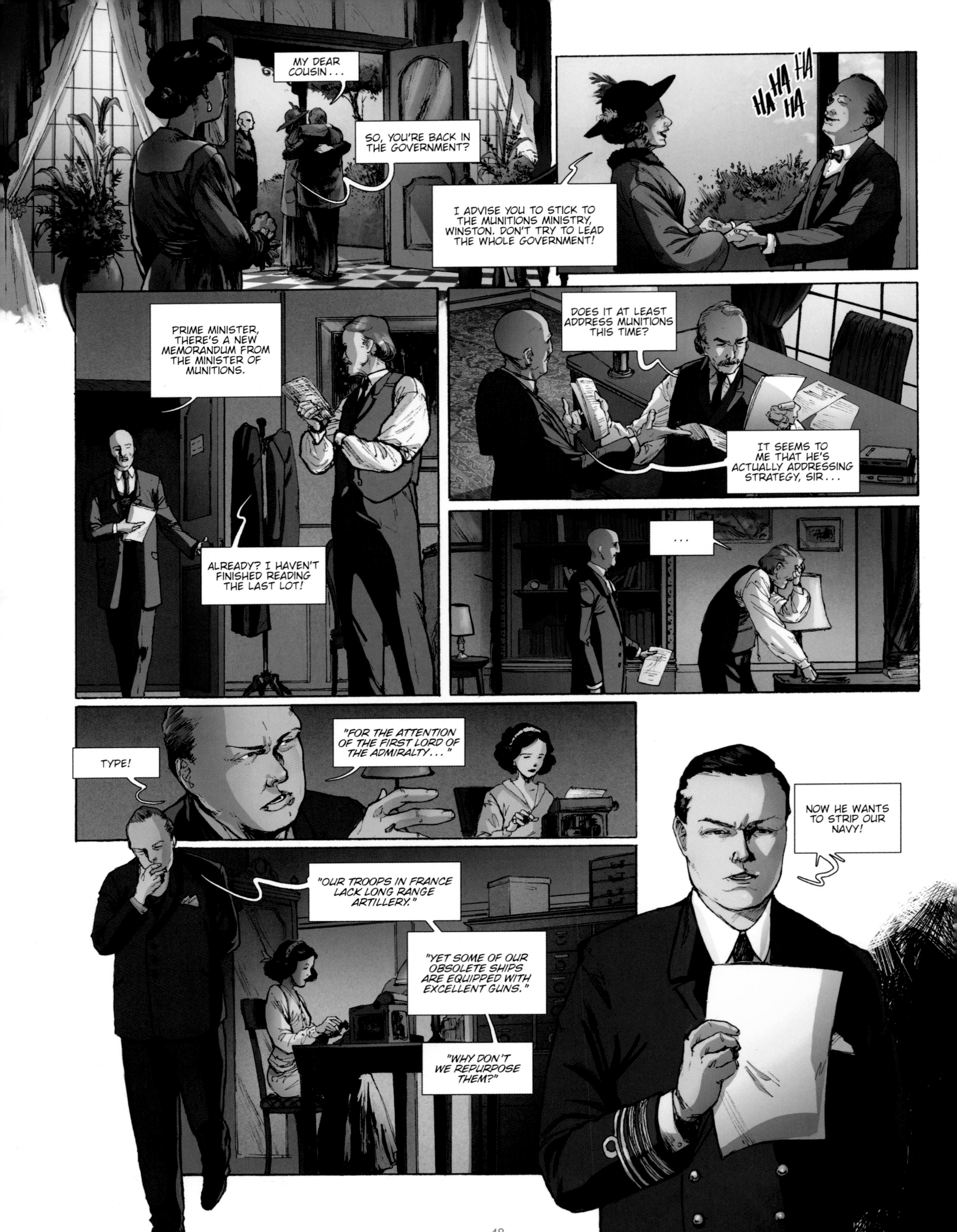
MY DEAR COUSIN . . .
SO, YOU'RE BACK IN THE GOVERNMENT?
I ADVISE YOU TO STICK TO THE MUNITIONS MINISTRY, WINSTON. DON'T TRY TO LEAD THE WHOLE GOVERNMENT!
HA HA HA HA
PRIME MINISTER, THERE'S A NEW MEMORANDUM FROM THE MINISTER OF MUNITIONS.
ALREADY? I HAVEN'T FINISHED READING THE LAST LOT!
DOES IT AT LEAST ADDRESS MUNITIONS THIS TIME?
IT SEEMS TO ME THAT HE'S ACTUALLY ADDRESSING STRATEGY, SIR . . .
. . .
TYPE!
"FOR THE ATTENTION OF THE FIRST LORD OF THE ADMIRALTY . . . "
"OUR TROOPS IN FRANCE LACK LONG RANGE ARTILLERY."
"YET SOME OF OUR OBSOLETE SHIPS ARE EQUIPPED WITH EXCELLENT GUNS."
"WHY DON'T WE REPURPOSE THEM?"
NOW HE WANTS TO STRIP OUR NAVY!

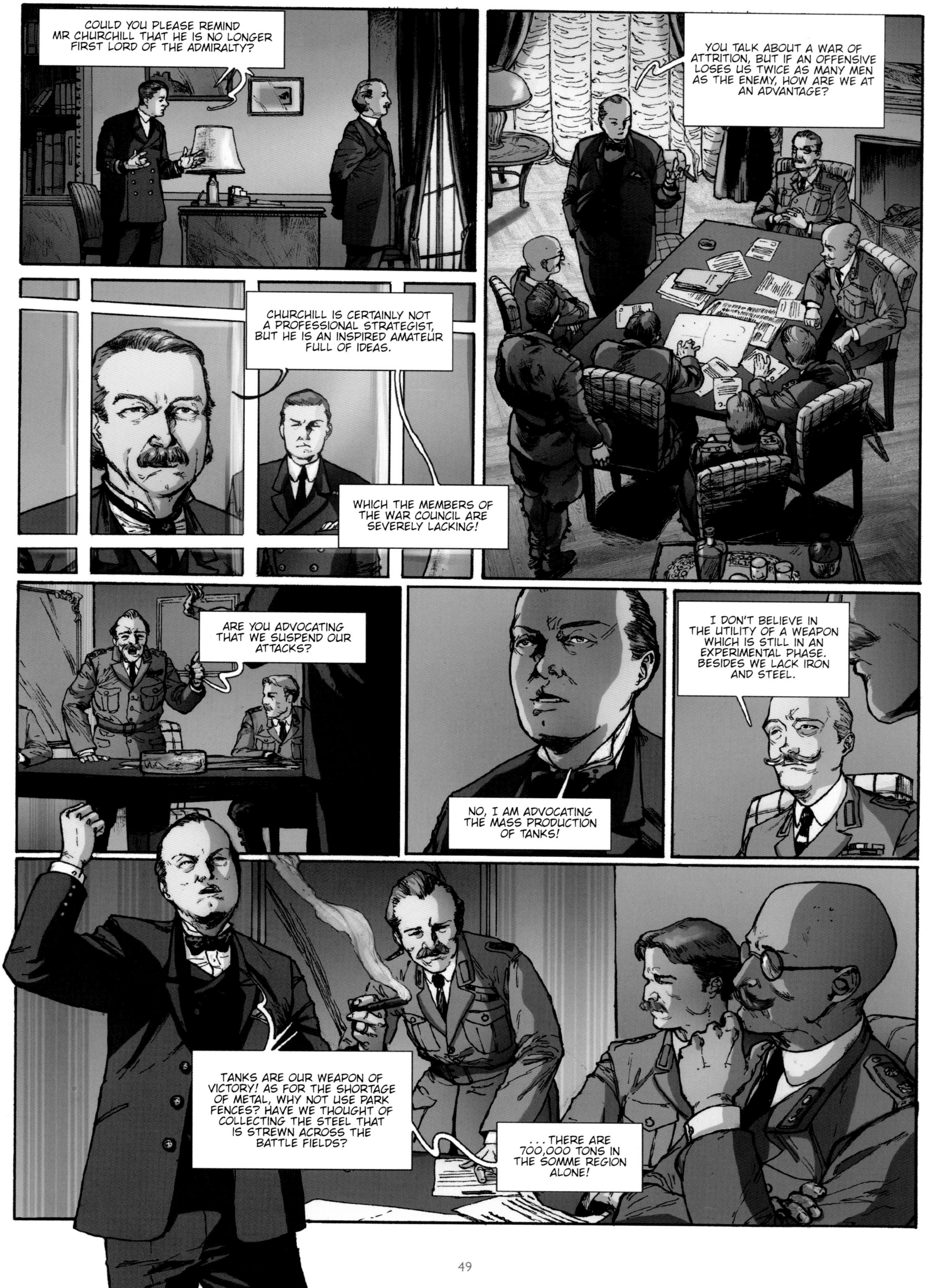

COULD YOU PLEASE REMIND MR CHURCHILL THAT HE IS NO LONGER FIRST LORD OF THE ADMIRALTY?
YOU TALK ABOUT A WAR OF ATTRITION, BUT IF AN OFFENSIVE LOSES US TWICE AS MANY MEN AS THE ENEMY, HOW ARE WE AT AN ADVANTAGE?
CHURCHILL IS CERTAINLY NOT A PROFESSIONAL STRATEGIST, BUT HE IS AN INSPIRED AMATEUR FULL OF IDEAS.
WHICH THE MEMBERS OF THE WAR COUNCIL ARE SEVERELY LACKING!
ARE YOU ADVOCATING THAT WE SUSPEND OUR ATTACKS?
NO, I AM ADVOCATING THE MASS PRODUCTION OF TANKS!
I DON'T BELIEVE IN THE UTILITY OF A WEAPON WHICH IS STILL IN AN EXPERIMENTAL PHASE. BESIDES WE LACK IRON AND STEEL.
TANKS ARE OUR WEAPON OF VICTORY! AS FOR THE SHORTAGE OF METAL, WHY NOT USE PARK FENCES? HAVE WE THOUGHT OF COLLECTING THE STEEL THAT IS STREWN ACROSS THE BATTLE FIELDS?
. . . THERE ARE 700,000 TONS IN THE SOMME REGION ALONE!

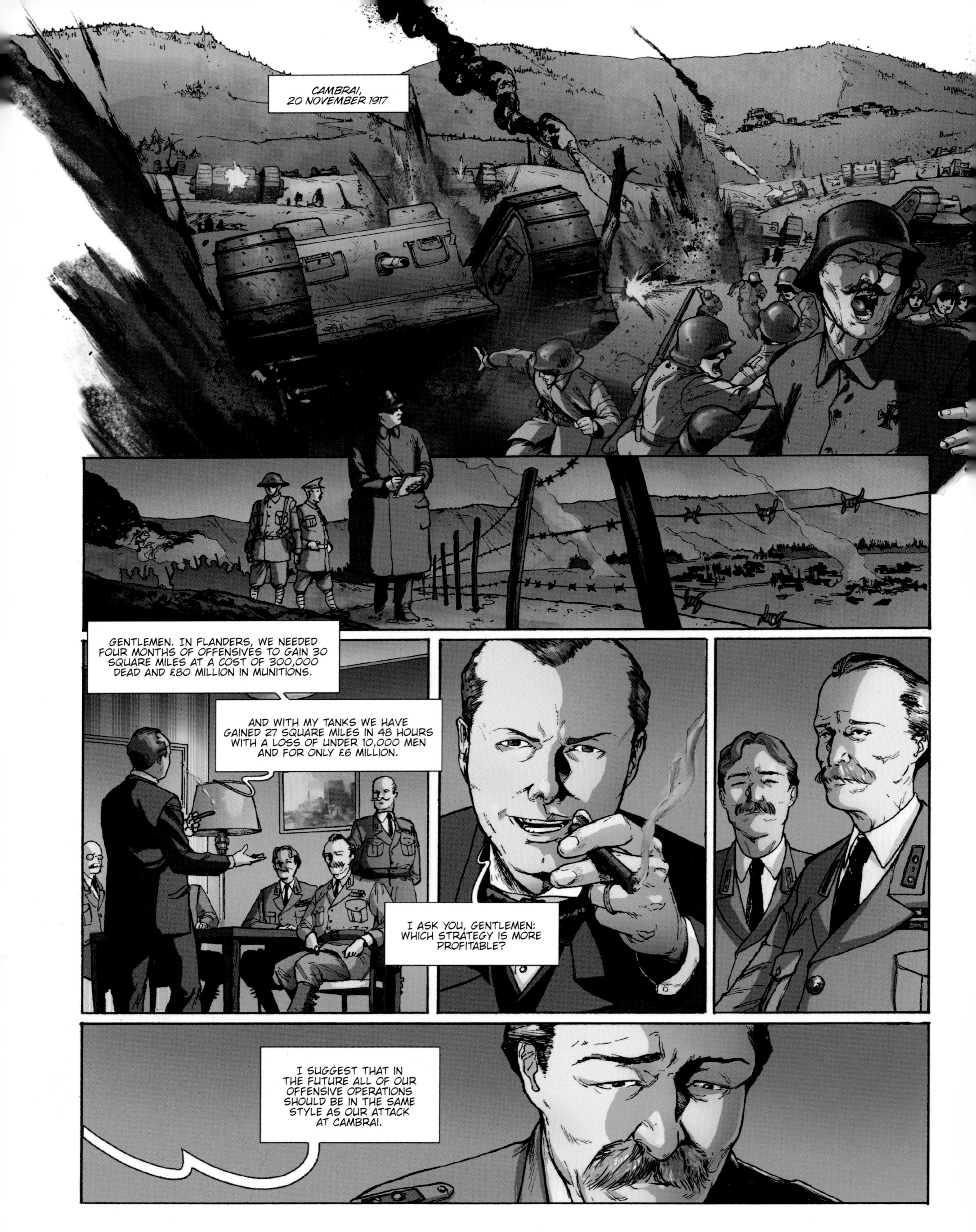
CAMBRAI,
20 NOVEMBER 1917
GENTLEMEN. IN FLANDERS, WE NEEDED FOUR MONTHS OF OFFENSIVES TO GAIN 30 SQUARE MILES AT A COST OF 300,000 DEAD AND £80 MILLION IN MUNITIONS.
AND WITH MY TANKS WE HAVE GAINED 27 SQUARE MILES IN 48 HOURS WITH A LOSS OF UNDER 10,000 MEN AND FOR ONLY £6 MILLION.
I ASK YOU, GENTLEMEN: WHICH STRATEGY IS MORE PROFITABLE?
I SUGGEST THAT IN THE FUTURE ALL OF OUR OFFENSIVE OPERATIONS SHOULD BE IN THE SAME STYLE AS OUR ATTACK AT CAMBRAI.

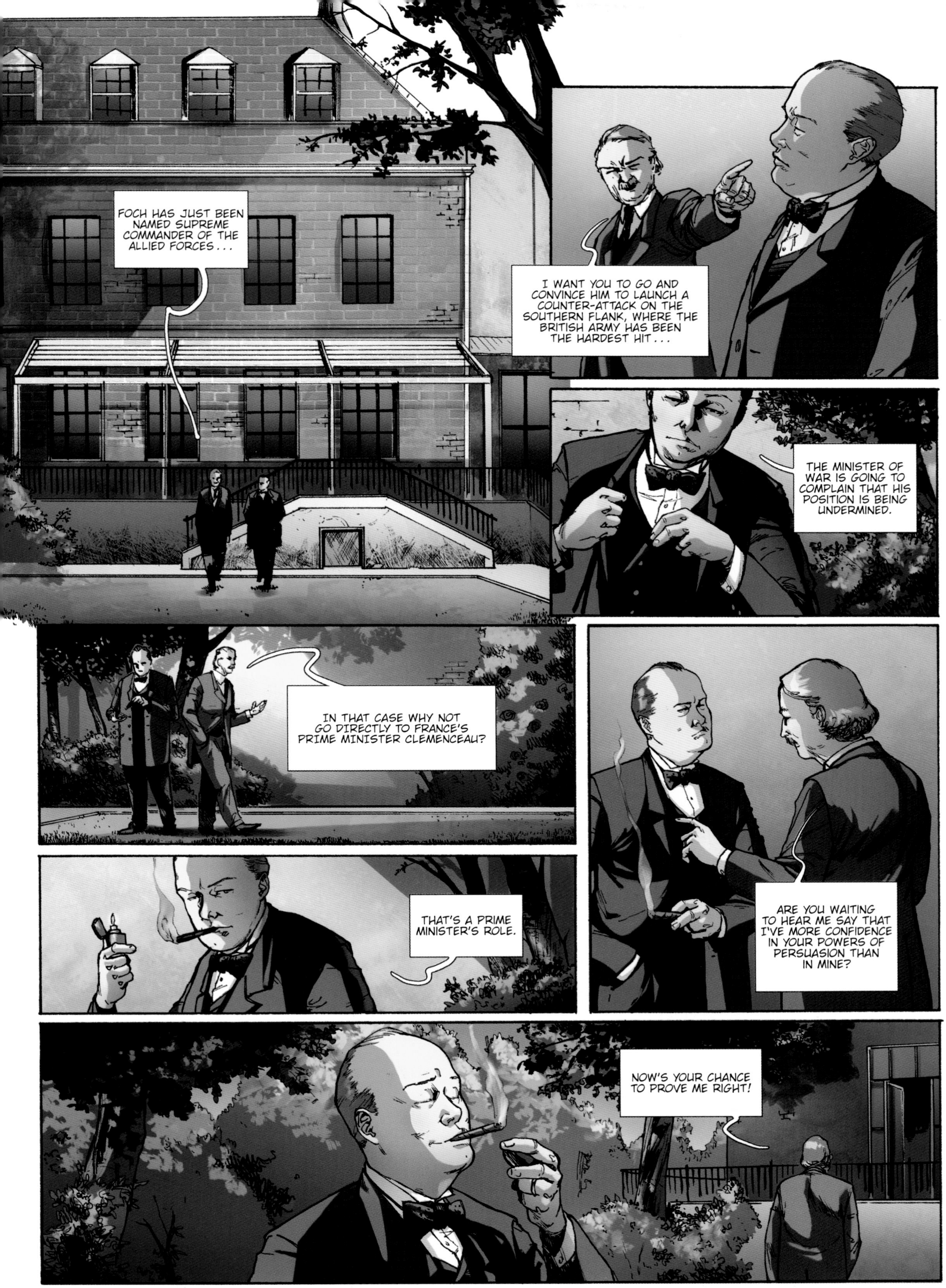
FOCH HAS JUST BEEN NAMED SUPREME COMMANDER OF THE ALLIED FORCES . . .
I WANT YOU TO GO AND CONVINCE HIM TO LAUNCH A COUNTER-ATTACK ON THE SOUTHERN FLANK, WHERE THE BRITISH ARMY HAS BEEN THE HARDEST HIT . . .
THE MINISTER OF WAR IS GOING TO COMPLAIN THAT HIS POSITION IS BEING UNDERMINED.
IN THAT CASE WHY NOT GO DIRECTLY TO FRANCE'S PRIME MINISTER CLEMENCEAU?
THAT'S A PRIME MINISTER'S ROLE.
ARE YOU WAITING TO HEAR ME SAY THAT I'VE MORE CONFIDENCE IN YOUR POWERS OF PERSUASION THAN IN MINE?
NOW'S YOUR CHANCE TO PROVE ME RIGHT!

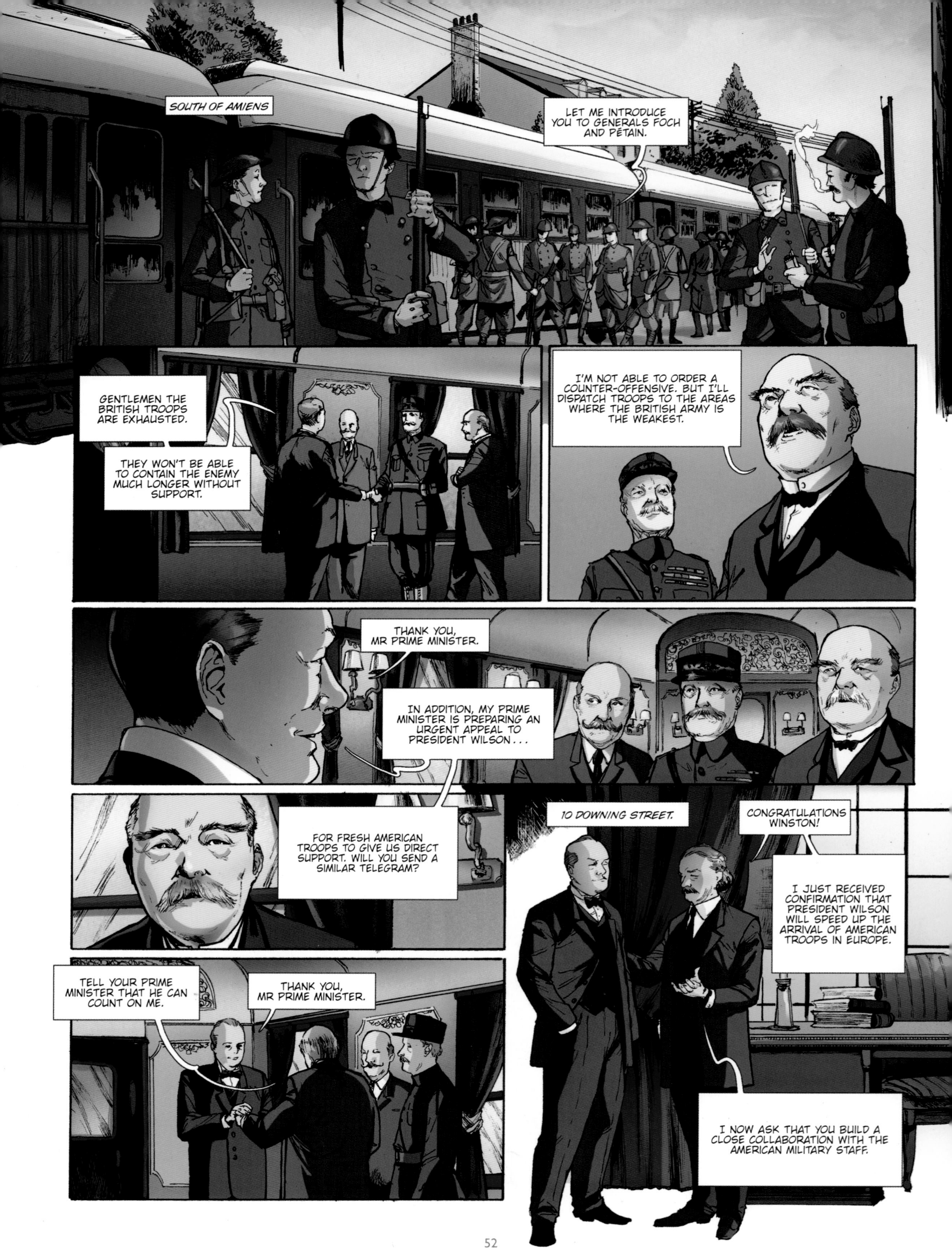

SOUTH OF AMIENS
LET ME INTRODUCE YOU TO GENERALS FOCH AND PÉTAIN.
GENTLEMEN THE BRITISH TROOPS ARE EXHAUSTED.
THEY WON'T BE ABLE TO CONTAIN THE ENEMY MUCH LONGER WITHOUT SUPPORT.
I'M NOT ABLE TO ORDER A COUNTER-OFFENSIVE. BUT I'LL DISPATCH TROOPS TO THE AREAS WHERE THE BRITISH ARMY IS THE WEAKEST.
THANK YOU, MR PRIME MINISTER.
IN ADDITION, MY PRIME MINISTER IS PREPARING AN URGENT APPEAL TO PRESIDENT WILSON . . .
FOR FRESH AMERICAN TROOPS TO GIVE US DIRECT SUPPORT. WILL YOU SEND A SIMILAR TELEGRAM?
TELL YOUR PRIME MINISTER THAT HE CAN COUNT ON ME.
THANK YOU, MR PRIME MINISTER.
10 DOWNING STREET.
CONGRATULATIONS WINSTON!
I JUST RECEIVED CONFIRMATION THAT PRESIDENT WILSON WILL SPEED UP THE ARRIVAL OF AMERICAN TROOPS IN EUROPE.
I NOW ASK THAT YOU BUILD A CLOSE COLLABORATION WITH THE AMERICAN MILITARY STAFF.

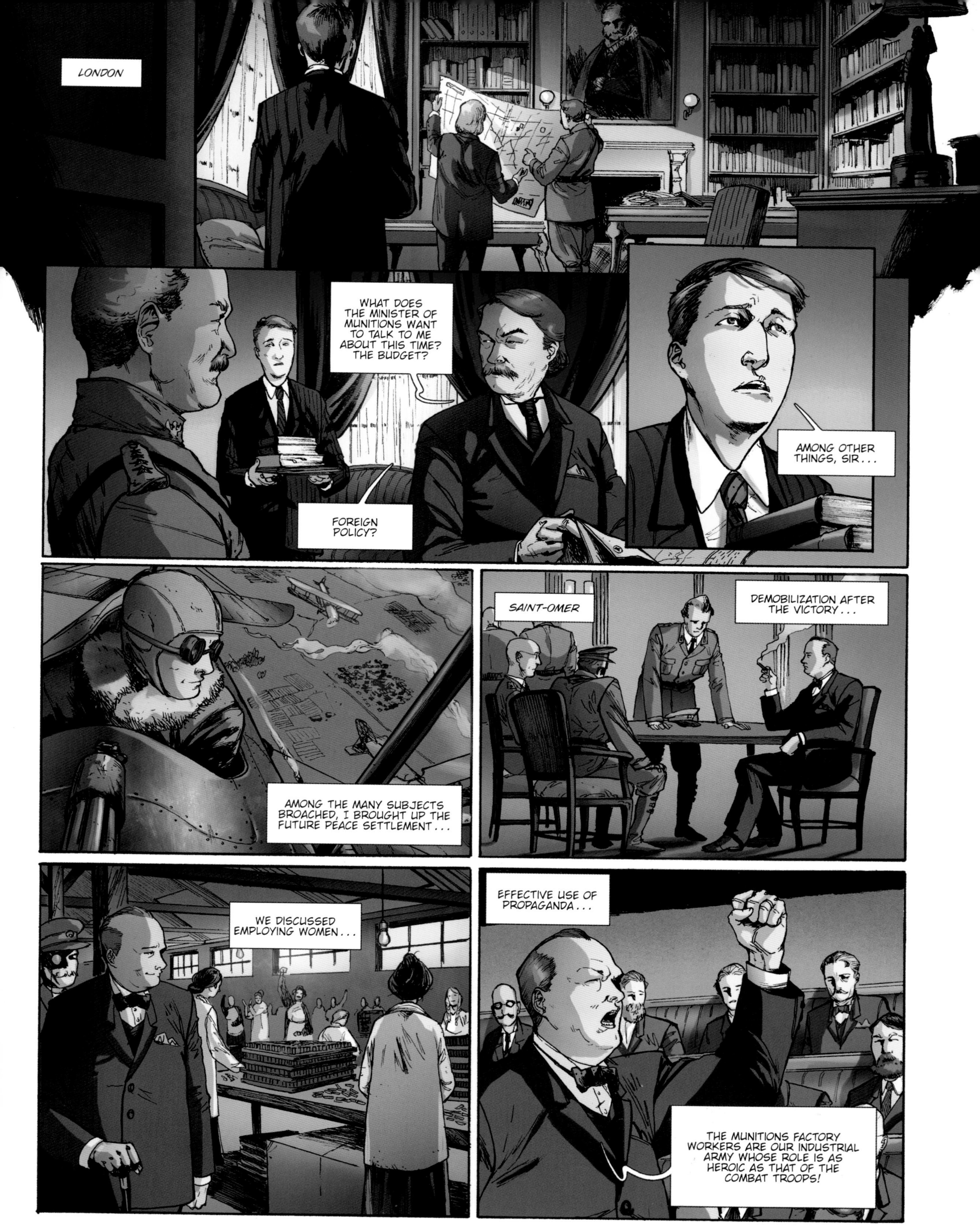
LONDON
WHAT DOES THE MINISTER OF MUNITIONS WANT TO TALK TO ME ABOUT THIS TIME? THE BUDGET?
FOREIGN POLICY?
AMONG OTHER THINGS, SIR...
AMONG THE MANY SUBJECTS BROACHED, I BROUGHT UP THE FUTURE PEACE SETTLEMENT...
SAINT-OMER
DEMOBILIZATION AFTER THE VICTORY...
WE DISCUSSED EMPLOYING WOMEN...
EFFECTIVE USE OF PROPAGANDA...
THE MUNITIONS FACTORY WORKERS ARE OUR INDUSTRIAL ARMY WHOSE ROLE IS AS HEROIC AS THAT OF THE COMBAT TROOPS!

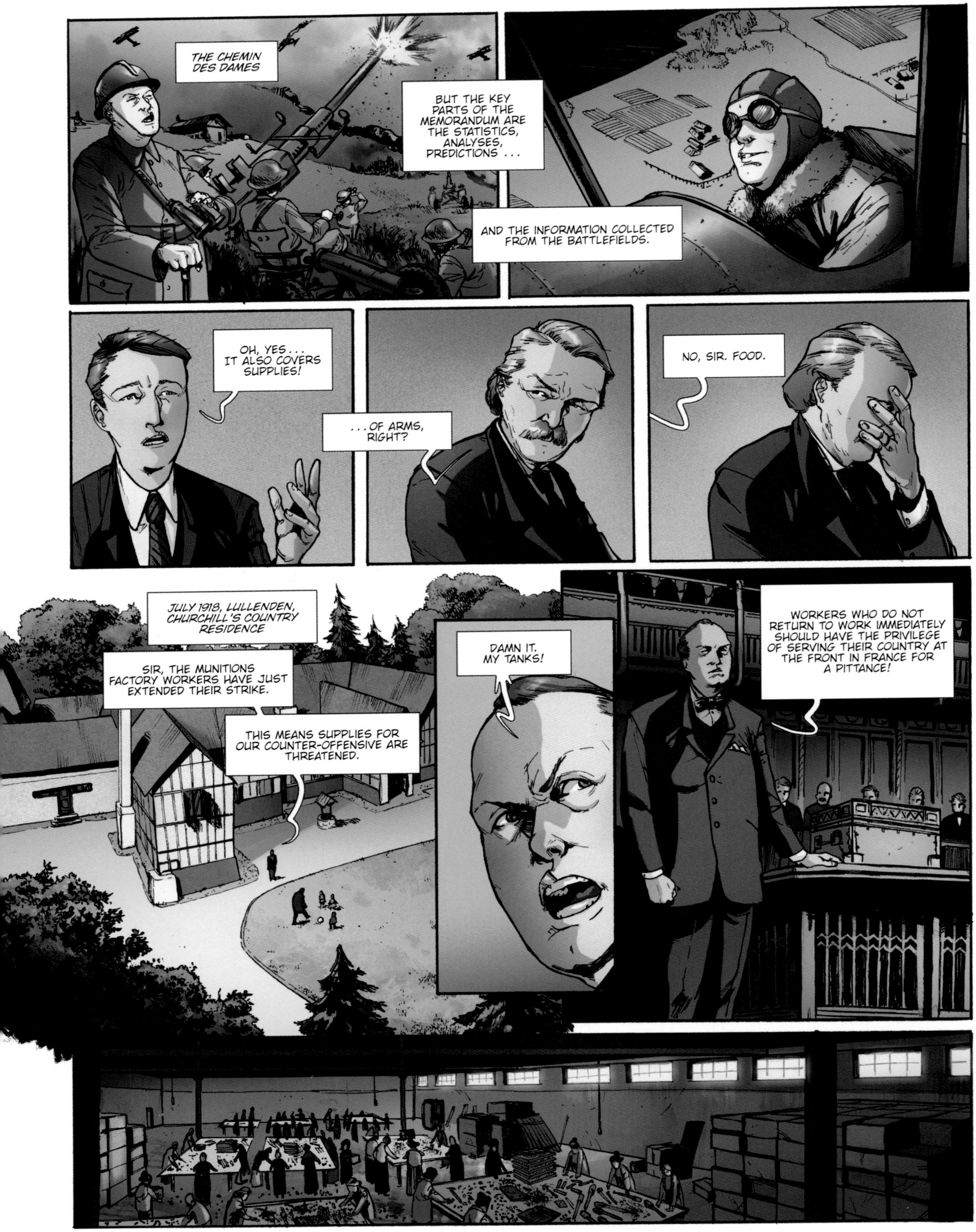
THE CHEMIN DES DAMES
BUT THE KEY PARTS OF THE MEMORANDUM ARE THE STATISTICS, ANALYSES, PREDICTIONS . . .
AND THE INFORMATION COLLECTED FROM THE BATTLEFIELDS.
OH, YES . . . IT ALSO COVERS SUPPLIES!
. . . OF ARMS, RIGHT?
NO, SIR. FOOD.
JULY 1918, LULLENDEN, CHURCHILL'S COUNTRY RESIDENCE
SIR, THE MUNITIONS FACTORY WORKERS HAVE JUST EXTENDED THEIR STRIKE.
THIS MEANS SUPPLIES FOR OUR COUNTER-OFFENSIVE ARE THREATENED.
DAMN IT. MY TANKS!
WORKERS WHO DO NOT RETURN TO WORK IMMEDIATELY SHOULD HAVE THE PRIVILEGE OF SERVING THEIR COUNTRY AT THE FRONT IN FRANCE FOR A PITTANCE!

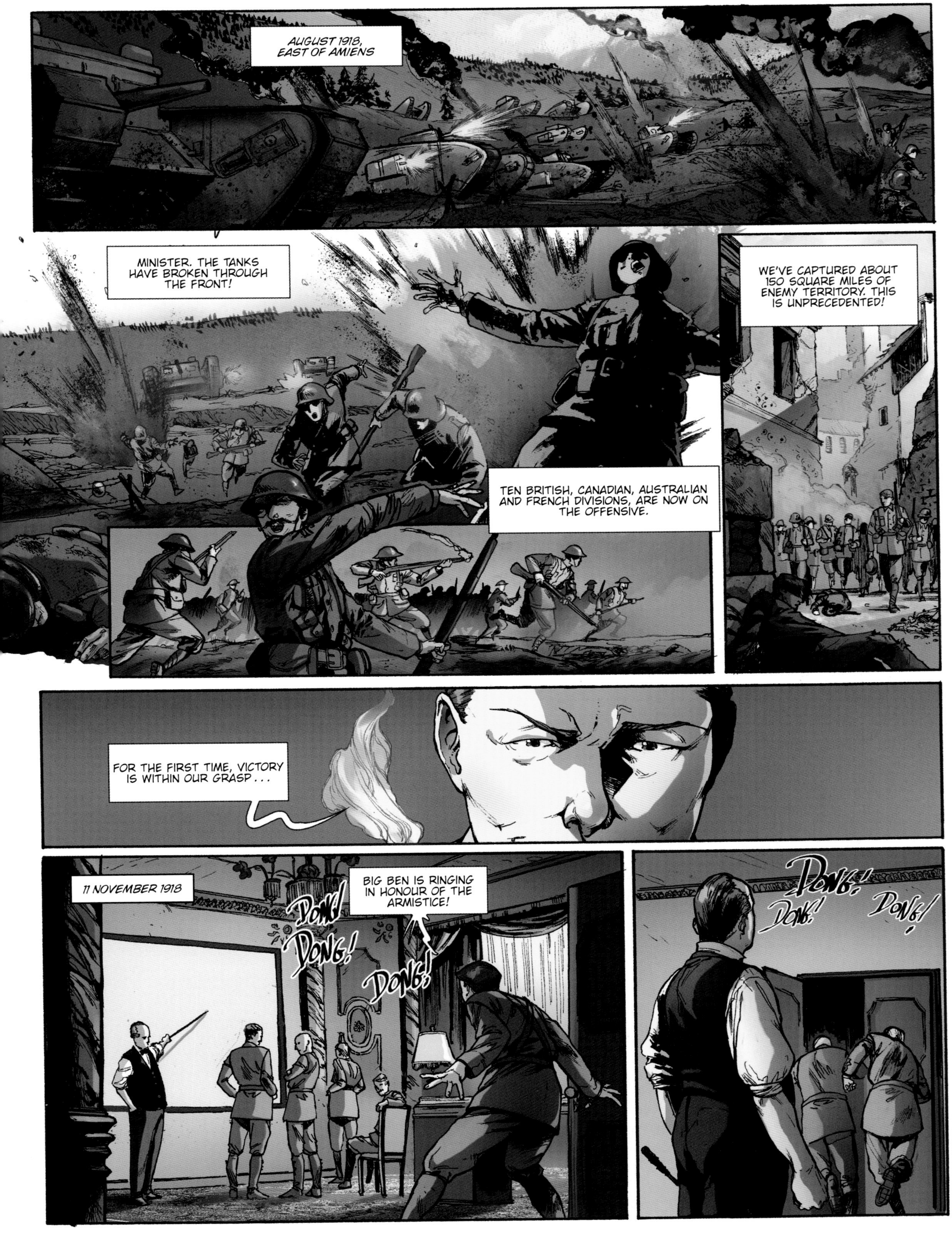
AUGUST 1918, EAST OF AMIENS
MINISTER. THE TANKS HAVE BROKEN THROUGH THE FRONT!
WE'VE CAPTURED ABOUT 150 SQUARE MILES OF ENEMY TERRITORY. THIS IS UNPRECEDENTED!
TEN BRITISH, CANADIAN, AUSTRALIAN AND FRENCH DIVISIONS, ARE NOW ON THE OFFENSIVE.
FOR THE FIRST TIME, VICTORY IS WITHIN OUR GRASP . . .
11 NOVEMBER 1918
BIG BEN IS RINGING IN HONOUR OF THE ARMISTICE!
DONG!
DONG!
DONG!
DONG!
DONG!
DONG!

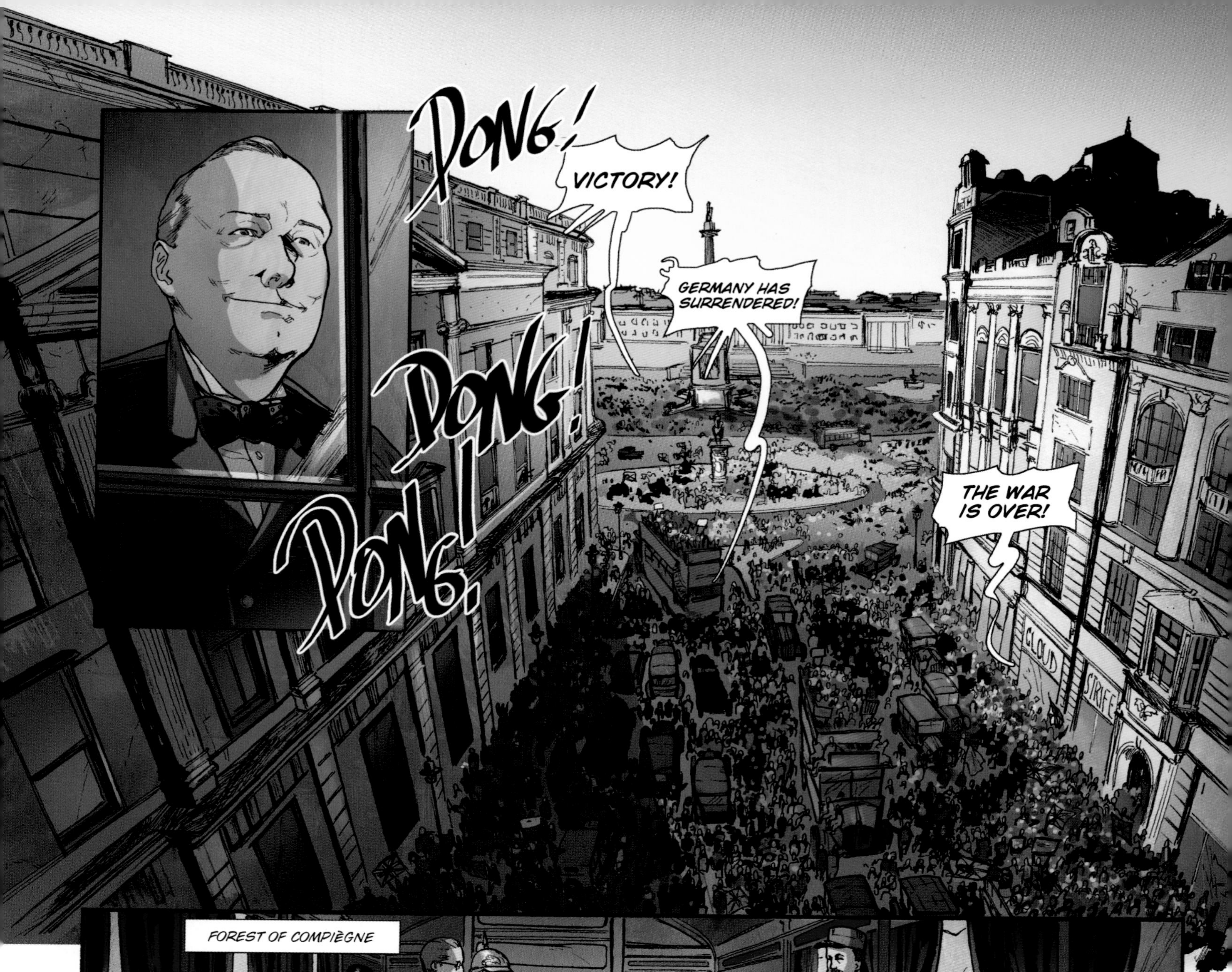
DONG!
VICTORY!
GERMANY HAS SURRENDERED!
DONG!
DONG!
THE WAR IS OVER!
GLOUD
STREE

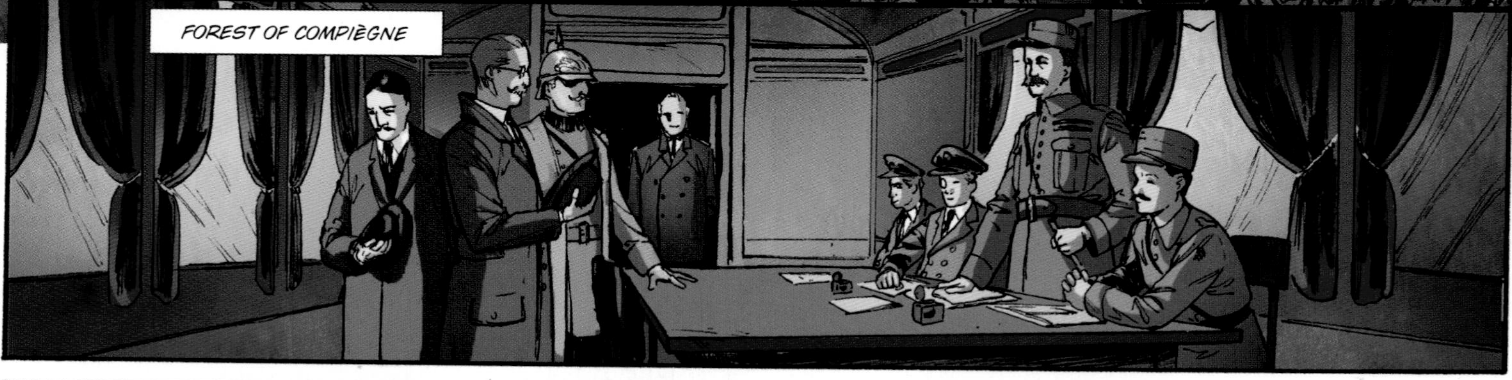
FOREST OF COMPIÈGNE

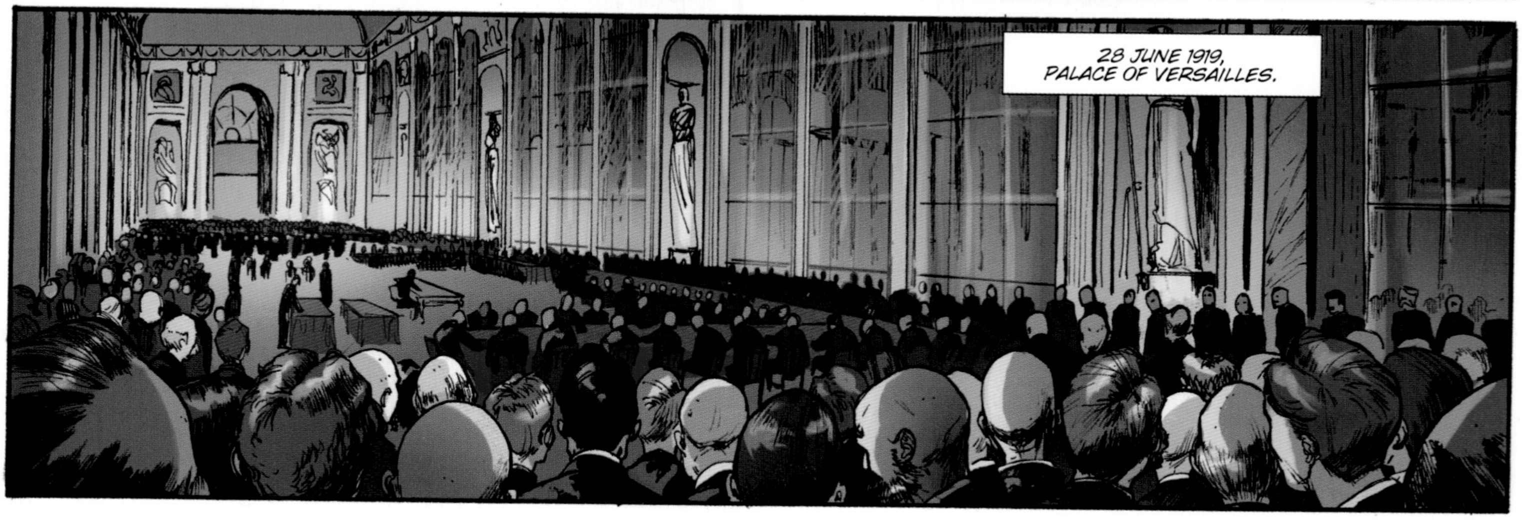
28 JUNE 1919, PALACE OF VERSAILLES.

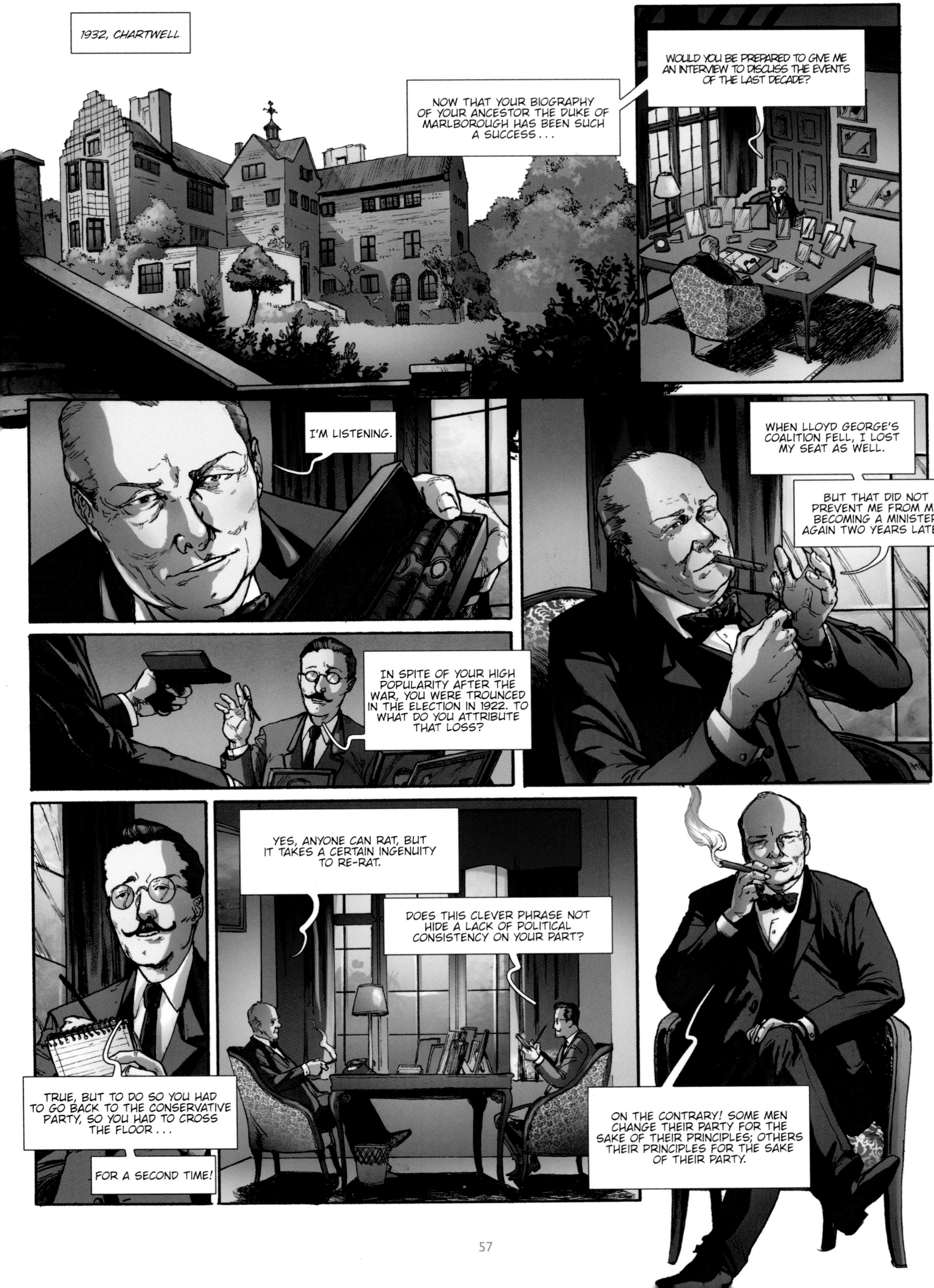
1932, CHARTWELL
NOW THAT YOUR BIOGRAPHY OF YOUR ANCESTOR THE DUKE OF MARLBOROUGH HAS BEEN SUCH A SUCCESS . . .
WOULD YOU BE PREPARED TO GIVE ME AN INTERVIEW TO DISCUSS THE EVENTS OF THE LAST DECADE?
I'M LISTENING.
IN SPITE OF YOUR HIGH POPULARITY AFTER THE WAR, YOU WERE TROUNCED IN THE ELECTION IN 1922. TO WHAT DO YOU ATTRIBUTE THAT LOSS?
WHEN LLOYD GEORGE'S COALITION FELL, I LOST MY SEAT AS WELL.
BUT THAT DID NOT PREVENT ME FROM MY BECOMING A MINISTER AGAIN TWO YEARS LATER.
TRUE, BUT TO DO SO YOU HAD TO GO BACK TO THE CONSERVATIVE PARTY, SO YOU HAD TO CROSS THE FLOOR . . .
FOR A SECOND TIME!
YES, ANYONE CAN RAT, BUT IT TAKES A CERTAIN INGENUITY TO RE-RAT.
DOES THIS CLEVER PHRASE NOT HIDE A LACK OF POLITICAL CONSISTENCY ON YOUR PART?
ON THE CONTRARY! SOME MEN CHANGE THEIR PARTY FOR THE SAKE OF THEIR PRINCIPLES; OTHERS THEIR PRINCIPLES FOR THE SAKE OF THEIR PARTY.

WHEN YOU WERE APPOINTED CHANCELLOR OF THE EXCHEQUER, A POSITION THAT YOUR FATHER HAD OCCUPIED, HOW DID YOU FEEL?

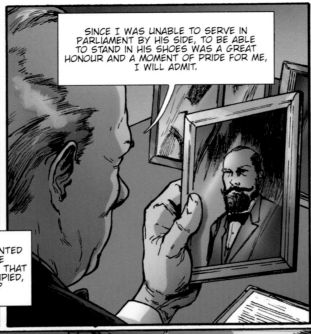

SINCE I WAS UNABLE TO SERVE IN PARLIAMENT BY HIS SIDE, TO BE ABLE TO STAND IN HIS SHOES WAS A GREAT HONOUR AND A MOMENT OF PRIDE FOR ME, I WILL ADMIT.

HOW DO YOU RESPOND TO THOSE WHO SAY THAT YOU WERE THE WORST CHANCELLOR THAT THIS COUNTRY HAS EVER KNOWN?

I FOLLOWED THE BEST ADVICE GIVEN!

I HAVE TO FIND A BETTER WAY TO SERVE THE BRITISH PEOPLE.

YOU ARE PRESENTLY WITHOUT A MINISTERIAL POSITION. WHAT DO YOU DO WITH YOUR DAYS?

I'M SPENDING TIME WITH MY FAMILY. I'M WRITING. I PAINT. I DO SOME BRICK-LAYING. I'M RAISING PIGS.

BUT I'M STILL PERFECTLY UP TO DATE ON WORLD NEWS!

IN CASE BRITAIN MIGHT CALL ON YOU AGAIN?

NO.

FOR THE DAY WHEN IT WILL!

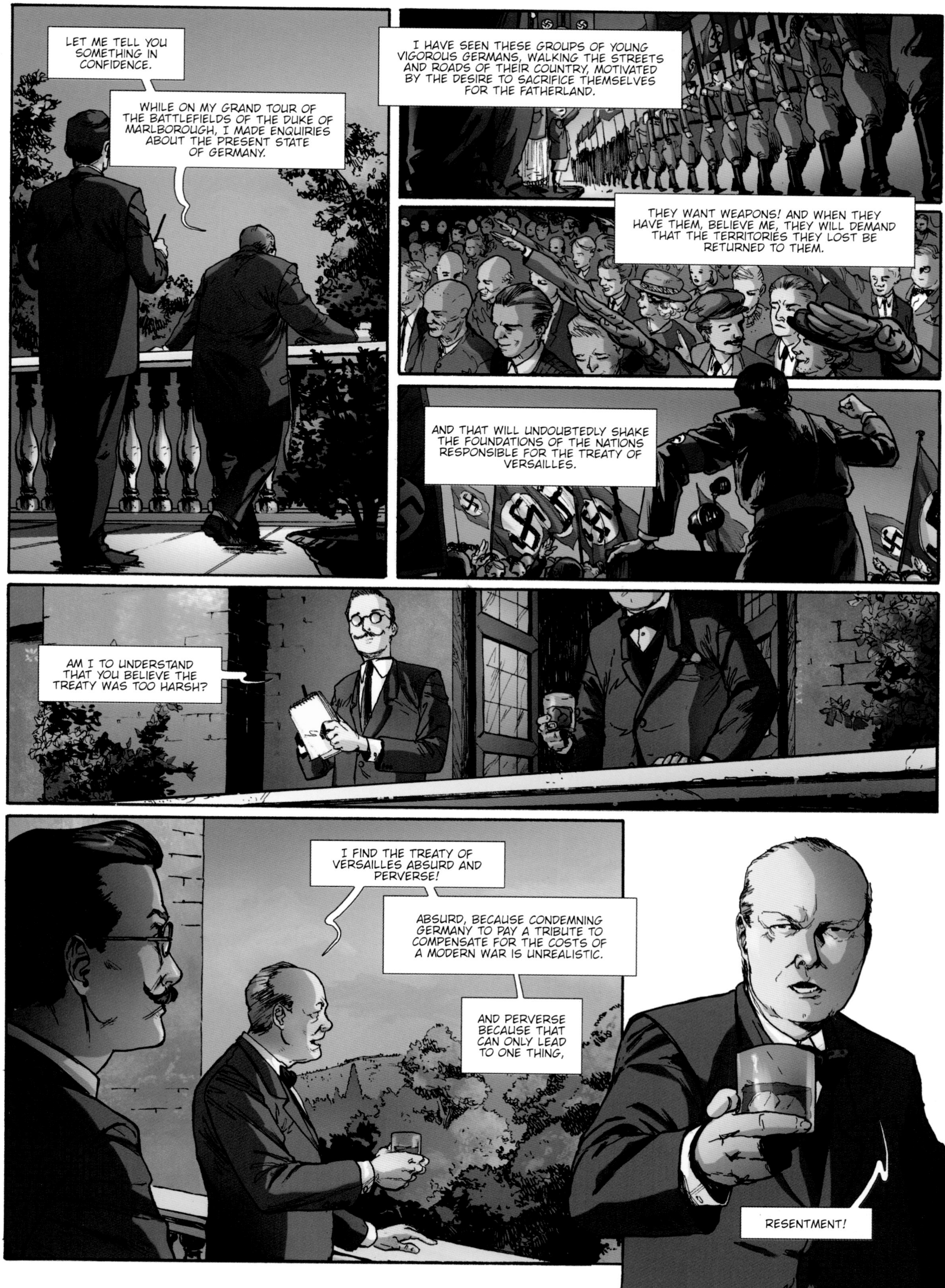
LET ME TELL YOU SOMETHING IN CONFIDENCE.
WHILE ON MY GRAND TOUR OF THE BATTLEFIELDS OF THE DUKE OF MARLBOROUGH, I MADE ENQUIRIES ABOUT THE PRESENT STATE OF GERMANY.
I HAVE SEEN THESE GROUPS OF YOUNG VIGOROUS GERMANS, WALKING THE STREETS AND ROADS OF THEIR COUNTRY, MOTIVATED BY THE DESIRE TO SACRIFICE THEMSELVES FOR THE FATHERLAND.
THEY WANT WEAPONS! AND WHEN THEY HAVE THEM, BELIEVE ME, THEY WILL DEMAND THAT THE TERRITORIES THEY LOST BE RETURNED TO THEM.
AND THAT WILL UNDOUBTEDLY SHAKE THE FOUNDATIONS OF THE NATIONS RESPONSIBLE FOR THE TREATY OF VERSAILLES.
AM I TO UNDERSTAND THAT YOU BELIEVE THE TREATY WAS TOO HARSH?
I FIND THE TREATY OF VERSAILLES ABSURD AND PERVERSE!
ABSURD, BECAUSE CONDEMNING GERMANY TO PAY A TRIBUTE TO COMPENSATE FOR THE COSTS OF A MODERN WAR IS UNREALISTIC.
AND PERVERSE BECAUSE THAT CAN ONLY LEAD TO ONE THING,
RESENTMENT!

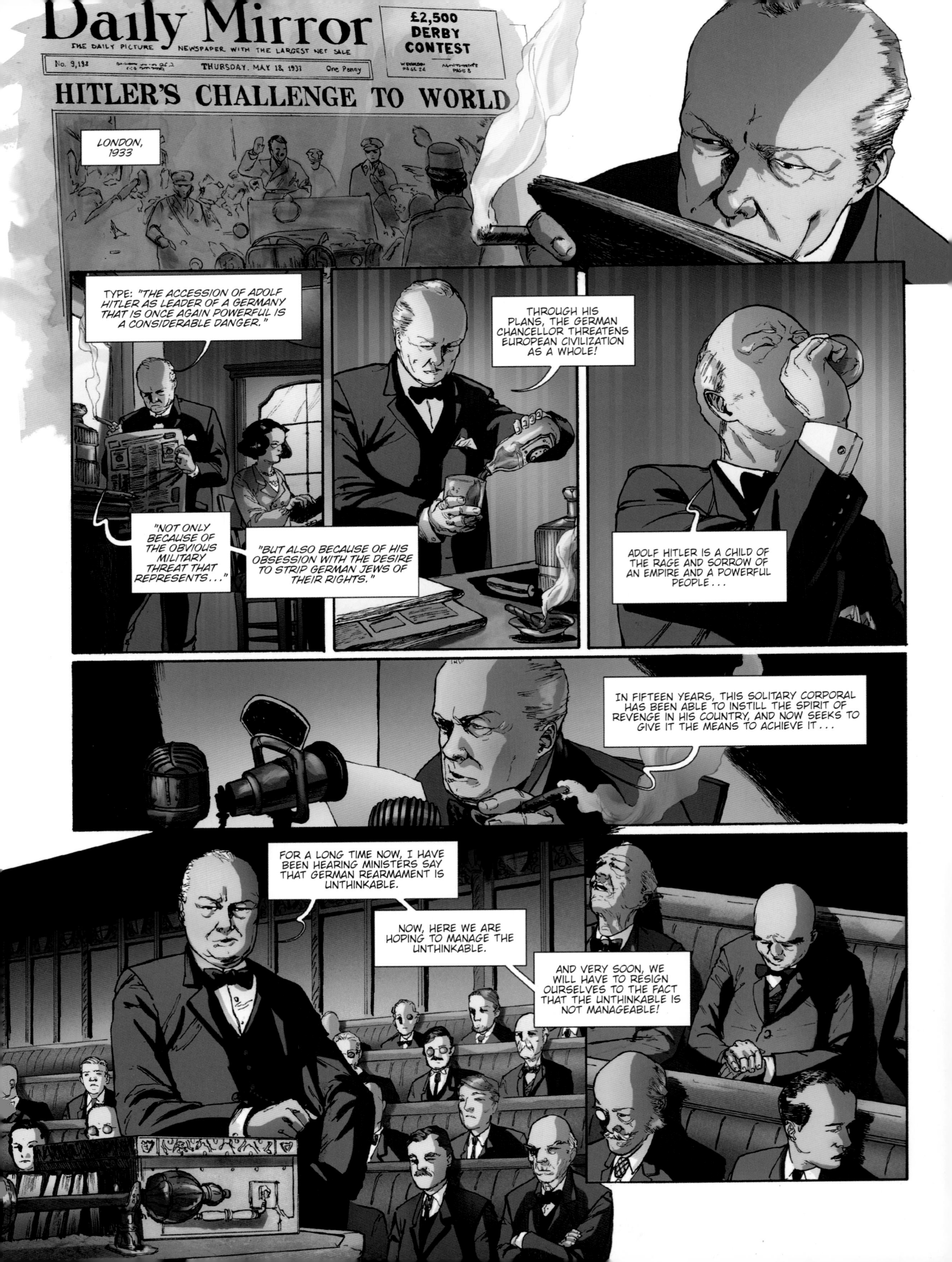
Daily Mirror
THE DAILY PICTURE NEWSPAPER WITH THE LARGEST NET SALE
No. 9,193
THURSDAY, MAY 18, 1933
One Penny
£2,500 DERBY CONTEST
HITLER'S CHALLENGE TO WORLD
LONDON, 1933
TYPE: "THE ACCESSION OF ADOLF HITLER AS LEADER OF A GERMANY THAT IS ONCE AGAIN POWERFUL IS A CONSIDERABLE DANGER."
"NOT ONLY BECAUSE OF THE OBVIOUS MILITARY THREAT THAT REPRESENTS . . ."
"BUT ALSO BECAUSE OF HIS OBSESSION WITH THE DESIRE TO STRIP GERMAN JEWS OF THEIR RIGHTS."
THROUGH HIS PLANS, THE GERMAN CHANCELLOR THREATENS EUROPEAN CIVILIZATION AS A WHOLE!
ADOLF HITLER IS A CHILD OF THE RAGE AND SORROW OF AN EMPIRE AND A POWERFUL PEOPLE . . .
IN FIFTEEN YEARS, THIS SOLITARY CORPORAL HAS BEEN ABLE TO INSTILL THE SPIRIT OF REVENGE IN HIS COUNTRY, AND NOW SEEKS TO GIVE IT THE MEANS TO ACHIEVE IT . . .
FOR A LONG TIME NOW, I HAVE BEEN HEARING MINISTERS SAY THAT GERMAN REARMAMENT IS UNTHINKABLE.
NOW, HERE WE ARE HOPING TO MANAGE THE UNTHINKABLE.
AND VERY SOON, WE WILL HAVE TO RESIGN OURSELVES TO THE FACT THAT THE UNTHINKABLE IS NOT MANAGEABLE!

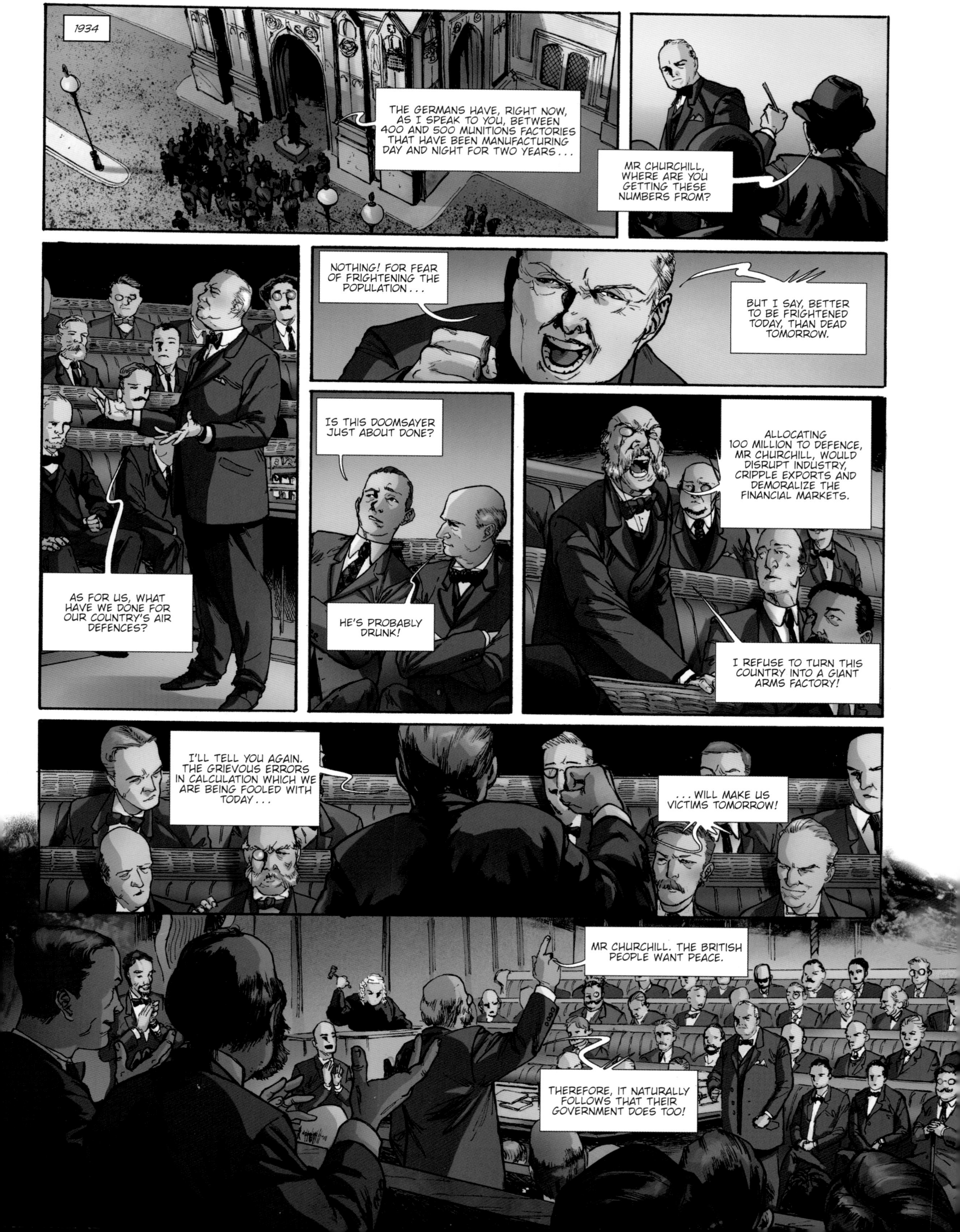

1934
THE GERMANS HAVE, RIGHT NOW, AS I SPEAK TO YOU, BETWEEN 400 AND 500 MUNITIONS FACTORIES THAT HAVE BEEN MANUFACTURING DAY AND NIGHT FOR TWO YEARS . . .
MR CHURCHILL, WHERE ARE YOU GETTING THESE NUMBERS FROM?
AS FOR US, WHAT HAVE WE DONE FOR OUR COUNTRY'S AIR DEFENCES?
NOTHING! FOR FEAR OF FRIGHTENING THE POPULATION . . .
BUT I SAY, BETTER TO BE FRIGHTENED TODAY, THAN DEAD TOMORROW.
IS THIS DOOMSAYER JUST ABOUT DONE?
HE'S PROBABLY DRUNK!
ALLOCATING 100 MILLION TO DEFENCE, MR CHURCHILL, WOULD DISRUPT INDUSTRY, CRIPPLE EXPORTS AND DEMORALIZE THE FINANCIAL MARKETS.
I REFUSE TO TURN THIS COUNTRY INTO A GIANT ARMS FACTORY!
I'LL TELL YOU AGAIN. THE GRIEVOUS ERRORS IN CALCULATION WHICH WE ARE BEING FOOLED WITH TODAY . . .
. . . WILL MAKE US VICTIMS TOMORROW!
MR CHURCHILL. THE BRITISH PEOPLE WANT PEACE.
THEREFORE, IT NATURALLY FOLLOWS THAT THEIR GOVERNMENT DOES TOO!

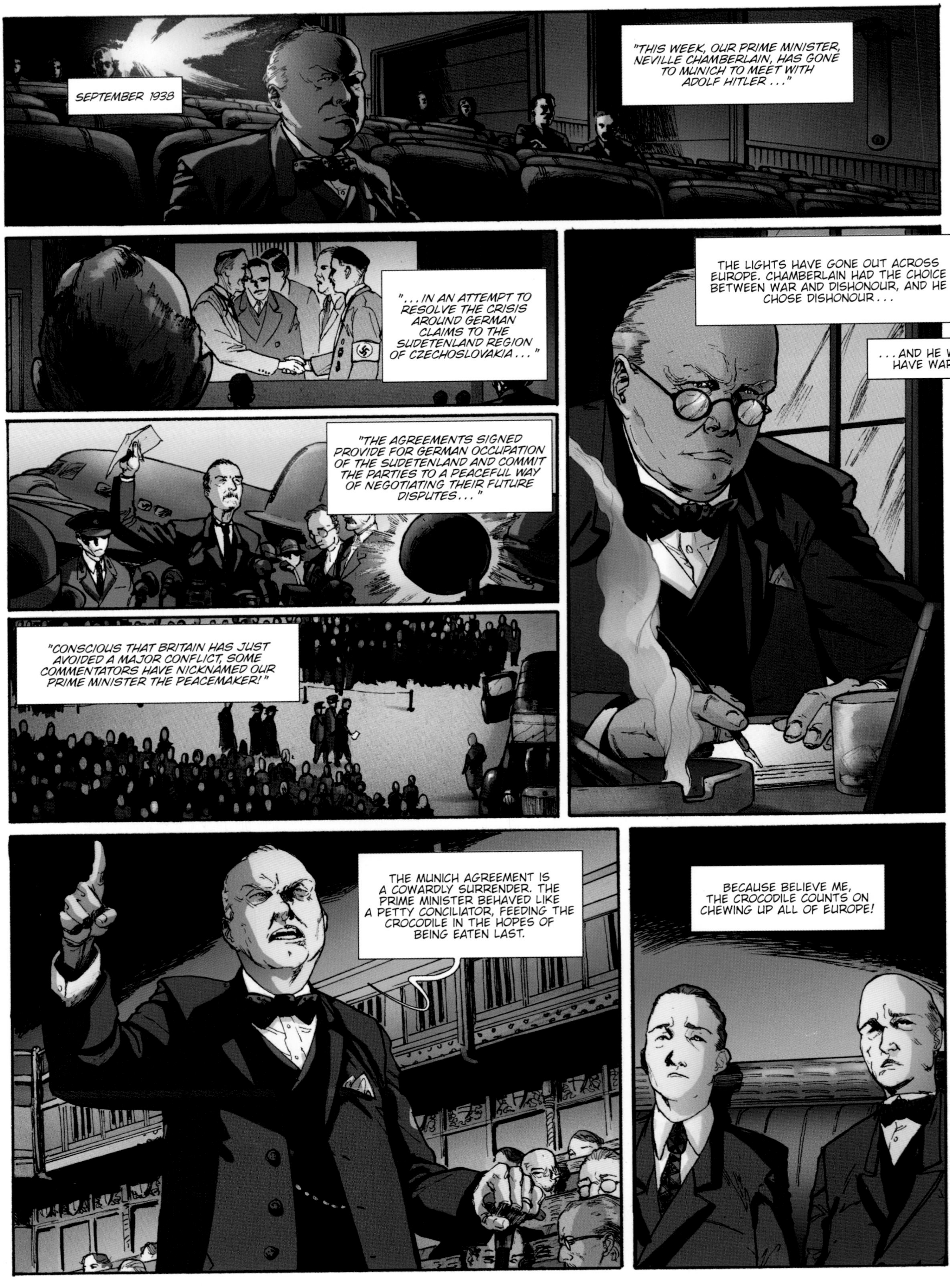

SEPTEMBER 1938
"THIS WEEK, OUR PRIME MINISTER, NEVILLE CHAMBERLAIN, HAS GONE TO MUNICH TO MEET WITH ADOLF HITLER . . ."
". . . IN AN ATTEMPT TO RESOLVE THE CRISIS AROUND GERMAN CLAIMS TO THE SUDETENLAND REGION OF CZECHOSLOVAKIA . . ."
"THE AGREEMENTS SIGNED PROVIDE FOR GERMAN OCCUPATION OF THE SUDETENLAND AND COMMIT THE PARTIES TO A PEACEFUL WAY OF NEGOTIATING THEIR FUTURE DISPUTES . . ."
"CONSCIOUS THAT BRITAIN HAS JUST AVOIDED A MAJOR CONFLICT, SOME COMMENTATORS HAVE NICKNAMED OUR PRIME MINISTER THE PEACEMAKER!"
THE LIGHTS HAVE GONE OUT ACROSS EUROPE. CHAMBERLAIN HAD THE CHOICE BETWEEN WAR AND DISHONOUR, AND HE CHOSE DISHONOUR . . .
. . . AND HE WILL HAVE WAR!
THE MUNICH AGREEMENT IS A COWARDLY SURRENDER. THE PRIME MINISTER BEHAVED LIKE A PETTY CONCILIATOR, FEEDING THE CROCODILE IN THE HOPES OF BEING EATEN LAST.
BECAUSE BELIEVE ME, THE CROCODILE COUNTS ON CHEWING UP ALL OF EUROPE!

WORLD WAR II

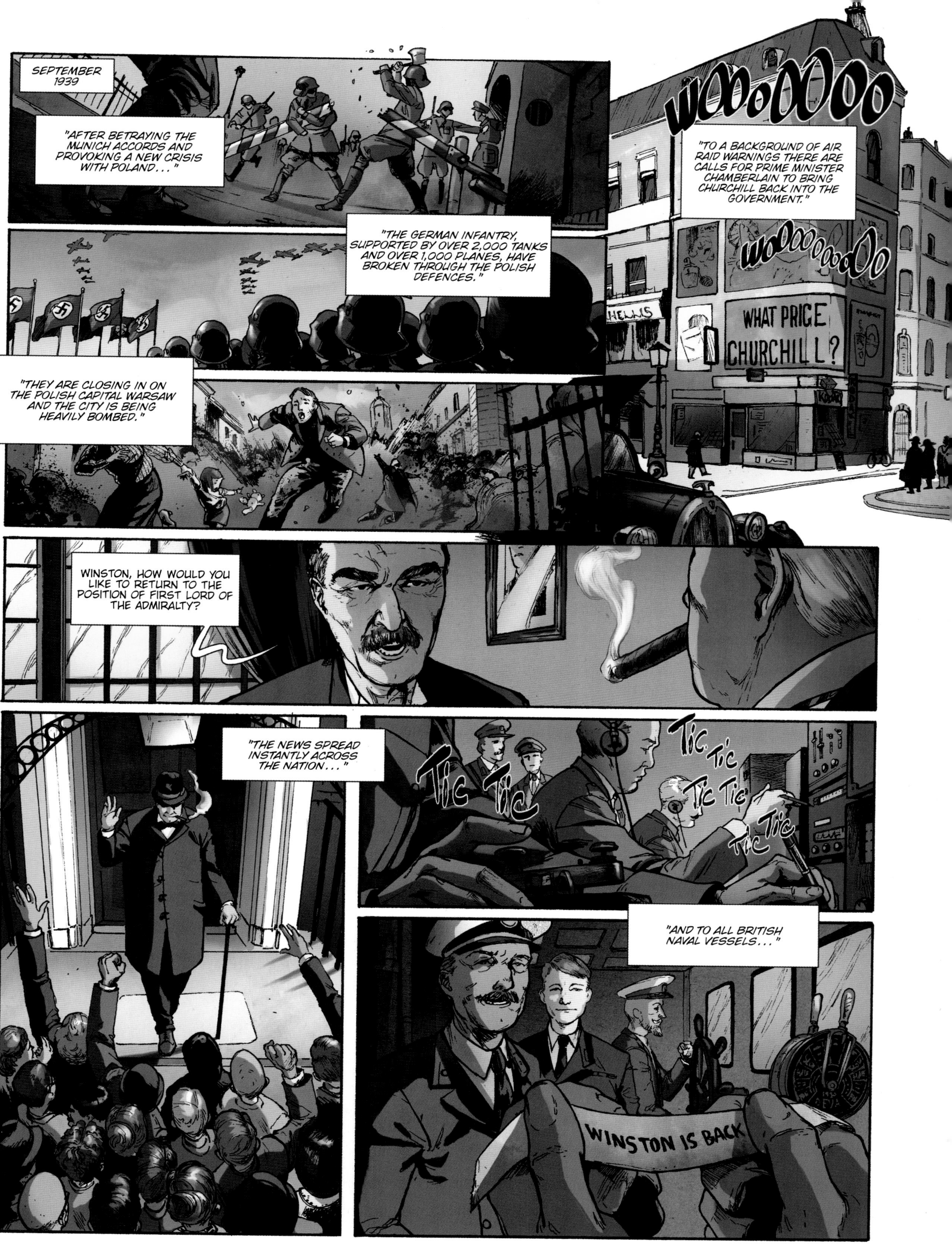
SEPTEMBER 1939
"AFTER BETRAYING THE MUNICH ACCORDS AND PROVOKING A NEW CRISIS WITH POLAND . . ."
"THE GERMAN INFANTRY, SUPPORTED BY OVER 2,000 TANKS AND OVER 1,000 PLANES, HAVE BROKEN THROUGH THE POLISH DEFENCES."
"THEY ARE CLOSING IN ON THE POLISH CAPITAL WARSAW AND THE CITY IS BEING HEAVILY BOMBED."
WOOoOOOO
"TO A BACKGROUND OF AIR RAID WARNINGS THERE ARE CALLS FOR PRIME MINISTER CHAMBERLAIN TO BRING CHURCHILL BACK INTO THE GOVERNMENT."
WOOOOOOOOO
WHAT PRICE CHURCHILL?
WINSTON, HOW WOULD YOU LIKE TO RETURN TO THE POSITION OF FIRST LORD OF THE ADMIRALTY?
"THE NEWS SPREAD INSTANTLY ACROSS THE NATION . . ."
TIC TIC
TIC TIC TIC TIC TIC TIC
"AND TO ALL BRITISH NAVAL VESSELS . . ."
WINSTON IS BACK

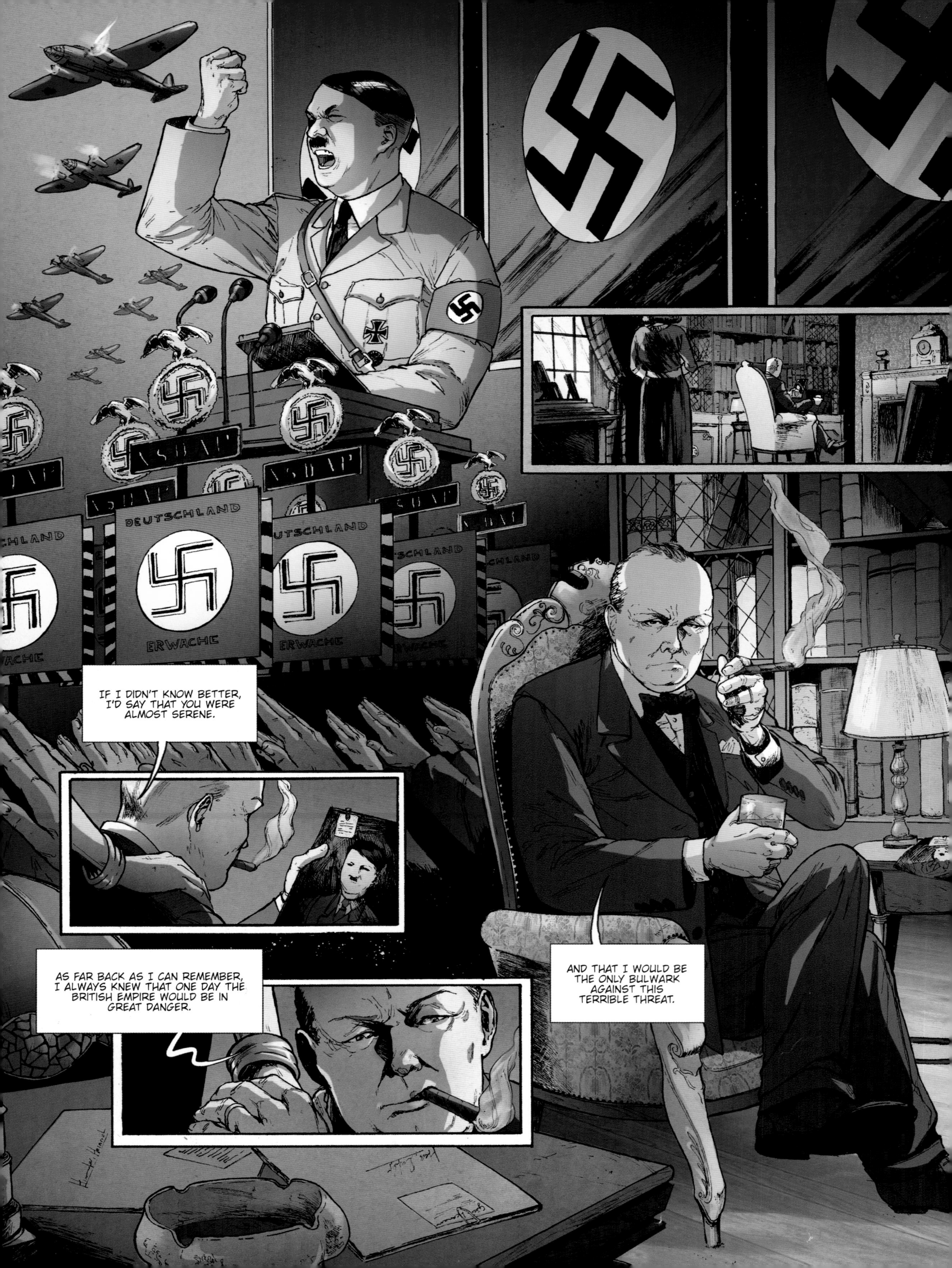
NSDAP
DEUTSCHLAND
ERWACHE
IF I DIDN'T KNOW BETTER, I'D SAY THAT YOU WERE ALMOST SERENE.
AS FAR BACK AS I CAN REMEMBER, I ALWAYS KNEW THAT ONE DAY THE BRITISH EMPIRE WOULD BE IN GREAT DANGER.
AND THAT I WOULD BE THE ONLY BULWARK AGAINST THIS TERRIBLE THREAT.

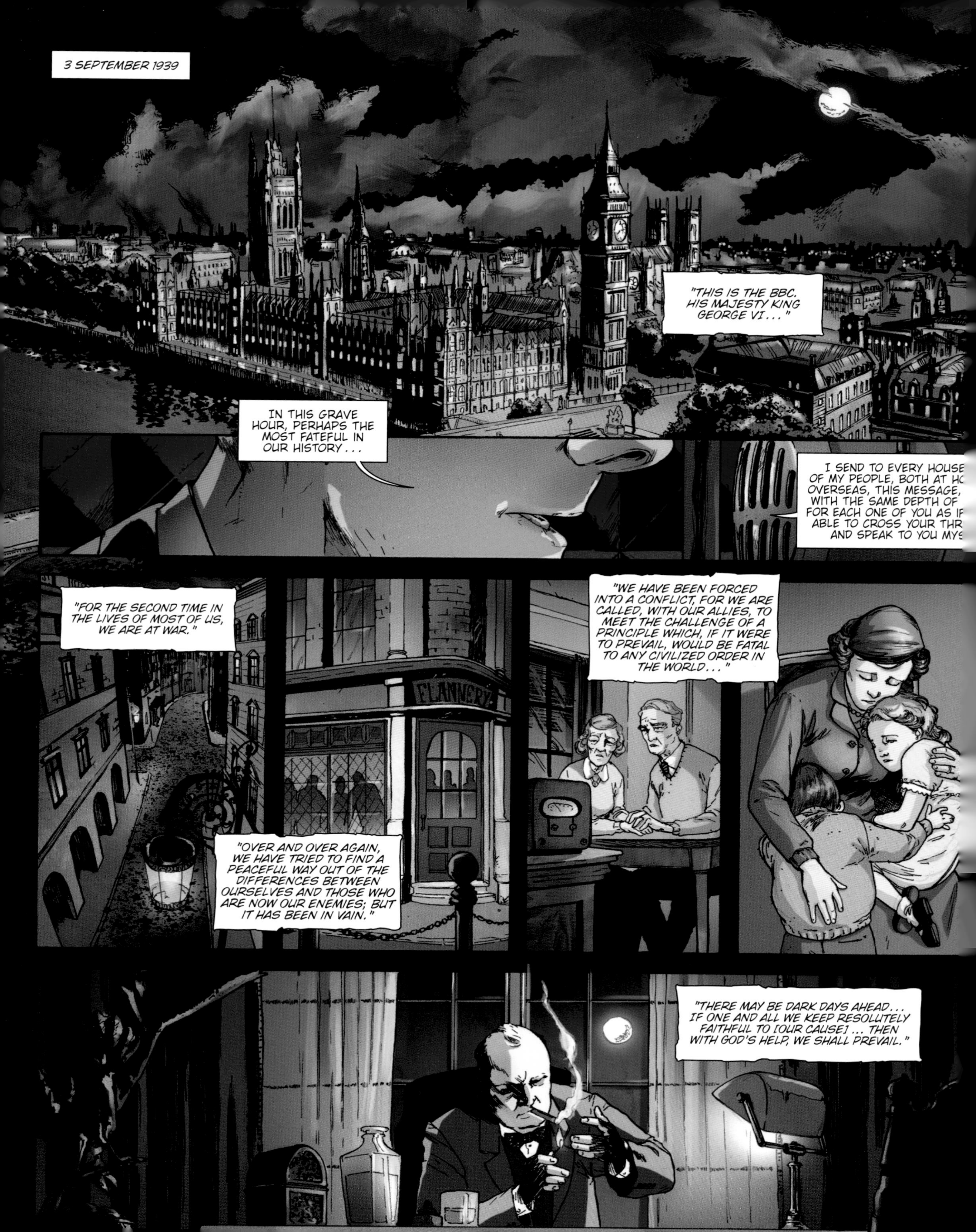
3 SEPTEMBER 1939
"THIS IS THE BBC. HIS MAJESTY KING GEORGE VI . . ."
IN THIS GRAVE HOUR, PERHAPS THE MOST FATEFUL IN OUR HISTORY . . .
I SEND TO EVERY HOUSE OF MY PEOPLE, BOTH AT HO OVERSEAS, THIS MESSAGE, WITH THE SAME DEPTH OF FOR EACH ONE OF YOU AS IF ABLE TO CROSS YOUR THR AND SPEAK TO YOU MYS
"FOR THE SECOND TIME IN THE LIVES OF MOST OF US, WE ARE AT WAR."
FLANNERY'S
"OVER AND OVER AGAIN, WE HAVE TRIED TO FIND A PEACEFUL WAY OUT OF THE DIFFERENCES BETWEEN OURSELVES AND THOSE WHO ARE NOW OUR ENEMIES; BUT IT HAS BEEN IN VAIN."
"WE HAVE BEEN FORCED INTO A CONFLICT, FOR WE ARE CALLED, WITH OUR ALLIES, TO MEET THE CHALLENGE OF A PRINCIPLE WHICH, IF IT WERE TO PREVAIL, WOULD BE FATAL TO ANY CIVILIZED ORDER IN THE WORLD . . ."
"THERE MAY BE DARK DAYS AHEAD . . . IF ONE AND ALL WE KEEP RESOLUTELY FAITHFUL TO [OUR CAUSE] . . . THEN WITH GOD'S HELP, WE SHALL PREVAIL."

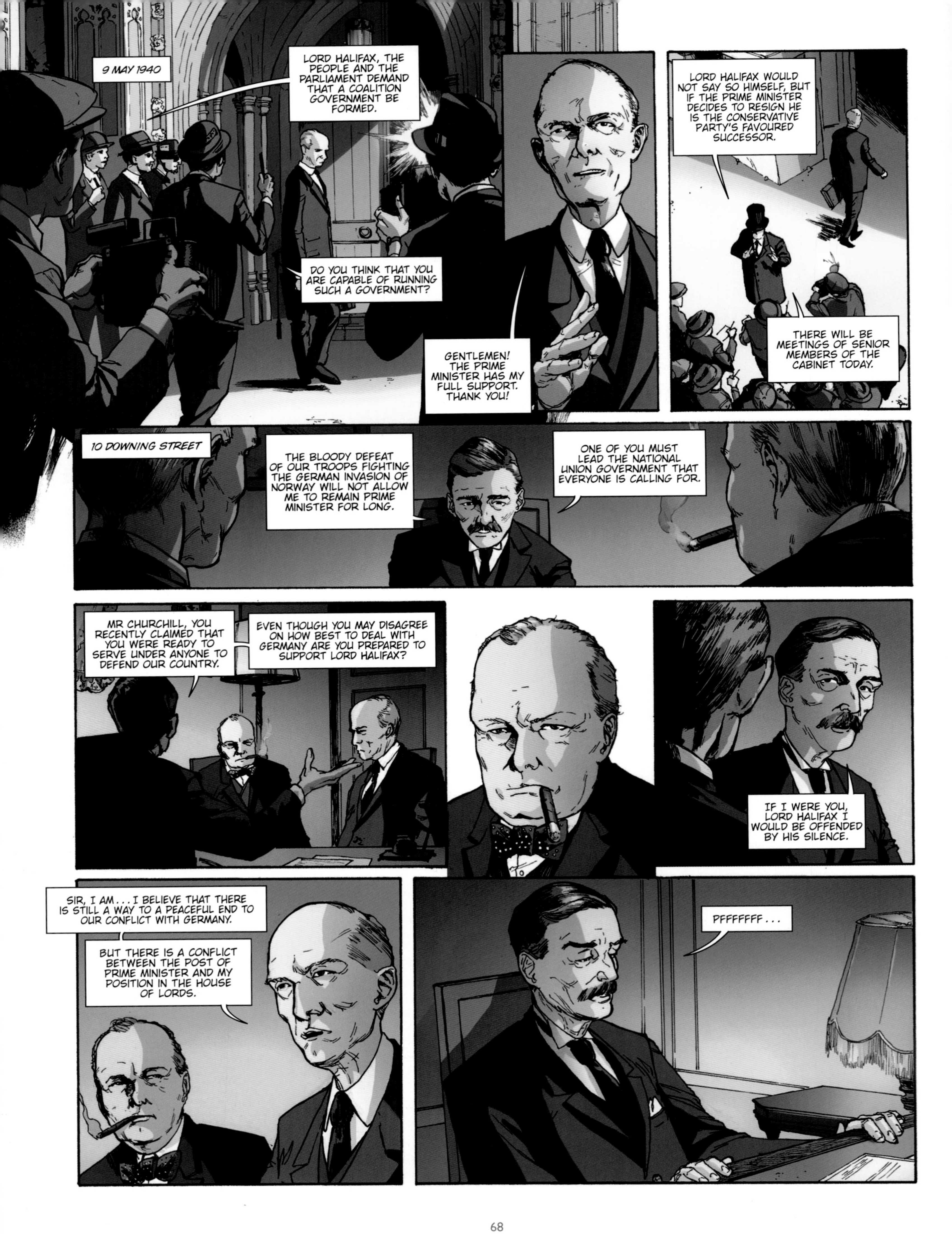
9 MAY 1940
LORD HALIFAX, THE PEOPLE AND THE PARLIAMENT DEMAND THAT A COALITION GOVERNMENT BE FORMED.
DO YOU THINK THAT YOU ARE CAPABLE OF RUNNING SUCH A GOVERNMENT?
GENTLEMEN! THE PRIME MINISTER HAS MY FULL SUPPORT. THANK YOU!
LORD HALIFAX WOULD NOT SAY SO HIMSELF, BUT IF THE PRIME MINISTER DECIDES TO RESIGN HE IS THE CONSERVATIVE PARTY'S FAVOURED SUCCESSOR.
THERE WILL BE MEETINGS OF SENIOR MEMBERS OF THE CABINET TODAY.
10 DOWNING STREET
THE BLOODY DEFEAT OF OUR TROOPS FIGHTING THE GERMAN INVASION OF NORWAY WILL NOT ALLOW ME TO REMAIN PRIME MINISTER FOR LONG.
ONE OF YOU MUST LEAD THE NATIONAL UNION GOVERNMENT THAT EVERYONE IS CALLING FOR.
MR CHURCHILL, YOU RECENTLY CLAIMED THAT YOU WERE READY TO SERVE UNDER ANYONE TO DEFEND OUR COUNTRY.
EVEN THOUGH YOU MAY DISAGREE ON HOW BEST TO DEAL WITH GERMANY ARE YOU PREPARED TO SUPPORT LORD HALIFAX?
IF I WERE YOU, LORD HALIFAX I WOULD BE OFFENDED BY HIS SILENCE.
SIR, I AM . . . I BELIEVE THAT THERE IS STILL A WAY TO A PEACEFUL END TO OUR CONFLICT WITH GERMANY.
BUT THERE IS A CONFLICT BETWEEN THE POST OF PRIME MINISTER AND MY POSITION IN THE HOUSE OF LORDS.
PFFFFFFF . . .

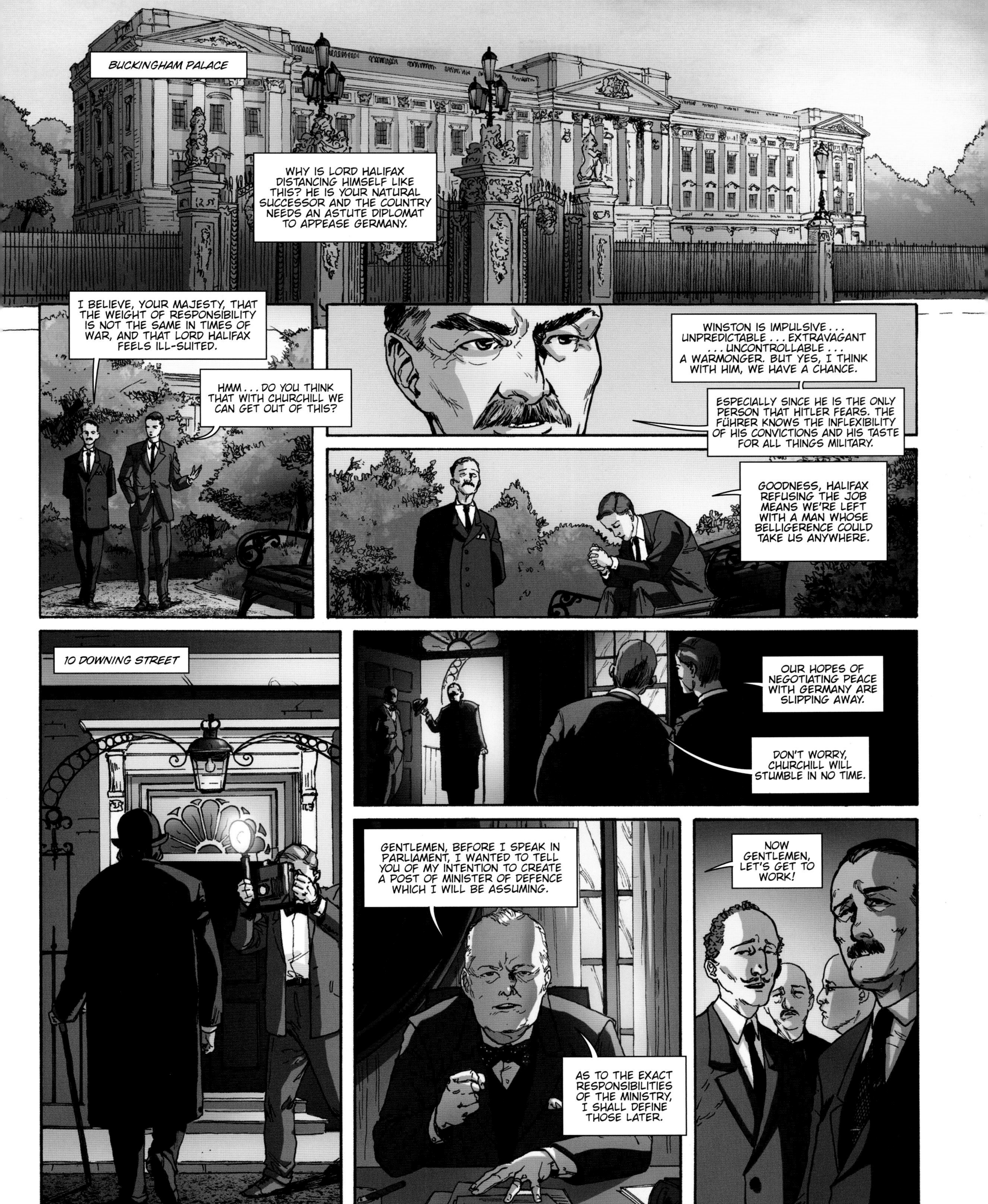
BUCKINGHAM PALACE
WHY IS LORD HALIFAX DISTANCING HIMSELF LIKE THIS? HE IS YOUR NATURAL SUCCESSOR AND THE COUNTRY NEEDS AN ASTUTE DIPLOMAT TO APPEASE GERMANY.
I BELIEVE, YOUR MAJESTY, THAT THE WEIGHT OF RESPONSIBILITY IS NOT THE SAME IN TIMES OF WAR, AND THAT LORD HALIFAX FEELS ILL-SUITED.
HMM . . . DO YOU THINK THAT WITH CHURCHILL WE CAN GET OUT OF THIS?
WINSTON IS IMPULSIVE . . . UNPREDICTABLE . . . EXTRAVAGANT . . . UNCONTROLLABLE . . . A WARMONGER. BUT YES, I THINK WITH HIM, WE HAVE A CHANCE.
ESPECIALLY SINCE HE IS THE ONLY PERSON THAT HITLER FEARS. THE FÜHRER KNOWS THE INFLEXIBILITY OF HIS CONVICTIONS AND HIS TASTE FOR ALL THINGS MILITARY.
GOODNESS, HALIFAX REFUSING THE JOB MEANS WE'RE LEFT WITH A MAN WHOSE BELLIGERENCE COULD TAKE US ANYWHERE.
10 DOWNING STREET
OUR HOPES OF NEGOTIATING PEACE WITH GERMANY ARE SLIPPING AWAY.
DON'T WORRY, CHURCHILL WILL STUMBLE IN NO TIME.
GENTLEMEN, BEFORE I SPEAK IN PARLIAMENT, I WANTED TO TELL YOU OF MY INTENTION TO CREATE A POST OF MINISTER OF DEFENCE WHICH I WILL BE ASSUMING.
AS TO THE EXACT RESPONSIBILITIES OF THE MINISTRY, I SHALL DEFINE THOSE LATER.
NOW GENTLEMEN, LET'S GET TO WORK!

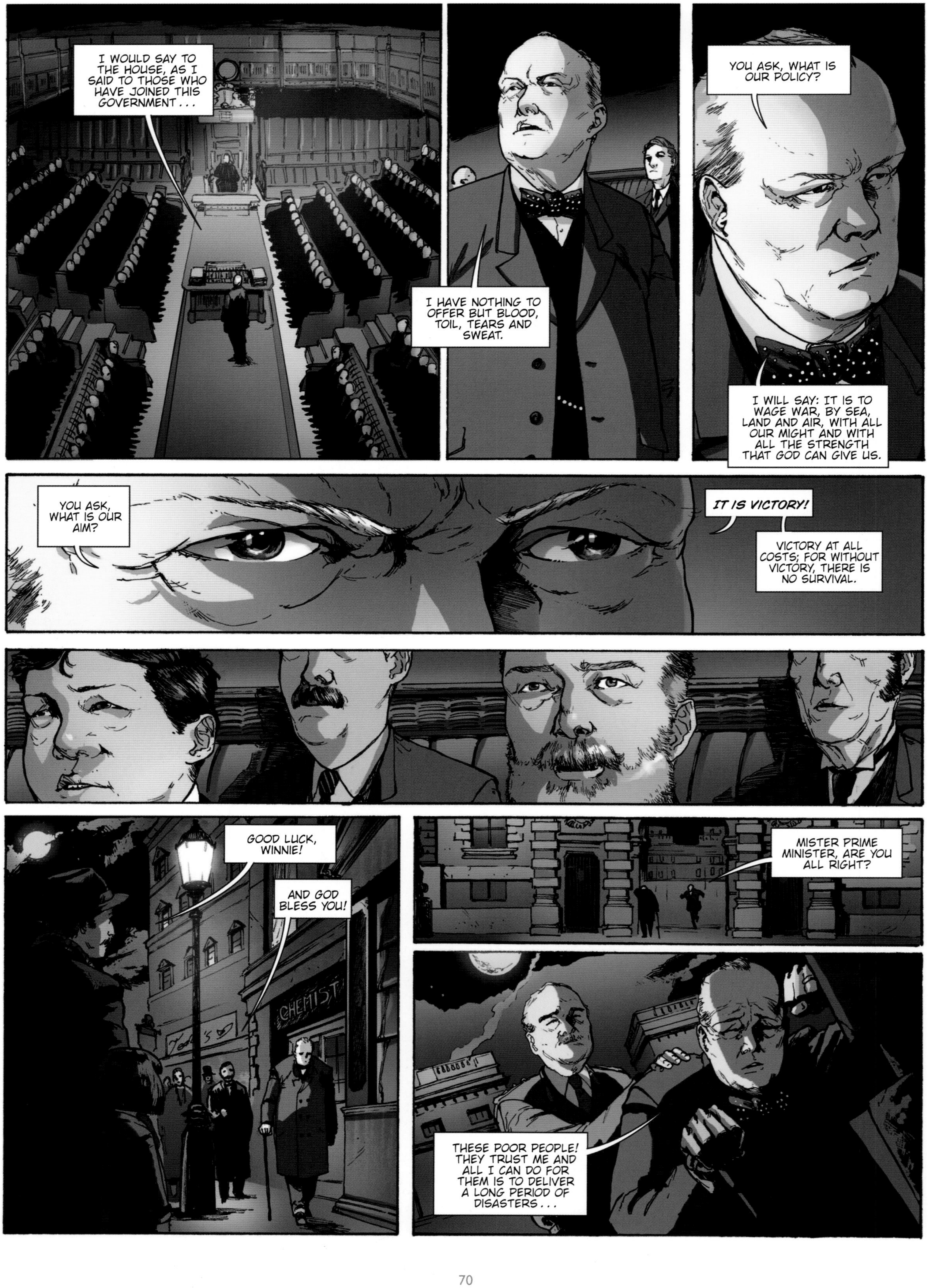
I WOULD SAY TO THE HOUSE, AS I SAID TO THOSE WHO HAVE JOINED THIS GOVERNMENT . . .
I HAVE NOTHING TO OFFER BUT BLOOD, TOIL, TEARS AND SWEAT.
YOU ASK, WHAT IS OUR POLICY?
I WILL SAY: IT IS TO WAGE WAR, BY SEA, LAND AND AIR, WITH ALL OUR MIGHT AND WITH ALL THE STRENGTH THAT GOD CAN GIVE US.
YOU ASK, WHAT IS OUR AIM?
IT IS VICTORY!
VICTORY AT ALL COSTS; FOR WITHOUT VICTORY, THERE IS NO SURVIVAL.
GOOD LUCK, WINNIE!
AND GOD BLESS YOU!
CHEMIST
MISTER PRIME MINISTER, ARE YOU ALL RIGHT?
THESE POOR PEOPLE! THEY TRUST ME AND ALL I CAN DO FOR THEM IS TO DELIVER A LONG PERIOD OF DISASTERS . . .

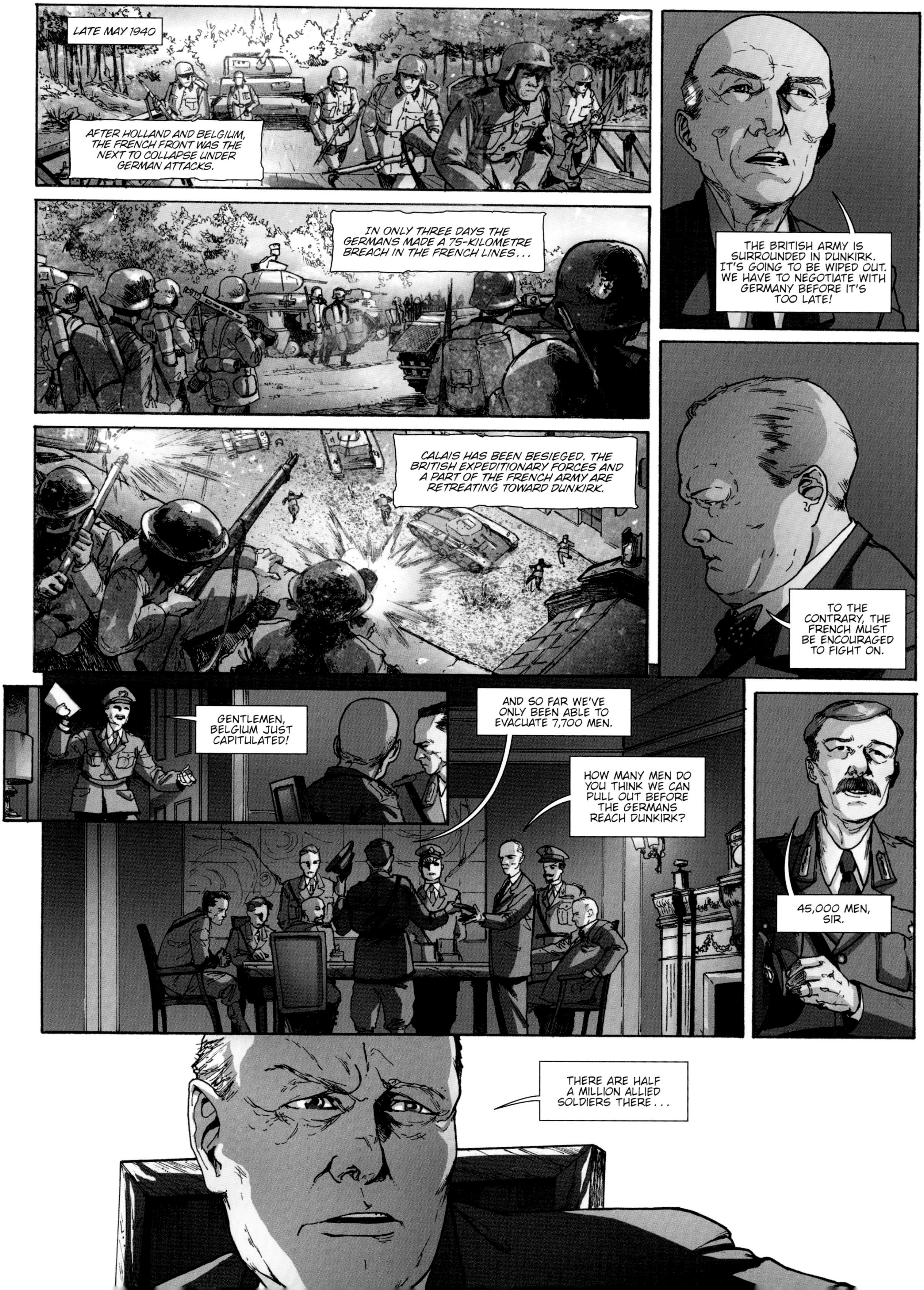
LATE MAY 1940
AFTER HOLLAND AND BELGIUM, THE FRENCH FRONT WAS THE NEXT TO COLLAPSE UNDER GERMAN ATTACKS.
THE BRITISH ARMY IS SURROUNDED IN DUNKIRK. IT'S GOING TO BE WIPED OUT. WE HAVE TO NEGOTIATE WITH GERMANY BEFORE IT'S TOO LATE!
IN ONLY THREE DAYS THE GERMANS MADE A 75-KILOMETRE BREACH IN THE FRENCH LINES . . .
CALAIS HAS BEEN BESIEGED. THE BRITISH EXPEDITIONARY FORCES AND A PART OF THE FRENCH ARMY ARE RETREATING TOWARD DUNKIRK.
TO THE CONTRARY, THE FRENCH MUST BE ENCOURAGED TO FIGHT ON.
GENTLEMEN, BELGIUM JUST CAPITULATED!
AND SO FAR WE'VE ONLY BEEN ABLE TO EVACUATE 7,700 MEN.
HOW MANY MEN DO YOU THINK WE CAN PULL OUT BEFORE THE GERMANS REACH DUNKIRK?
45,000 MEN, SIR.
THERE ARE HALF A MILLION ALLIED SOLDIERS THERE . . .

WE WILL GET MUCH BETTER CONDITIONS OF PEACE BEFORE FRANCE PULLS OUT OF THE WAR.

I REFUSE TO SIT DOWN AT A TABLE WITH HITLER. ONCE WE DO, WE WILL FIND THAT THE CONDITIONS THAT WE ARE OFFERED WILL PUT US AT HIS MERCY.

AND THE DETERMINATION THAT WE HAVE NOW WILL DISAPPEAR!

AND EVEN IF WE ARE DEFEATED, THE CONDITIONS WILL NOT BE WORSE THAN THOSE WE WILL BE OFFERED NOW.

I'M GOING TO ORDER THE BRITISH DIVISIONS THAT ARE TRAPPED IN DUNKIRK TO FIGHT TO THE LAST MAN.

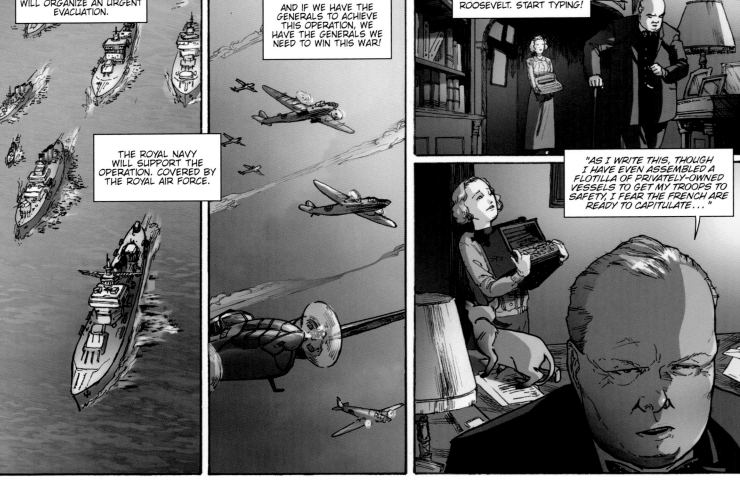

AND WE, IN THE MEANTIME, WILL ORGANIZE AN URGENT EVACUATION.

AND IF WE HAVE THE GENERALS TO ACHIEVE THIS OPERATION, WE HAVE THE GENERALS WE NEED TO WIN THIS WAR!

THE ROYAL NAVY WILL SUPPORT THE OPERATION. COVERED BY THE ROYAL AIR FORCE.

TELEGRAM TO PRESIDENT ROOSEVELT. START TYPING!

"AS I WRITE THIS, THOUGH I HAVE EVEN ASSEMBLED A FLOTILLA OF PRIVATELY-OWNED VESSELS TO GET MY TROOPS TO SAFETY, I FEAR THE FRENCH ARE READY TO CAPITULATE..."

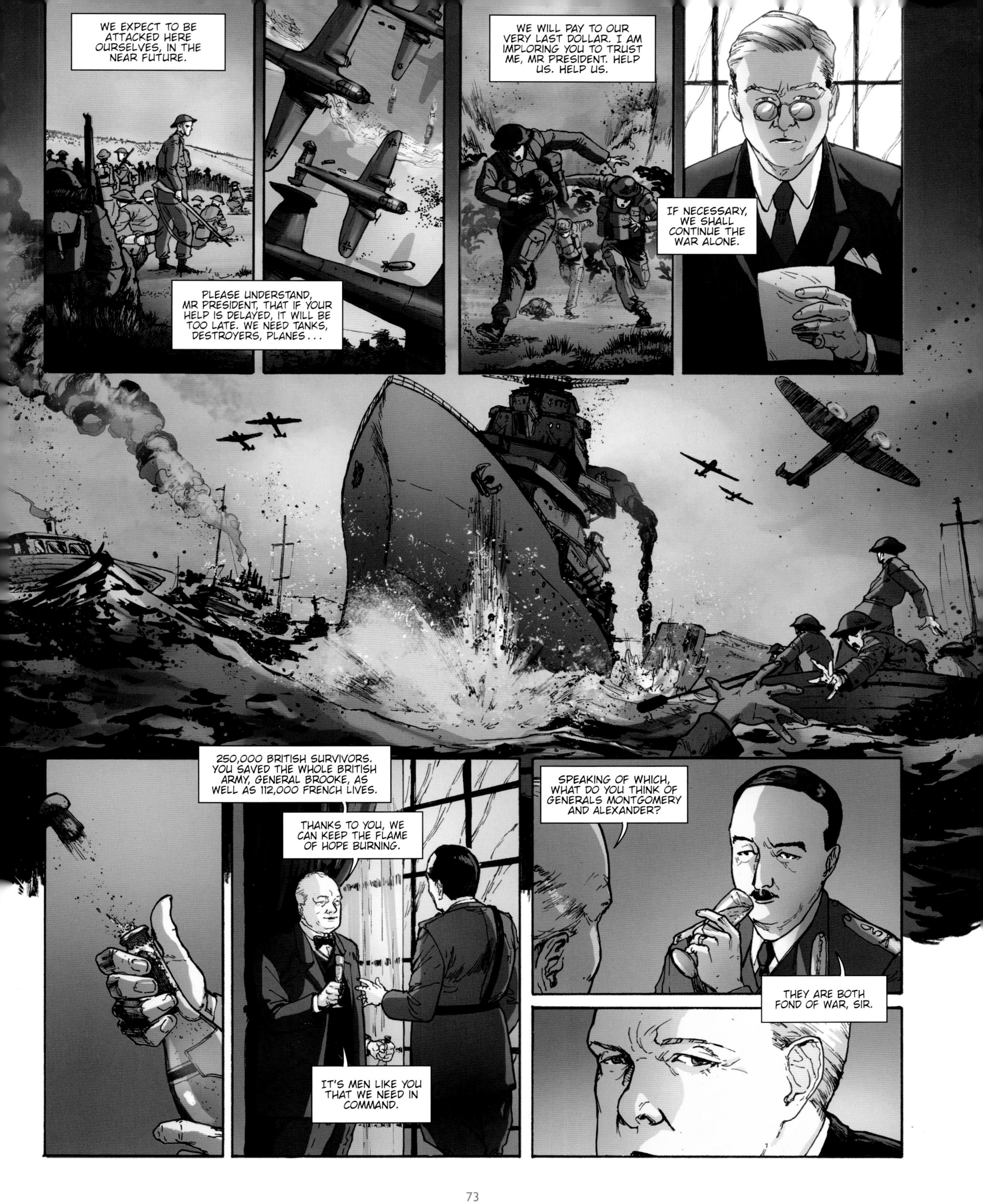
WE EXPECT TO BE ATTACKED HERE OURSELVES, IN THE NEAR FUTURE.
PLEASE UNDERSTAND, MR PRESIDENT, THAT IF YOUR HELP IS DELAYED, IT WILL BE TOO LATE. WE NEED TANKS, DESTROYERS, PLANES . . .
WE WILL PAY TO OUR VERY LAST DOLLAR. I AM IMPLORING YOU TO TRUST ME, MR PRESIDENT. HELP US. HELP US.
IF NECESSARY, WE SHALL CONTINUE THE WAR ALONE.
250,000 BRITISH SURVIVORS. YOU SAVED THE WHOLE BRITISH ARMY, GENERAL BROOKE, AS WELL AS 112,000 FRENCH LIVES.
THANKS TO YOU, WE CAN KEEP THE FLAME OF HOPE BURNING.
IT'S MEN LIKE YOU THAT WE NEED IN COMMAND.
SPEAKING OF WHICH, WHAT DO YOU THINK OF GENERALS MONTGOMERY AND ALEXANDER?
THEY ARE BOTH FOND OF WAR, SIR.

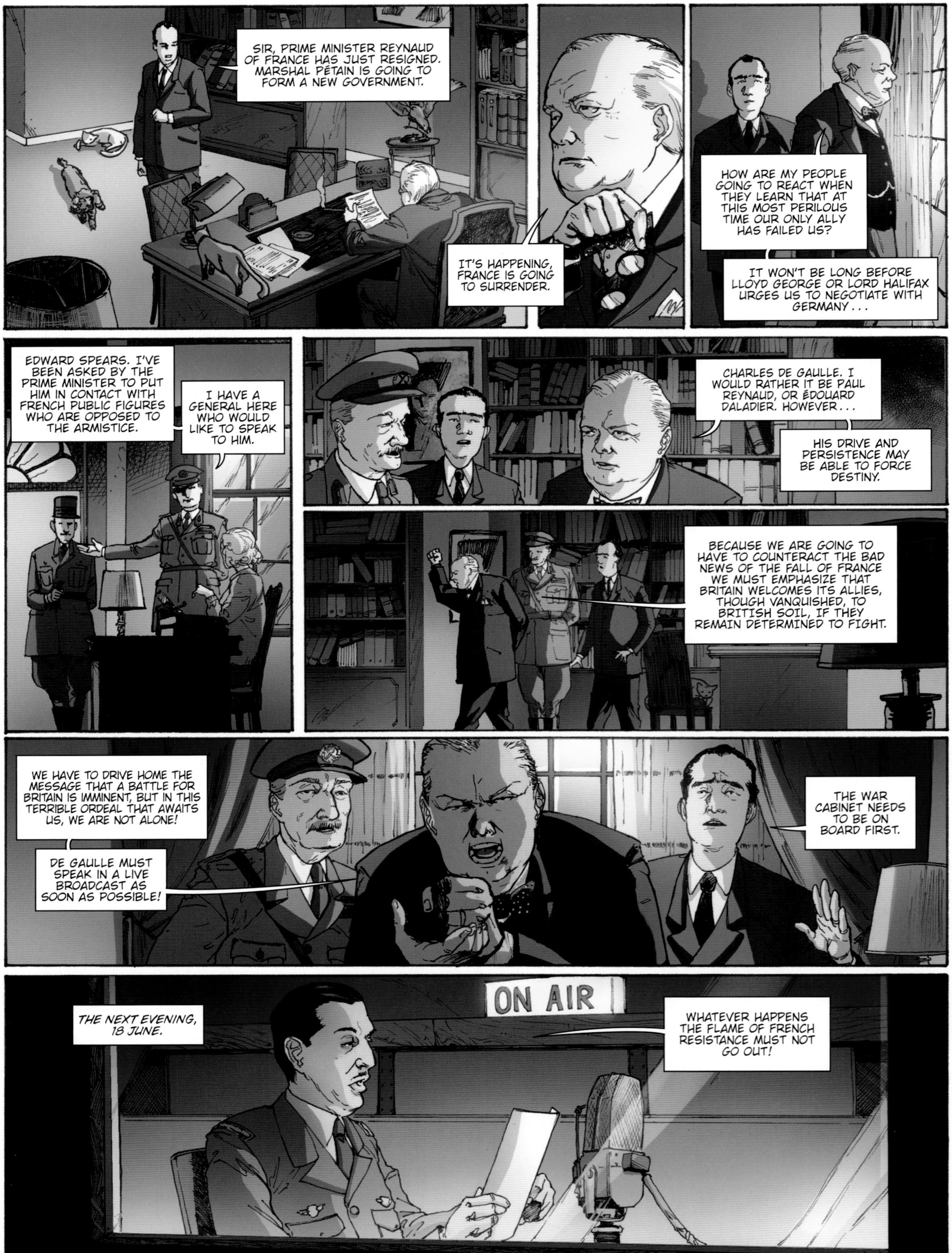
SIR, PRIME MINISTER REYNAUD OF FRANCE HAS JUST RESIGNED. MARSHAL PÉTAIN IS GOING TO FORM A NEW GOVERNMENT.
IT'S HAPPENING, FRANCE IS GOING TO SURRENDER.
HOW ARE MY PEOPLE GOING TO REACT WHEN THEY LEARN THAT AT THIS MOST PERILOUS TIME OUR ONLY ALLY HAS FAILED US?
IT WON'T BE LONG BEFORE LLOYD GEORGE OR LORD HALIFAX URGES US TO NEGOTIATE WITH GERMANY . . .
EDWARD SPEARS. I'VE BEEN ASKED BY THE PRIME MINISTER TO PUT HIM IN CONTACT WITH FRENCH PUBLIC FIGURES WHO ARE OPPOSED TO THE ARMISTICE.
I HAVE A GENERAL HERE WHO WOULD LIKE TO SPEAK TO HIM.
CHARLES DE GAULLE. I WOULD RATHER IT BE PAUL REYNAUD, OR ÉDOUARD DALADIER. HOWEVER . . .
HIS DRIVE AND PERSISTENCE MAY BE ABLE TO FORCE DESTINY.
BECAUSE WE ARE GOING TO HAVE TO COUNTERACT THE BAD NEWS OF THE FALL OF FRANCE WE MUST EMPHASIZE THAT BRITAIN WELCOMES ITS ALLIES, THOUGH VANQUISHED, TO BRITISH SOIL, IF THEY REMAIN DETERMINED TO FIGHT.
WE HAVE TO DRIVE HOME THE MESSAGE THAT A BATTLE FOR BRITAIN IS IMMINENT, BUT IN THIS TERRIBLE ORDEAL THAT AWAITS US, WE ARE NOT ALONE!
DE GAULLE MUST SPEAK IN A LIVE BROADCAST AS SOON AS POSSIBLE!
THE WAR CABINET NEEDS TO BE ON BOARD FIRST.
ON AIR
THE NEXT EVENING, 18 JUNE.
WHATEVER HAPPENS THE FLAME OF FRENCH RESISTANCE MUST NOT GO OUT!

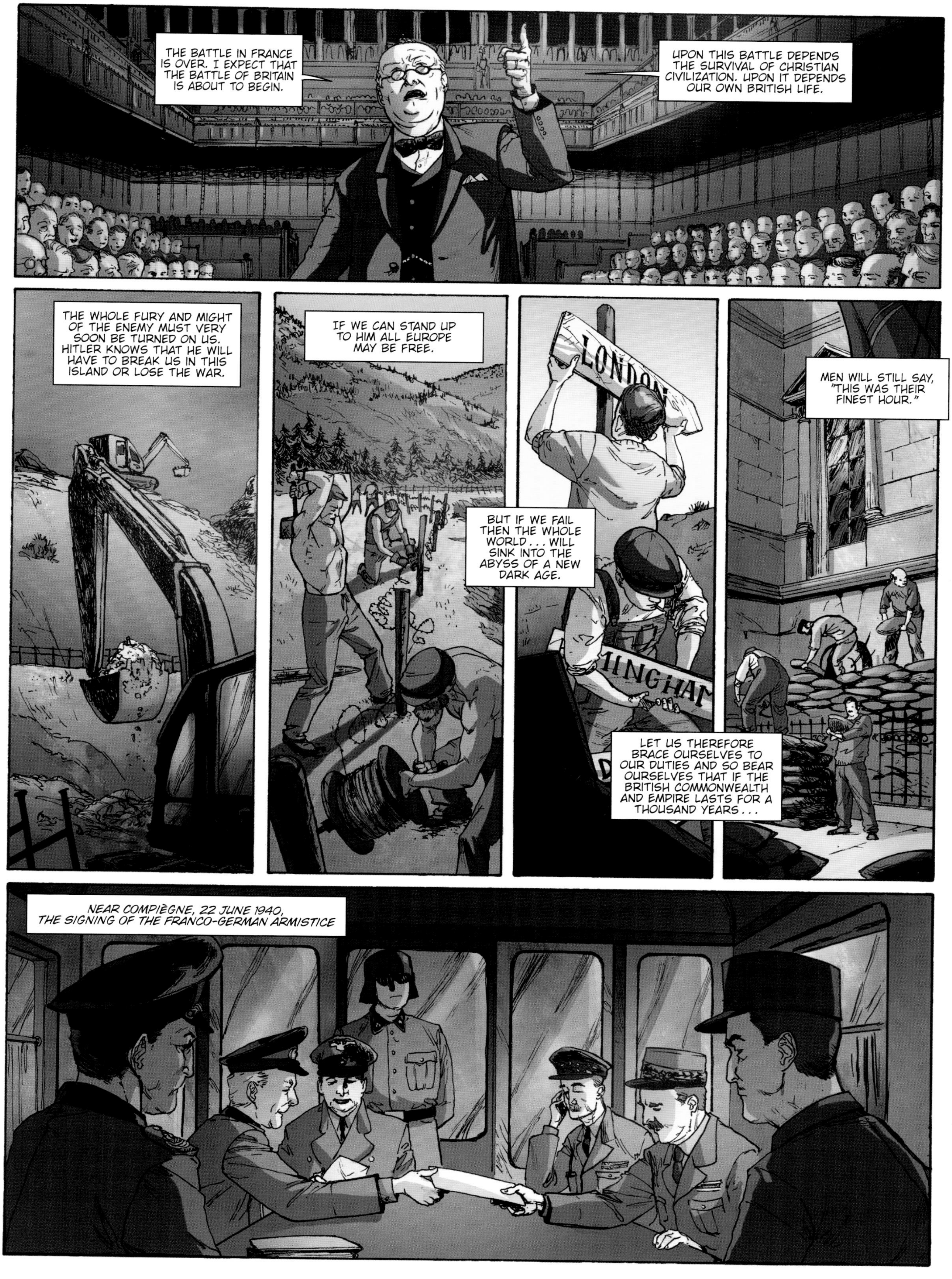

THE BATTLE IN FRANCE IS OVER. I EXPECT THAT THE BATTLE OF BRITAIN IS ABOUT TO BEGIN.
UPON THIS BATTLE DEPENDS THE SURVIVAL OF CHRISTIAN CIVILIZATION. UPON IT DEPENDS OUR OWN BRITISH LIFE.
THE WHOLE FURY AND MIGHT OF THE ENEMY MUST VERY SOON BE TURNED ON US. HITLER KNOWS THAT HE WILL HAVE TO BREAK US IN THIS ISLAND OR LOSE THE WAR.
IF WE CAN STAND UP TO HIM ALL EUROPE MAY BE FREE.
LONDON
BUT IF WE FAIL THEN THE WHOLE WORLD . . . WILL SINK INTO THE ABYSS OF A NEW DARK AGE.
LET US THEREFORE BRACE OURSELVES TO OUR DUTIES AND SO BEAR OURSELVES THAT IF THE BRITISH COMMONWEALTH AND EMPIRE LASTS FOR A THOUSAND YEARS . . .
MEN WILL STILL SAY, "THIS WAS THEIR FINEST HOUR."
NEAR COMPIÈGNE, 22 JUNE 1940, THE SIGNING OF THE FRANCO-GERMAN ARMISTICE

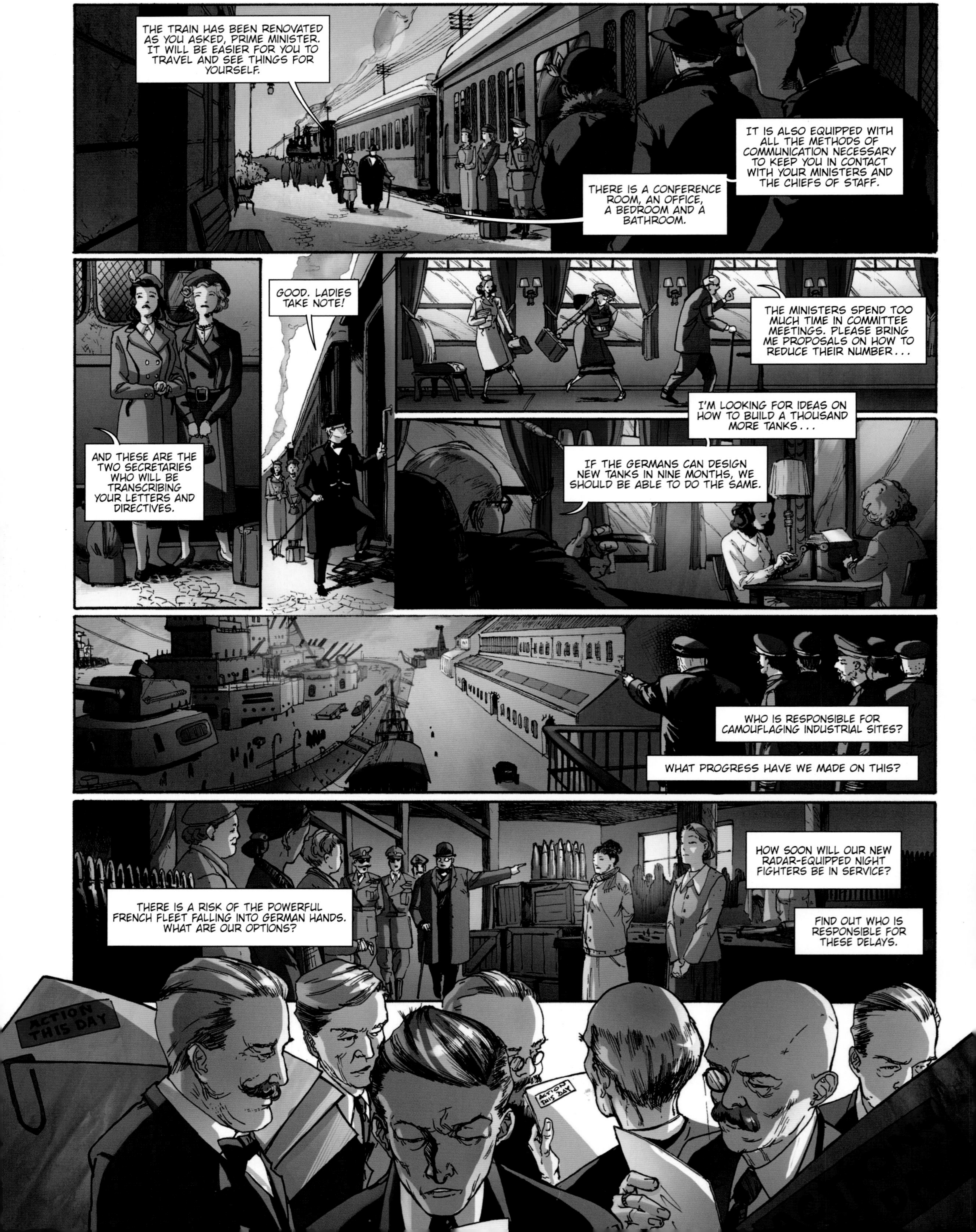

THE TRAIN HAS BEEN RENOVATED AS YOU ASKED, PRIME MINISTER. IT WILL BE EASIER FOR YOU TO TRAVEL AND SEE THINGS FOR YOURSELF.
IT IS ALSO EQUIPPED WITH ALL THE METHODS OF COMMUNICATION NECESSARY TO KEEP YOU IN CONTACT WITH YOUR MINISTERS AND THE CHIEFS OF STAFF.
THERE IS A CONFERENCE ROOM, AN OFFICE, A BEDROOM AND A BATHROOM.
AND THESE ARE THE TWO SECRETARIES WHO WILL BE TRANSCRIBING YOUR LETTERS AND DIRECTIVES.
GOOD. LADIES TAKE NOTE!
THE MINISTERS SPEND TOO MUCH TIME IN COMMITTEE MEETINGS. PLEASE BRING ME PROPOSALS ON HOW TO REDUCE THEIR NUMBER . . .
I'M LOOKING FOR IDEAS ON HOW TO BUILD A THOUSAND MORE TANKS . . .
IF THE GERMANS CAN DESIGN NEW TANKS IN NINE MONTHS, WE SHOULD BE ABLE TO DO THE SAME.
WHO IS RESPONSIBLE FOR CAMOUFLAGING INDUSTRIAL SITES?
WHAT PROGRESS HAVE WE MADE ON THIS?
THERE IS A RISK OF THE POWERFUL FRENCH FLEET FALLING INTO GERMAN HANDS. WHAT ARE OUR OPTIONS?
HOW SOON WILL OUR NEW RADAR-EQUIPPED NIGHT FIGHTERS BE IN SERVICE?
FIND OUT WHO IS RESPONSIBLE FOR THESE DELAYS.
ACTION THIS DAY
ACTION THIS DAY

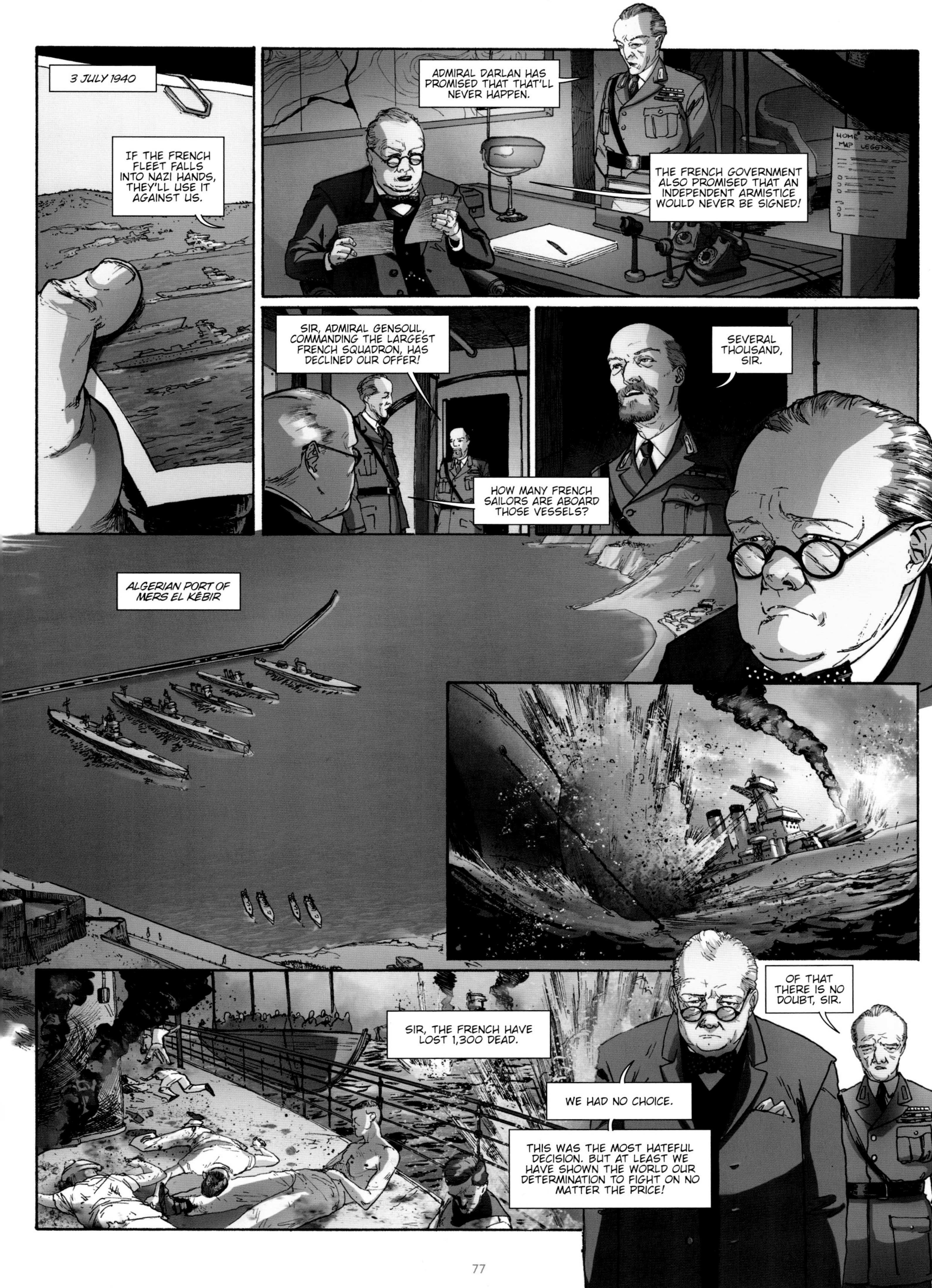
3 JULY 1940
IF THE FRENCH FLEET FALLS INTO NAZI HANDS, THEY'LL USE IT AGAINST US.
ADMIRAL DARLAN HAS PROMISED THAT THAT'LL NEVER HAPPEN.
THE FRENCH GOVERNMENT ALSO PROMISED THAT AN INDEPENDENT ARMISTICE WOULD NEVER BE SIGNED!
SIR, ADMIRAL GENSOUL, COMMANDING THE LARGEST FRENCH SQUADRON, HAS DECLINED OUR OFFER!
HOW MANY FRENCH SAILORS ARE ABOARD THOSE VESSELS?
SEVERAL THOUSAND, SIR.
ALGERIAN PORT OF MERS EL KÉBIR
SIR, THE FRENCH HAVE LOST 1,300 DEAD.
OF THAT THERE IS NO DOUBT, SIR.
WE HAD NO CHOICE.
THIS WAS THE MOST HATEFUL DECISION. BUT AT LEAST WE HAVE SHOWN THE WORLD OUR DETERMINATION TO FIGHT ON NO MATTER THE PRICE!

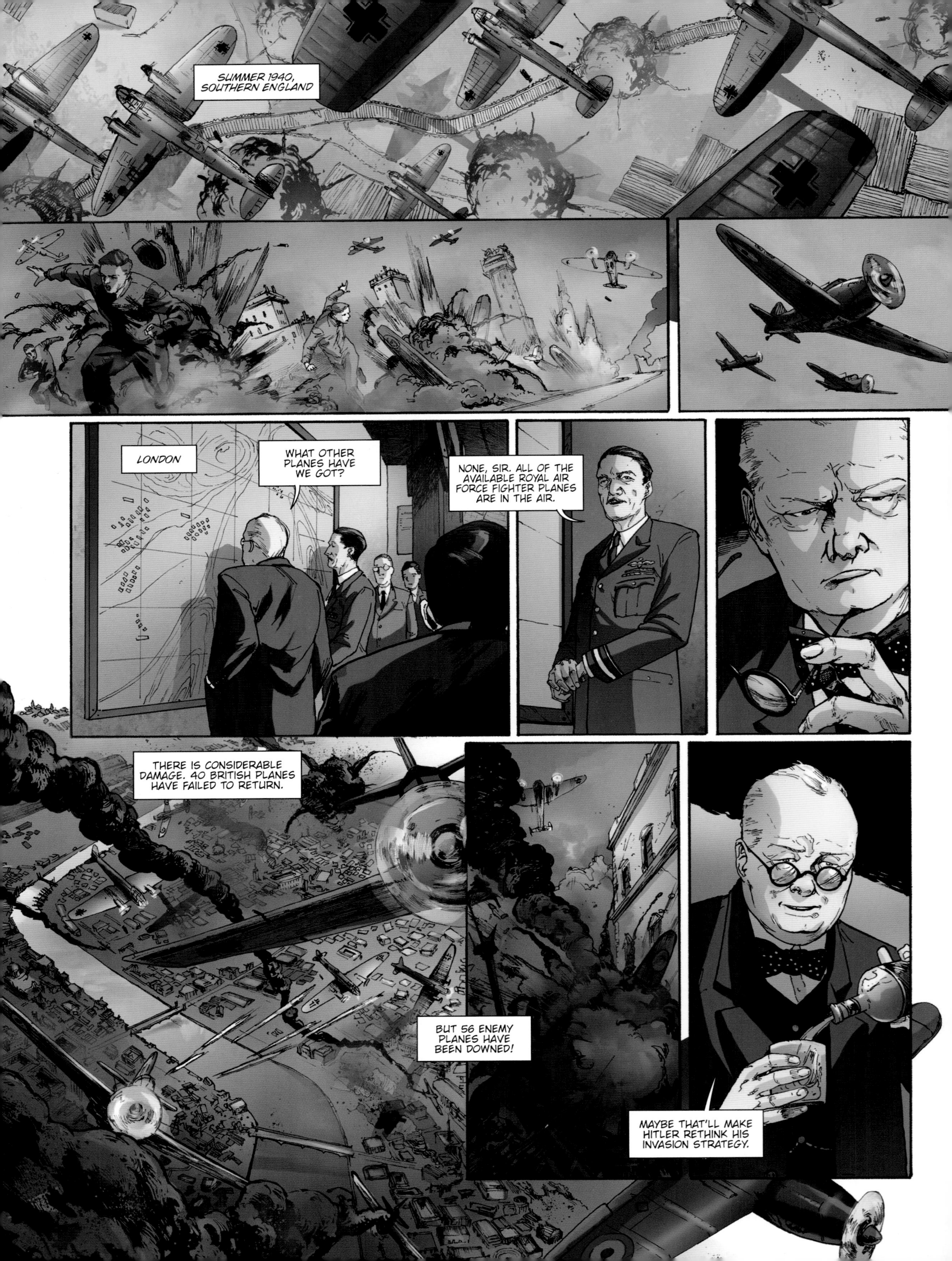
SUMMER 1940, SOUTHERN ENGLAND
LONDON
WHAT OTHER PLANES HAVE WE GOT?
NONE, SIR. ALL OF THE AVAILABLE ROYAL AIR FORCE FIGHTER PLANES ARE IN THE AIR.
THERE IS CONSIDERABLE DAMAGE. 40 BRITISH PLANES HAVE FAILED TO RETURN.
BUT 56 ENEMY PLANES HAVE BEEN DOWNED!
MAYBE THAT'LL MAKE HITLER RETHINK HIS INVASION STRATEGY.

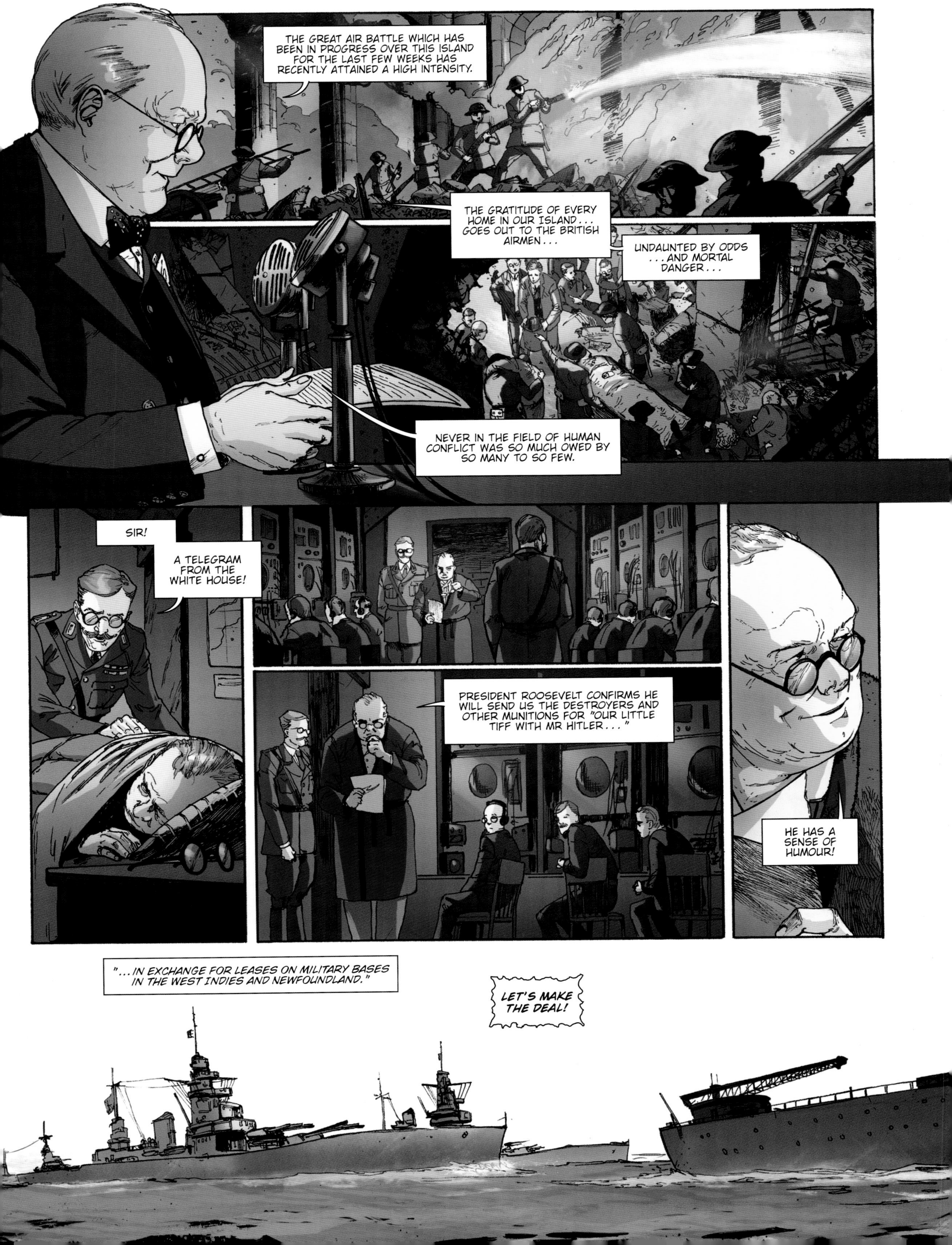
THE GREAT AIR BATTLE WHICH HAS BEEN IN PROGRESS OVER THIS ISLAND FOR THE LAST FEW WEEKS HAS RECENTLY ATTAINED A HIGH INTENSITY.
THE GRATITUDE OF EVERY HOME IN OUR ISLAND... GOES OUT TO THE BRITISH AIRMEN...
UNDAUNTED BY ODDS ...AND MORTAL DANGER...
NEVER IN THE FIELD OF HUMAN CONFLICT WAS SO MUCH OWED BY SO MANY TO SO FEW.
SIR!
A TELEGRAM FROM THE WHITE HOUSE!
PRESIDENT ROOSEVELT CONFIRMS HE WILL SEND US THE DESTROYERS AND OTHER MUNITIONS FOR "OUR LITTLE TIFF WITH MR HITLER..."
HE HAS A SENSE OF HUMOUR!
"...IN EXCHANGE FOR LEASES ON MILITARY BASES IN THE WEST INDIES AND NEWFOUNDLAND."
LET'S MAKE THE DEAL!

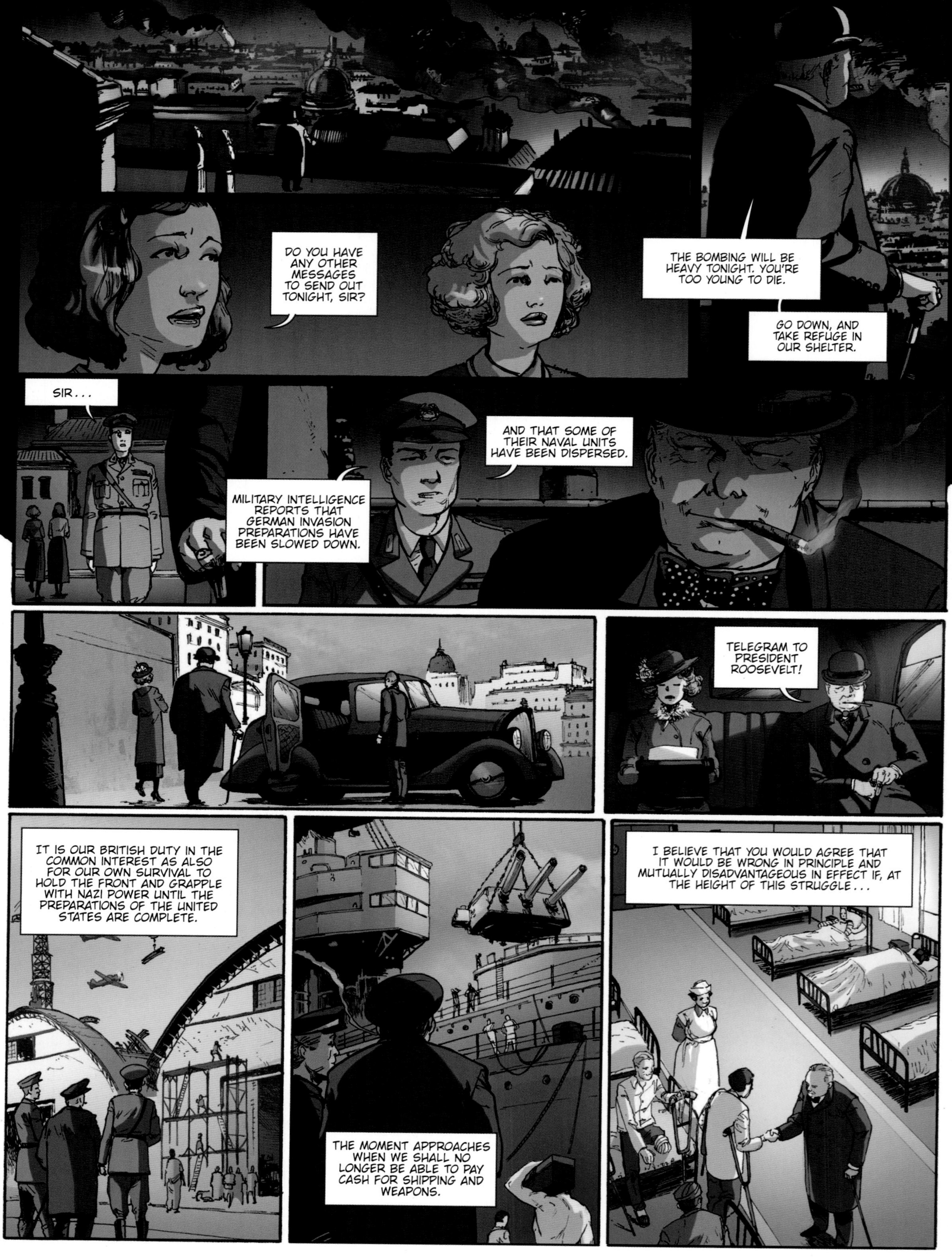
DO YOU HAVE ANY OTHER MESSAGES TO SEND OUT TONIGHT, SIR?
THE BOMBING WILL BE HEAVY TONIGHT. YOU'RE TOO YOUNG TO DIE.
GO DOWN, AND TAKE REFUGE IN OUR SHELTER.
SIR...
MILITARY INTELLIGENCE REPORTS THAT GERMAN INVASION PREPARATIONS HAVE BEEN SLOWED DOWN.
AND THAT SOME OF THEIR NAVAL UNITS HAVE BEEN DISPERSED.
TELEGRAM TO PRESIDENT ROOSEVELT!
IT IS OUR BRITISH DUTY IN THE COMMON INTEREST AS ALSO FOR OUR OWN SURVIVAL TO HOLD THE FRONT AND GRAPPLE WITH NAZI POWER UNTIL THE PREPARATIONS OF THE UNITED STATES ARE COMPLETE.
THE MOMENT APPROACHES WHEN WE SHALL NO LONGER BE ABLE TO PAY CASH FOR SHIPPING AND WEAPONS.
I BELIEVE THAT YOU WOULD AGREE THAT IT WOULD BE WRONG IN PRINCIPLE AND MUTUALLY DISADVANTAGEOUS IN EFFECT IF, AT THE HEIGHT OF THIS STRUGGLE...

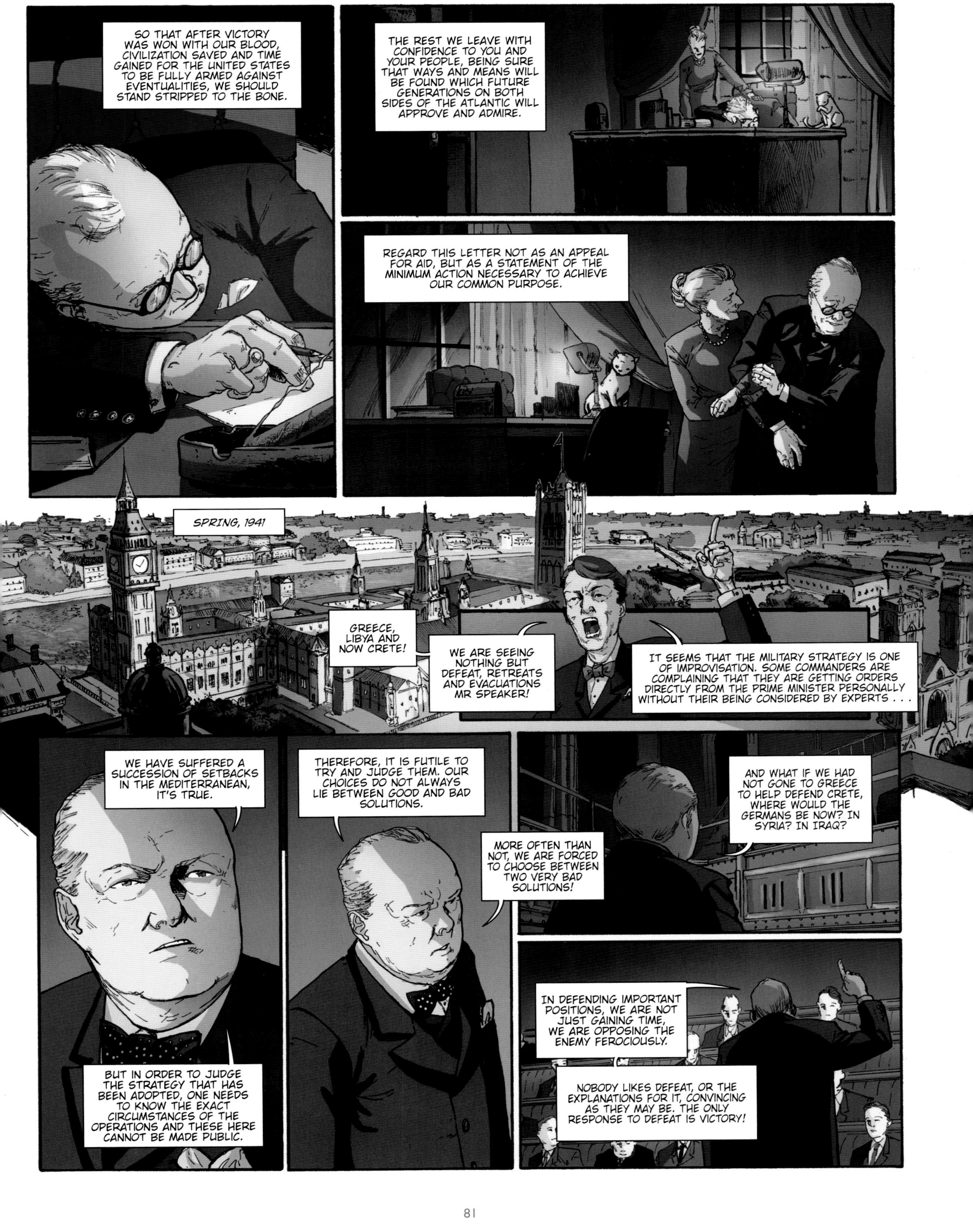
SO THAT AFTER VICTORY WAS WON WITH OUR BLOOD, CIVILIZATION SAVED AND TIME GAINED FOR THE UNITED STATES TO BE FULLY ARMED AGAINST EVENTUALITIES, WE SHOULD STAND STRIPPED TO THE BONE.
THE REST WE LEAVE WITH CONFIDENCE TO YOU AND YOUR PEOPLE, BEING SURE THAT WAYS AND MEANS WILL BE FOUND WHICH FUTURE GENERATIONS ON BOTH SIDES OF THE ATLANTIC WILL APPROVE AND ADMIRE.
REGARD THIS LETTER NOT AS AN APPEAL FOR AID, BUT AS A STATEMENT OF THE MINIMUM ACTION NECESSARY TO ACHIEVE OUR COMMON PURPOSE.
SPRING, 1941
GREECE, LIBYA AND NOW CRETE!
WE ARE SEEING NOTHING BUT DEFEAT, RETREATS AND EVACUATIONS MR SPEAKER!
IT SEEMS THAT THE MILITARY STRATEGY IS ONE OF IMPROVISATION. SOME COMMANDERS ARE COMPLAINING THAT THEY ARE GETTING ORDERS DIRECTLY FROM THE PRIME MINISTER PERSONALLY WITHOUT THEIR BEING CONSIDERED BY EXPERTS . . .
WE HAVE SUFFERED A SUCCESSION OF SETBACKS IN THE MEDITERRANEAN, IT'S TRUE.
BUT IN ORDER TO JUDGE THE STRATEGY THAT HAS BEEN ADOPTED, ONE NEEDS TO KNOW THE EXACT CIRCUMSTANCES OF THE OPERATIONS AND THESE HERE CANNOT BE MADE PUBLIC.
THEREFORE, IT IS FUTILE TO TRY AND JUDGE THEM. OUR CHOICES DO NOT ALWAYS LIE BETWEEN GOOD AND BAD SOLUTIONS.
MORE OFTEN THAN NOT, WE ARE FORCED TO CHOOSE BETWEEN TWO VERY BAD SOLUTIONS!
AND WHAT IF WE HAD NOT GONE TO GREECE TO HELP DEFEND CRETE, WHERE WOULD THE GERMANS BE NOW? IN SYRIA? IN IRAQ?
IN DEFENDING IMPORTANT POSITIONS, WE ARE NOT JUST GAINING TIME, WE ARE OPPOSING THE ENEMY FEROCIOUSLY.
NOBODY LIKES DEFEAT, OR THE EXPLANATIONS FOR IT, CONVINCING AS THEY MAY BE. THE ONLY RESPONSE TO DEFEAT IS VICTORY!

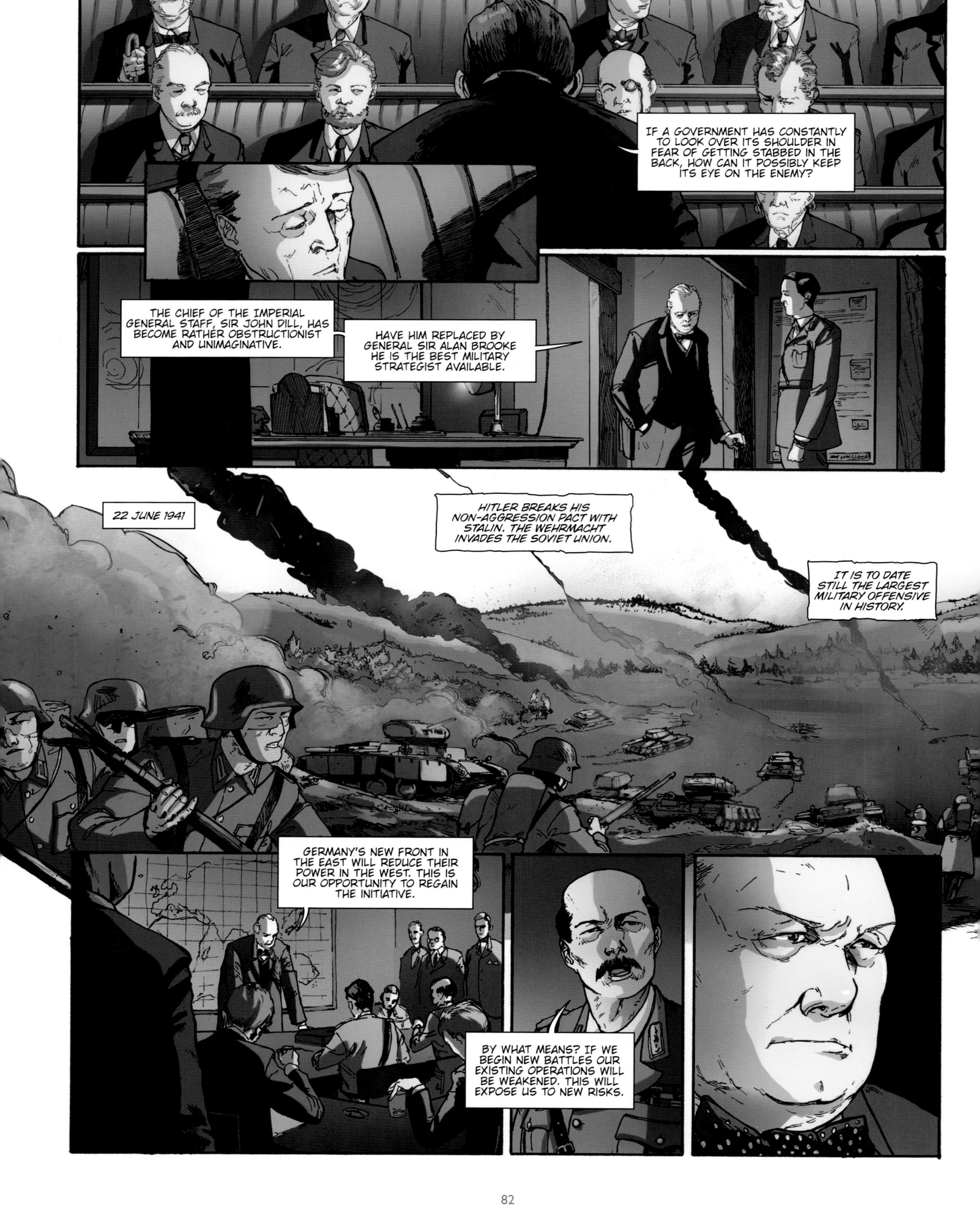
IF A GOVERNMENT HAS CONSTANTLY TO LOOK OVER ITS SHOULDER IN FEAR OF GETTING STABBED IN THE BACK, HOW CAN IT POSSIBLY KEEP ITS EYE ON THE ENEMY?
THE CHIEF OF THE IMPERIAL GENERAL STAFF, SIR JOHN DILL, HAS BECOME RATHER OBSTRUCTIONIST AND UNIMAGINATIVE.
HAVE HIM REPLACED BY GENERAL SIR ALAN BROOKE HE IS THE BEST MILITARY STRATEGIST AVAILABLE.
22 JUNE 1941
HITLER BREAKS HIS NON-AGGRESSION PACT WITH STALIN. THE WEHRMACHT INVADES THE SOVIET UNION.
IT IS TO DATE STILL THE LARGEST MILITARY OFFENSIVE IN HISTORY.
GERMANY'S NEW FRONT IN THE EAST WILL REDUCE THEIR POWER IN THE WEST. THIS IS OUR OPPORTUNITY TO REGAIN THE INITIATIVE.
BY WHAT MEANS? IF WE BEGIN NEW BATTLES OUR EXISTING OPERATIONS WILL BE WEAKENED. THIS WILL EXPOSE US TO NEW RISKS.

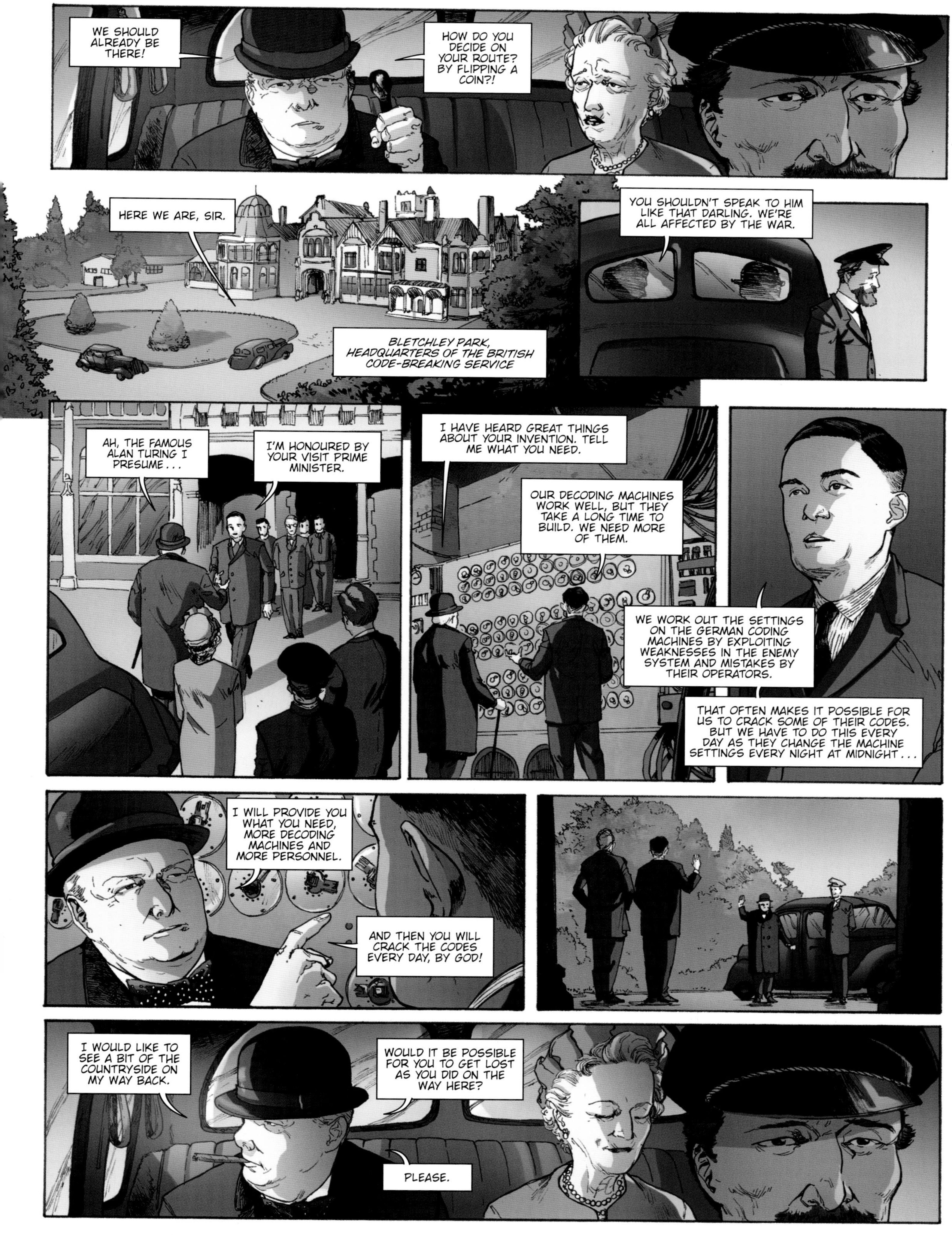
WE SHOULD ALREADY BE THERE!
HOW DO YOU DECIDE ON YOUR ROUTE? BY FLIPPING A COIN?!
HERE WE ARE, SIR.
BLETCHLEY PARK, HEADQUARTERS OF THE BRITISH CODE-BREAKING SERVICE
YOU SHOULDN'T SPEAK TO HIM LIKE THAT DARLING. WE'RE ALL AFFECTED BY THE WAR.
AH, THE FAMOUS ALAN TURING I PRESUME . . .
I'M HONOURED BY YOUR VISIT PRIME MINISTER.
I HAVE HEARD GREAT THINGS ABOUT YOUR INVENTION. TELL ME WHAT YOU NEED.
OUR DECODING MACHINES WORK WELL, BUT THEY TAKE A LONG TIME TO BUILD. WE NEED MORE OF THEM.
WE WORK OUT THE SETTINGS ON THE GERMAN CODING MACHINES BY EXPLOITING WEAKNESSES IN THE ENEMY SYSTEM AND MISTAKES BY THEIR OPERATORS.
THAT OFTEN MAKES IT POSSIBLE FOR US TO CRACK SOME OF THEIR CODES. BUT WE HAVE TO DO THIS EVERY DAY AS THEY CHANGE THE MACHINE SETTINGS EVERY NIGHT AT MIDNIGHT . . .
I WILL PROVIDE YOU WHAT YOU NEED, MORE DECODING MACHINES AND MORE PERSONNEL.
AND THEN YOU WILL CRACK THE CODES EVERY DAY, BY GOD!
I WOULD LIKE TO SEE A BIT OF THE COUNTRYSIDE ON MY WAY BACK.
WOULD IT BE POSSIBLE FOR YOU TO GET LOST AS YOU DID ON THE WAY HERE?
PLEASE.

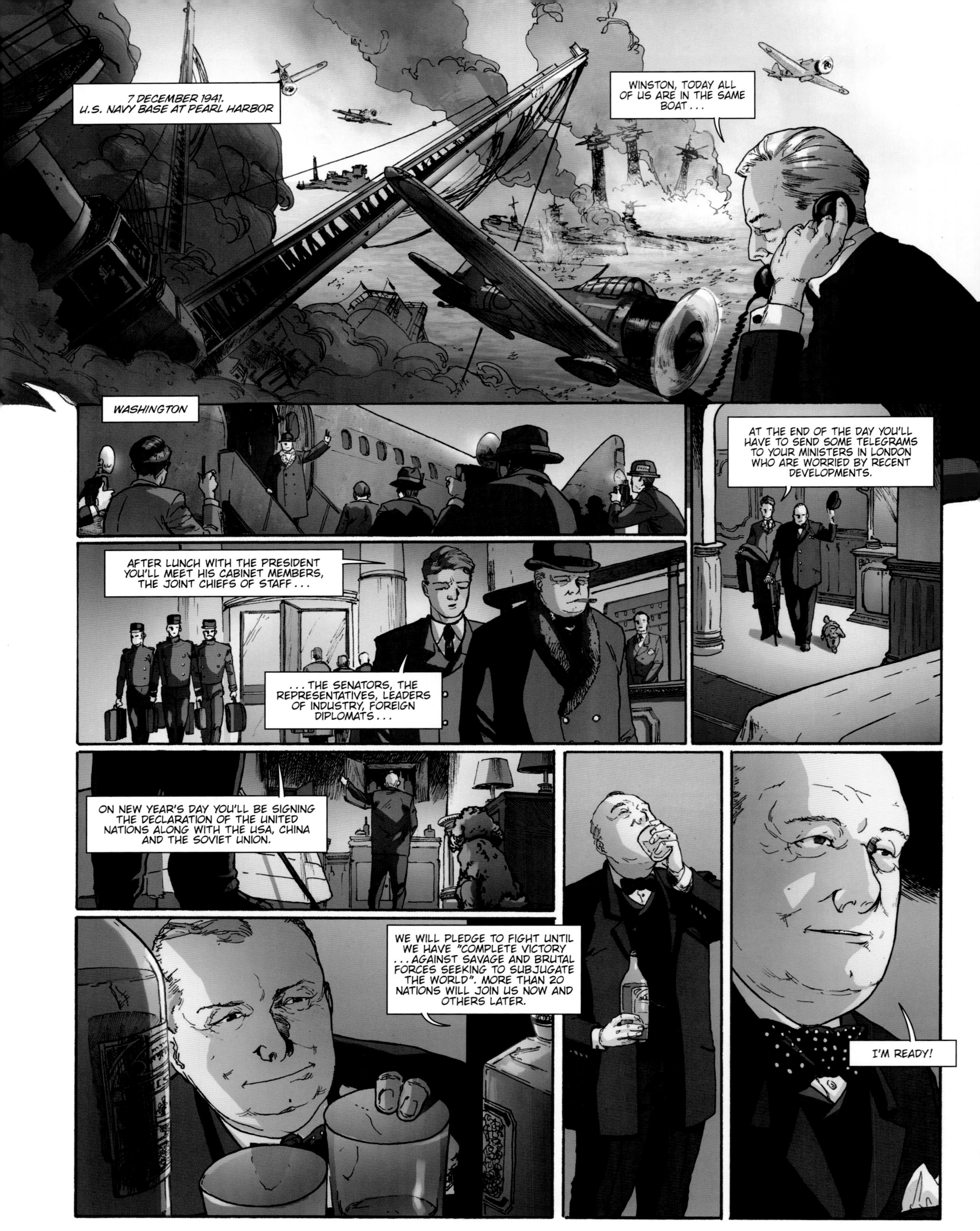
7 DECEMBER 1941. U.S. NAVY BASE AT PEARL HARBOR
WINSTON, TODAY ALL OF US ARE IN THE SAME BOAT . . .
WASHINGTON
AT THE END OF THE DAY YOU'LL HAVE TO SEND SOME TELEGRAMS TO YOUR MINISTERS IN LONDON WHO ARE WORRIED BY RECENT DEVELOPMENTS.
AFTER LUNCH WITH THE PRESIDENT YOU'LL MEET HIS CABINET MEMBERS, THE JOINT CHIEFS OF STAFF . . .
. . . THE SENATORS, THE REPRESENTATIVES, LEADERS OF INDUSTRY, FOREIGN DIPLOMATS . . .
ON NEW YEAR'S DAY YOU'LL BE SIGNING THE DECLARATION OF THE UNITED NATIONS ALONG WITH THE USA, CHINA AND THE SOVIET UNION.
WE WILL PLEDGE TO FIGHT UNTIL WE HAVE "COMPLETE VICTORY . . . AGAINST SAVAGE AND BRUTAL FORCES SEEKING TO SUBJUGATE THE WORLD". MORE THAN 20 NATIONS WILL JOIN US NOW AND OTHERS LATER.
I'M READY!

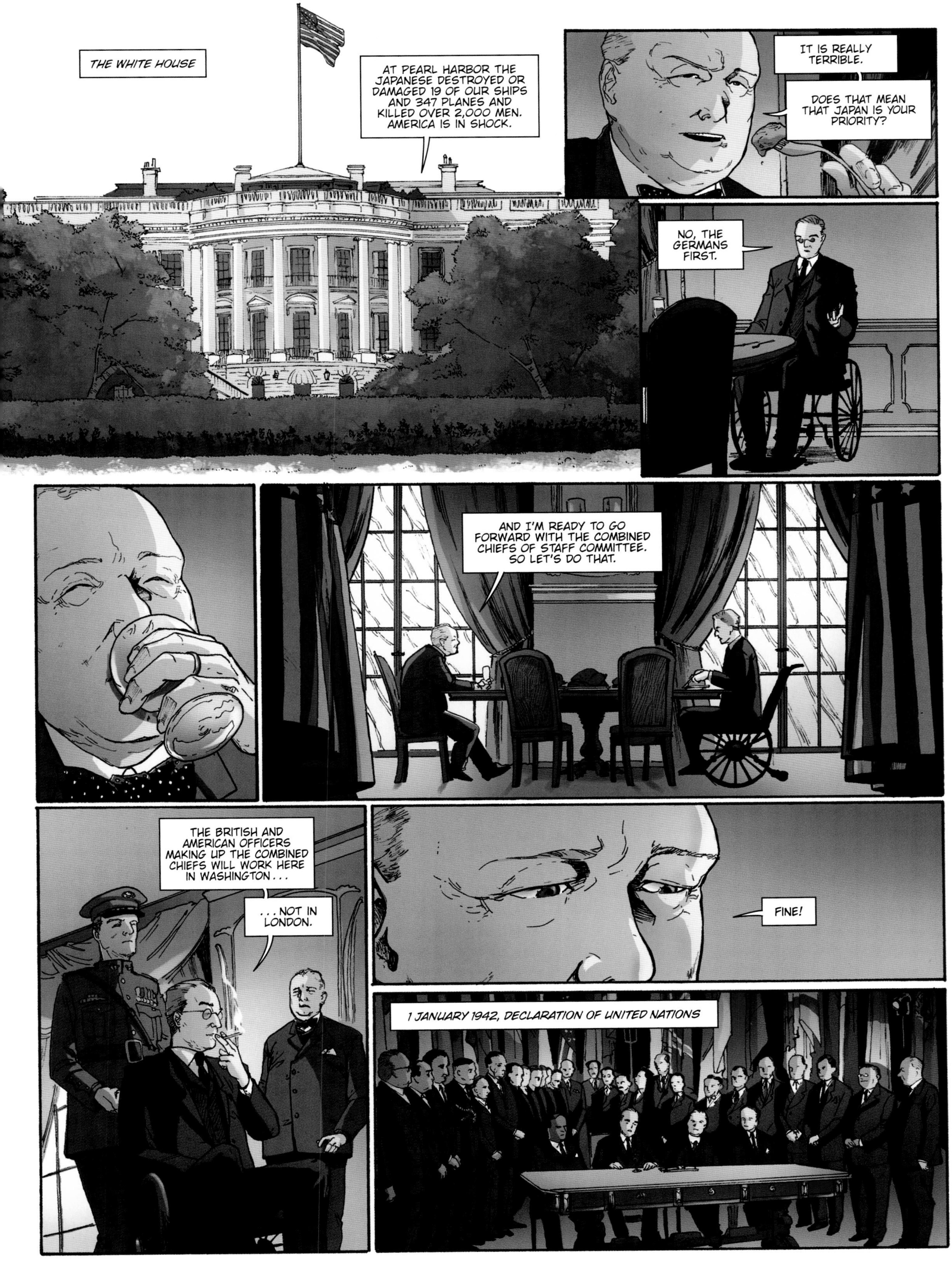
THE WHITE HOUSE
AT PEARL HARBOR THE JAPANESE DESTROYED OR DAMAGED 19 OF OUR SHIPS AND 347 PLANES AND KILLED OVER 2,000 MEN. AMERICA IS IN SHOCK.
IT IS REALLY TERRIBLE.
DOES THAT MEAN THAT JAPAN IS YOUR PRIORITY?
NO, THE GERMANS FIRST.
AND I'M READY TO GO FORWARD WITH THE COMBINED CHIEFS OF STAFF COMMITTEE. SO LET'S DO THAT.
THE BRITISH AND AMERICAN OFFICERS MAKING UP THE COMBINED CHIEFS WILL WORK HERE IN WASHINGTON . . .
. . . NOT IN LONDON.
FINE!
1 JANUARY 1942, DECLARATION OF UNITED NATIONS

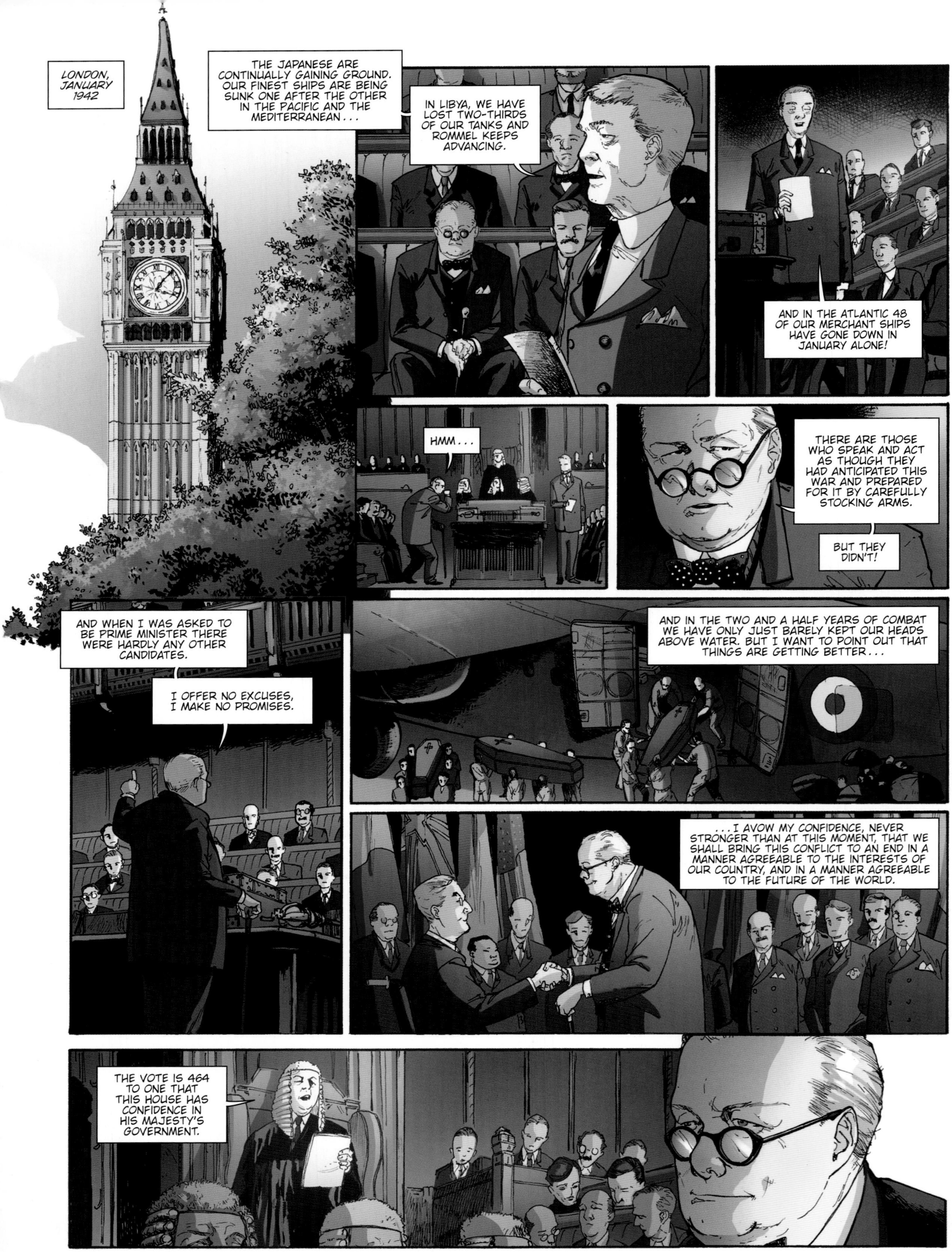
LONDON, JANUARY 1942
THE JAPANESE ARE CONTINUALLY GAINING GROUND. OUR FINEST SHIPS ARE BEING SUNK ONE AFTER THE OTHER IN THE PACIFIC AND THE MEDITERRANEAN . . .
IN LIBYA, WE HAVE LOST TWO-THIRDS OF OUR TANKS AND ROMMEL KEEPS ADVANCING.
AND IN THE ATLANTIC 48 OF OUR MERCHANT SHIPS HAVE GONE DOWN IN JANUARY ALONE!
HMM . . .
THERE ARE THOSE WHO SPEAK AND ACT AS THOUGH THEY HAD ANTICIPATED THIS WAR AND PREPARED FOR IT BY CAREFULLY STOCKING ARMS.
BUT THEY DIDN'T!
AND WHEN I WAS ASKED TO BE PRIME MINISTER THERE WERE HARDLY ANY OTHER CANDIDATES.
I OFFER NO EXCUSES, I MAKE NO PROMISES.
AND IN THE TWO AND A HALF YEARS OF COMBAT WE HAVE ONLY JUST BARELY KEPT OUR HEADS ABOVE WATER. BUT I WANT TO POINT OUT THAT THINGS ARE GETTING BETTER . . .
. . . I AVOW MY CONFIDENCE, NEVER STRONGER THAN AT THIS MOMENT, THAT WE SHALL BRING THIS CONFLICT TO AN END IN A MANNER AGREEABLE TO THE INTERESTS OF OUR COUNTRY, AND IN A MANNER AGREEABLE TO THE FUTURE OF THE WORLD.
THE VOTE IS 464 TO ONE THAT THIS HOUSE HAS CONFIDENCE IN HIS MAJESTY'S GOVERNMENT.

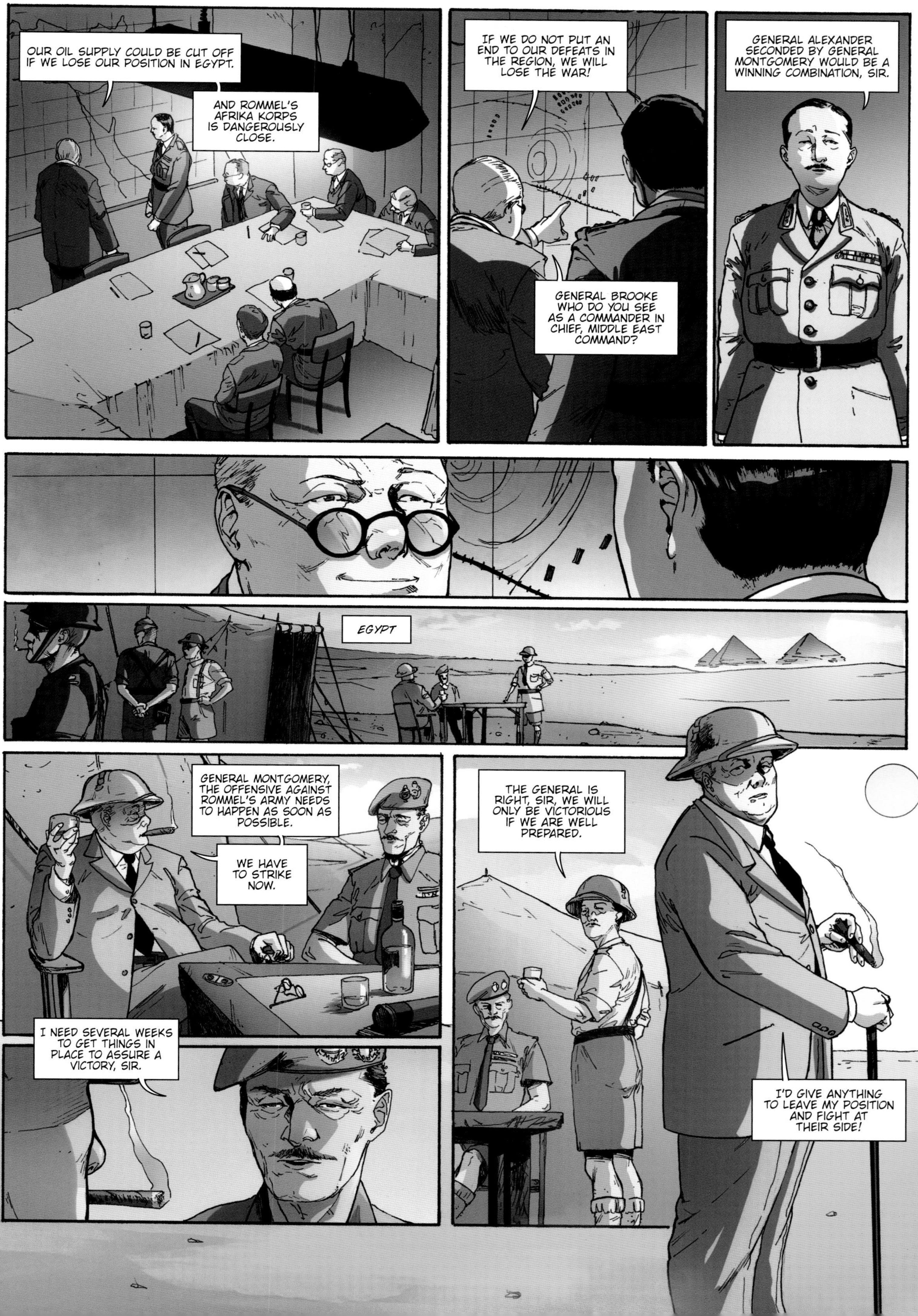
OUR OIL SUPPLY COULD BE CUT OFF IF WE LOSE OUR POSITION IN EGYPT.
AND ROMMEL'S AFRIKA KORPS IS DANGEROUSLY CLOSE.
IF WE DO NOT PUT AN END TO OUR DEFEATS IN THE REGION, WE WILL LOSE THE WAR!
GENERAL BROOKE WHO DO YOU SEE AS A COMMANDER IN CHIEF, MIDDLE EAST COMMAND?
GENERAL ALEXANDER SECONDED BY GENERAL MONTGOMERY WOULD BE A WINNING COMBINATION, SIR.
EGYPT
GENERAL MONTGOMERY, THE OFFENSIVE AGAINST ROMMEL'S ARMY NEEDS TO HAPPEN AS SOON AS POSSIBLE.
WE HAVE TO STRIKE NOW.
I NEED SEVERAL WEEKS TO GET THINGS IN PLACE TO ASSURE A VICTORY, SIR.
THE GENERAL IS RIGHT, SIR, WE WILL ONLY BE VICTORIOUS IF WE ARE WELL PREPARED.
I'D GIVE ANYTHING TO LEAVE MY POSITION AND FIGHT AT THEIR SIDE!

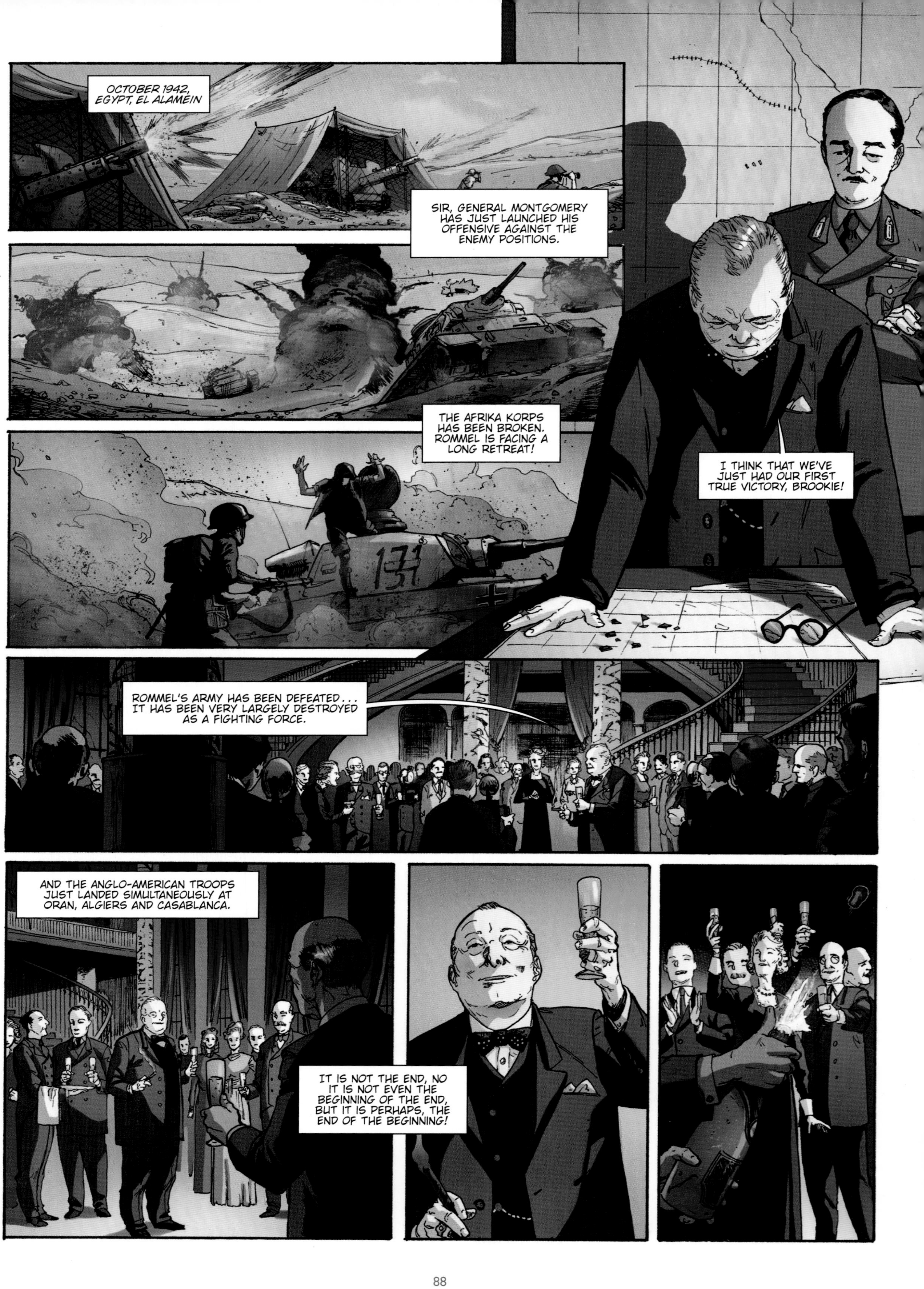
OCTOBER 1942, EGYPT, EL ALAMEIN
SIR, GENERAL MONTGOMERY HAS JUST LAUNCHED HIS OFFENSIVE AGAINST THE ENEMY POSITIONS.
THE AFRIKA KORPS HAS BEEN BROKEN. ROMMEL IS FACING A LONG RETREAT!
I THINK THAT WE'VE JUST HAD OUR FIRST TRUE VICTORY, BROOKIE!
ROMMEL'S ARMY HAS BEEN DEFEATED... IT HAS BEEN VERY LARGELY DESTROYED AS A FIGHTING FORCE.
AND THE ANGLO-AMERICAN TROOPS JUST LANDED SIMULTANEOUSLY AT ORAN, ALGIERS AND CASABLANCA.
IT IS NOT THE END, NO IT IS NOT EVEN THE BEGINNING OF THE END, BUT IT IS PERHAPS, THE END OF THE BEGINNING!

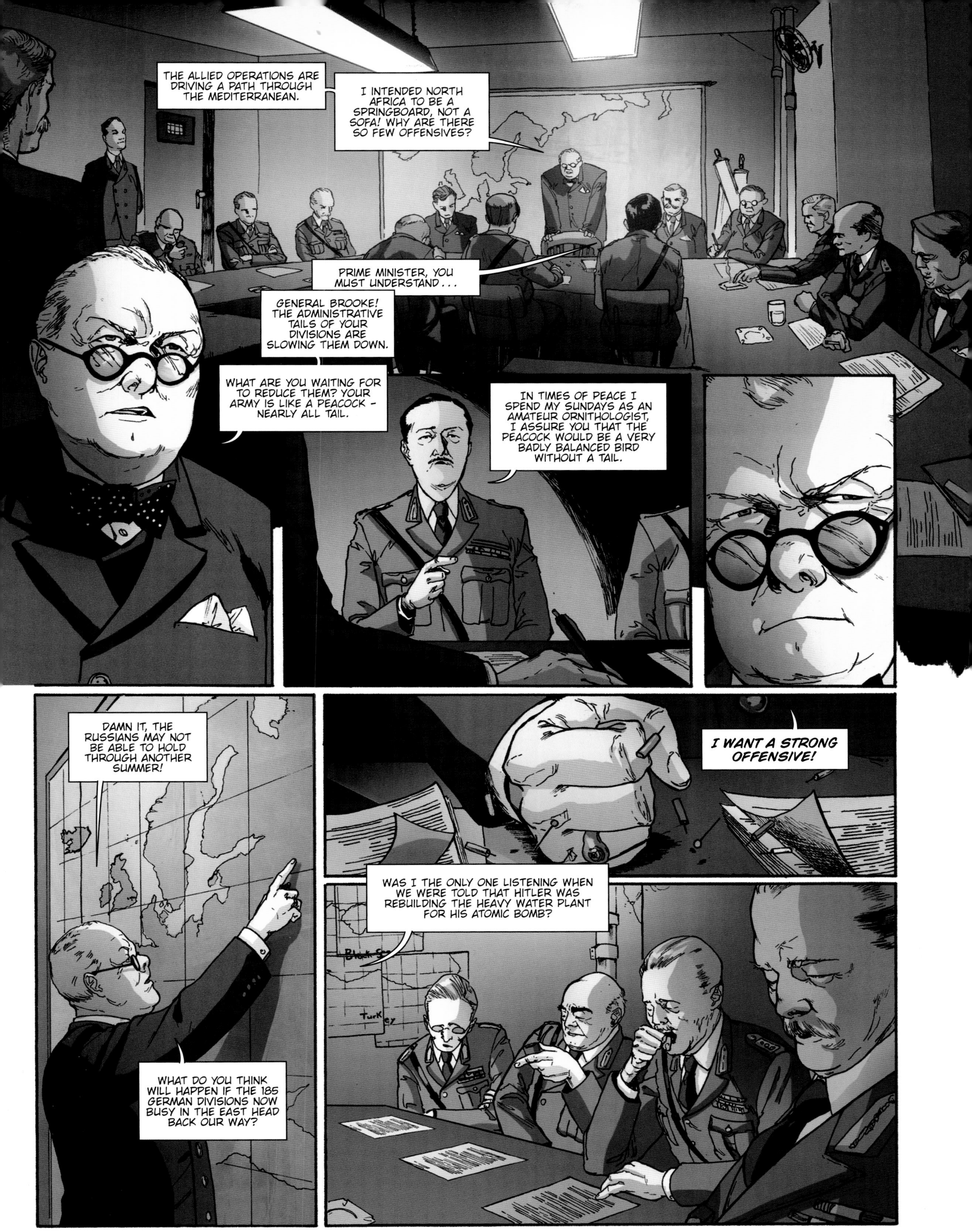
THE ALLIED OPERATIONS ARE DRIVING A PATH THROUGH THE MEDITERRANEAN.
I INTENDED NORTH AFRICA TO BE A SPRINGBOARD, NOT A SOFA! WHY ARE THERE SO FEW OFFENSIVES?
PRIME MINISTER, YOU MUST UNDERSTAND . . .
GENERAL BROOKE! THE ADMINISTRATIVE TAILS OF YOUR DIVISIONS ARE SLOWING THEM DOWN.
WHAT ARE YOU WAITING FOR TO REDUCE THEM? YOUR ARMY IS LIKE A PEACOCK - NEARLY ALL TAIL.
IN TIMES OF PEACE I SPEND MY SUNDAYS AS AN AMATEUR ORNITHOLOGIST, I ASSURE YOU THAT THE PEACOCK WOULD BE A VERY BADLY BALANCED BIRD WITHOUT A TAIL.
DAMN IT, THE RUSSIANS MAY NOT BE ABLE TO HOLD THROUGH ANOTHER SUMMER!
WHAT DO YOU THINK WILL HAPPEN IF THE 185 GERMAN DIVISIONS NOW BUSY IN THE EAST HEAD BACK OUR WAY?
I WANT A STRONG OFFENSIVE!
WAS I THE ONLY ONE LISTENING WHEN WE WERE TOLD THAT HITLER WAS REBUILDING THE HEAVY WATER PLANT FOR HIS ATOMIC BOMB?
Turkey

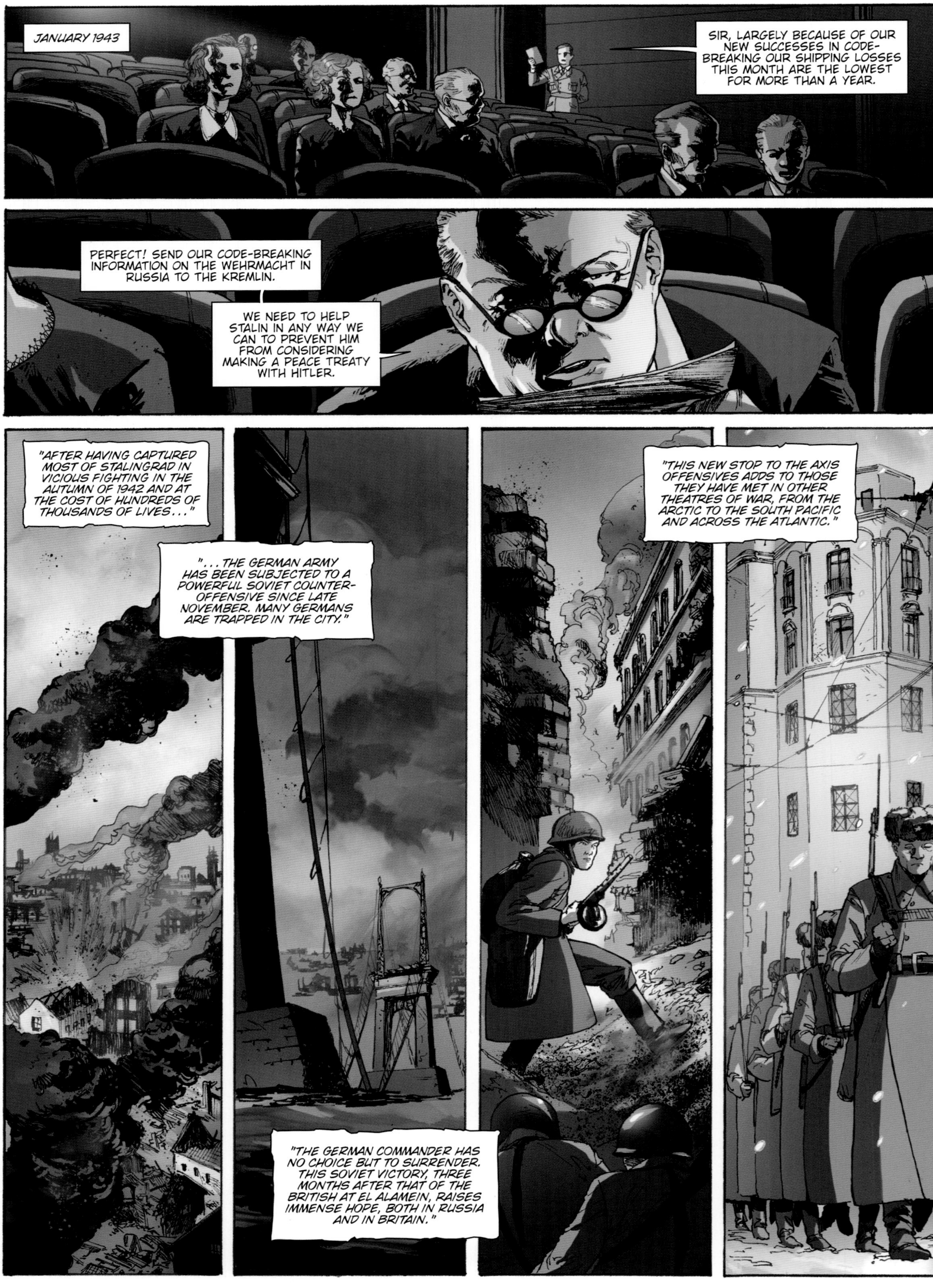

JANUARY 1943
SIR, LARGELY BECAUSE OF OUR NEW SUCCESSES IN CODE-BREAKING OUR SHIPPING LOSSES THIS MONTH ARE THE LOWEST FOR MORE THAN A YEAR.
PERFECT! SEND OUR CODE-BREAKING INFORMATION ON THE WEHRMACHT IN RUSSIA TO THE KREMLIN.
WE NEED TO HELP STALIN IN ANY WAY WE CAN TO PREVENT HIM FROM CONSIDERING MAKING A PEACE TREATY WITH HITLER.
"AFTER HAVING CAPTURED MOST OF STALINGRAD IN VICIOUS FIGHTING IN THE AUTUMN OF 1942 AND AT THE COST OF HUNDREDS OF THOUSANDS OF LIVES..."
"...THE GERMAN ARMY HAS BEEN SUBJECTED TO A POWERFUL SOVIET COUNTER-OFFENSIVE SINCE LATE NOVEMBER. MANY GERMANS ARE TRAPPED IN THE CITY."
"THE GERMAN COMMANDER HAS NO CHOICE BUT TO SURRENDER. THIS SOVIET VICTORY, THREE MONTHS AFTER THAT OF THE BRITISH AT EL ALAMEIN, RAISES IMMENSE HOPE, BOTH IN RUSSIA AND IN BRITAIN."
"THIS NEW STOP TO THE AXIS OFFENSIVES ADDS TO THOSE THEY HAVE MET IN OTHER THEATRES OF WAR, FROM THE ARCTIC TO THE SOUTH PACIFIC AND ACROSS THE ATLANTIC."

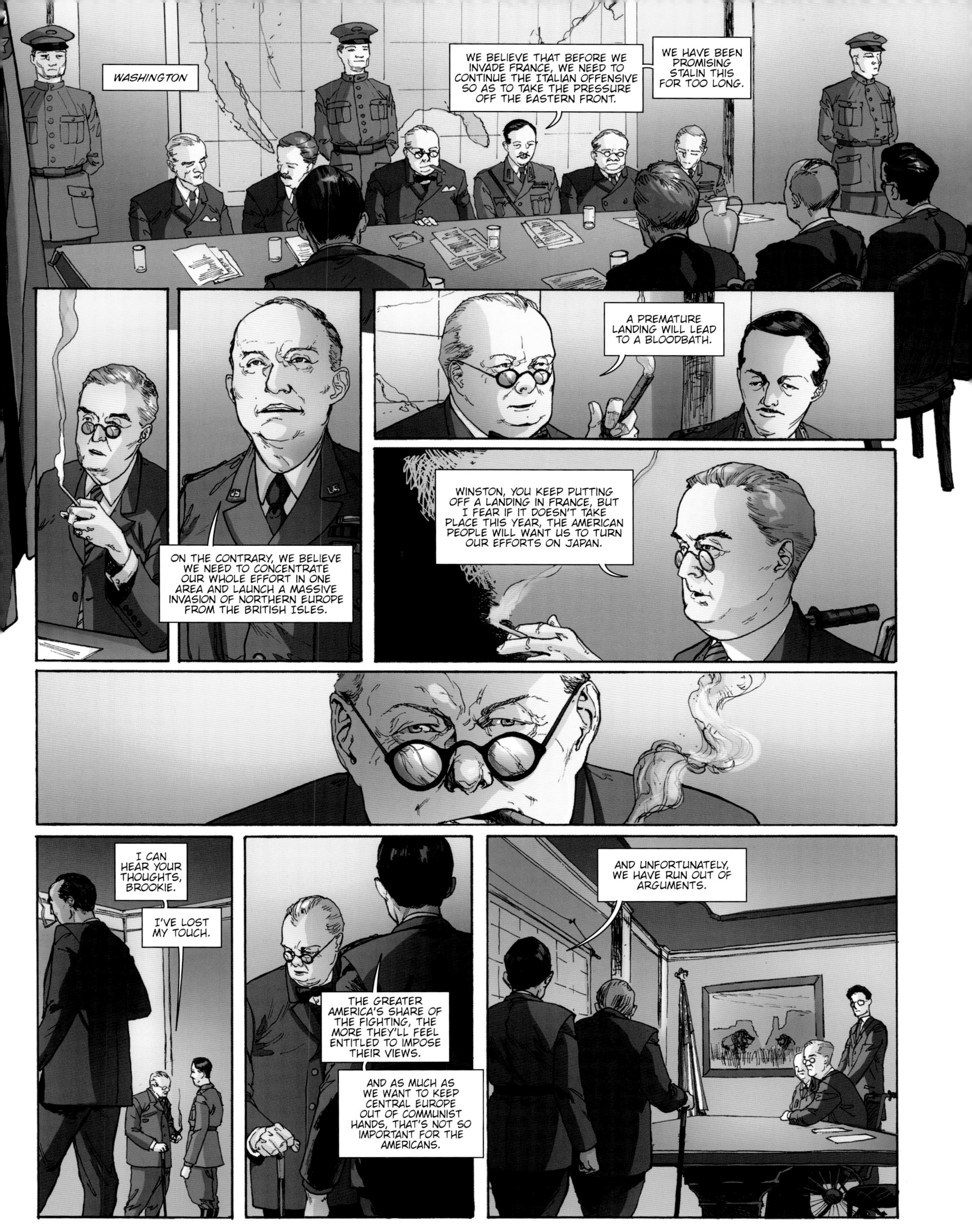

WASHINGTON
WE BELIEVE THAT BEFORE WE INVADE FRANCE, WE NEED TO CONTINUE THE ITALIAN OFFENSIVE SO AS TO TAKE THE PRESSURE OFF THE EASTERN FRONT.
WE HAVE BEEN PROMISING STALIN THIS FOR TOO LONG.
ON THE CONTRARY, WE BELIEVE WE NEED TO CONCENTRATE OUR WHOLE EFFORT IN ONE AREA AND LAUNCH A MASSIVE INVASION OF NORTHERN EUROPE FROM THE BRITISH ISLES.
A PREMATURE LANDING WILL LEAD TO A BLOODBATH.
WINSTON, YOU KEEP PUTTING OFF A LANDING IN FRANCE, BUT I FEAR IF IT DOESN'T TAKE PLACE THIS YEAR, THE AMERICAN PEOPLE WILL WANT US TO TURN OUR EFFORTS ON JAPAN.
I CAN HEAR YOUR THOUGHTS, BROOKIE.
I'VE LOST MY TOUCH.
THE GREATER AMERICA'S SHARE OF THE FIGHTING, THE MORE THEY'LL FEEL ENTITLED TO IMPOSE THEIR VIEWS.
AND AS MUCH AS WE WANT TO KEEP CENTRAL EUROPE OUT OF COMMUNIST HANDS, THAT'S NOT SO IMPORTANT FOR THE AMERICANS.
AND UNFORTUNATELY, WE HAVE RUN OUT OF ARGUMENTS.

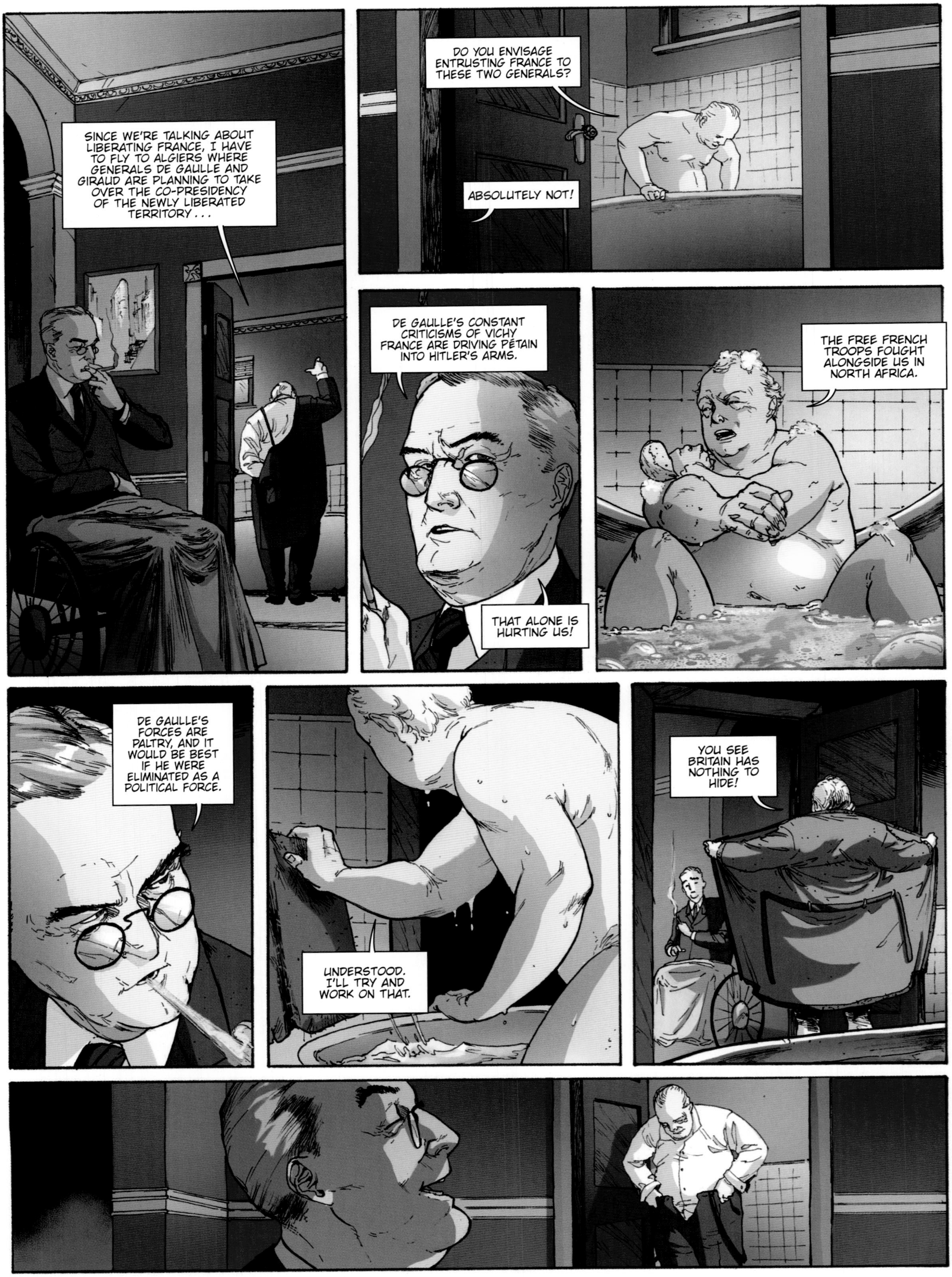

SINCE WE'RE TALKING ABOUT LIBERATING FRANCE, I HAVE TO FLY TO ALGIERS WHERE GENERALS DE GAULLE AND GIRAUD ARE PLANNING TO TAKE OVER THE CO-PRESIDENCY OF THE NEWLY LIBERATED TERRITORY . . .
DO YOU ENVISAGE ENTRUSTING FRANCE TO THESE TWO GENERALS?
ABSOLUTELY NOT!
DE GAULLE'S CONSTANT CRITICISMS OF VICHY FRANCE ARE DRIVING PÉTAIN INTO HITLER'S ARMS.
THAT ALONE IS HURTING US!
THE FREE FRENCH TROOPS FOUGHT ALONGSIDE US IN NORTH AFRICA.
DE GAULLE'S FORCES ARE PALTRY, AND IT WOULD BE BEST IF HE WERE ELIMINATED AS A POLITICAL FORCE.
UNDERSTOOD. I'LL TRY AND WORK ON THAT.
YOU SEE BRITAIN HAS NOTHING TO HIDE!

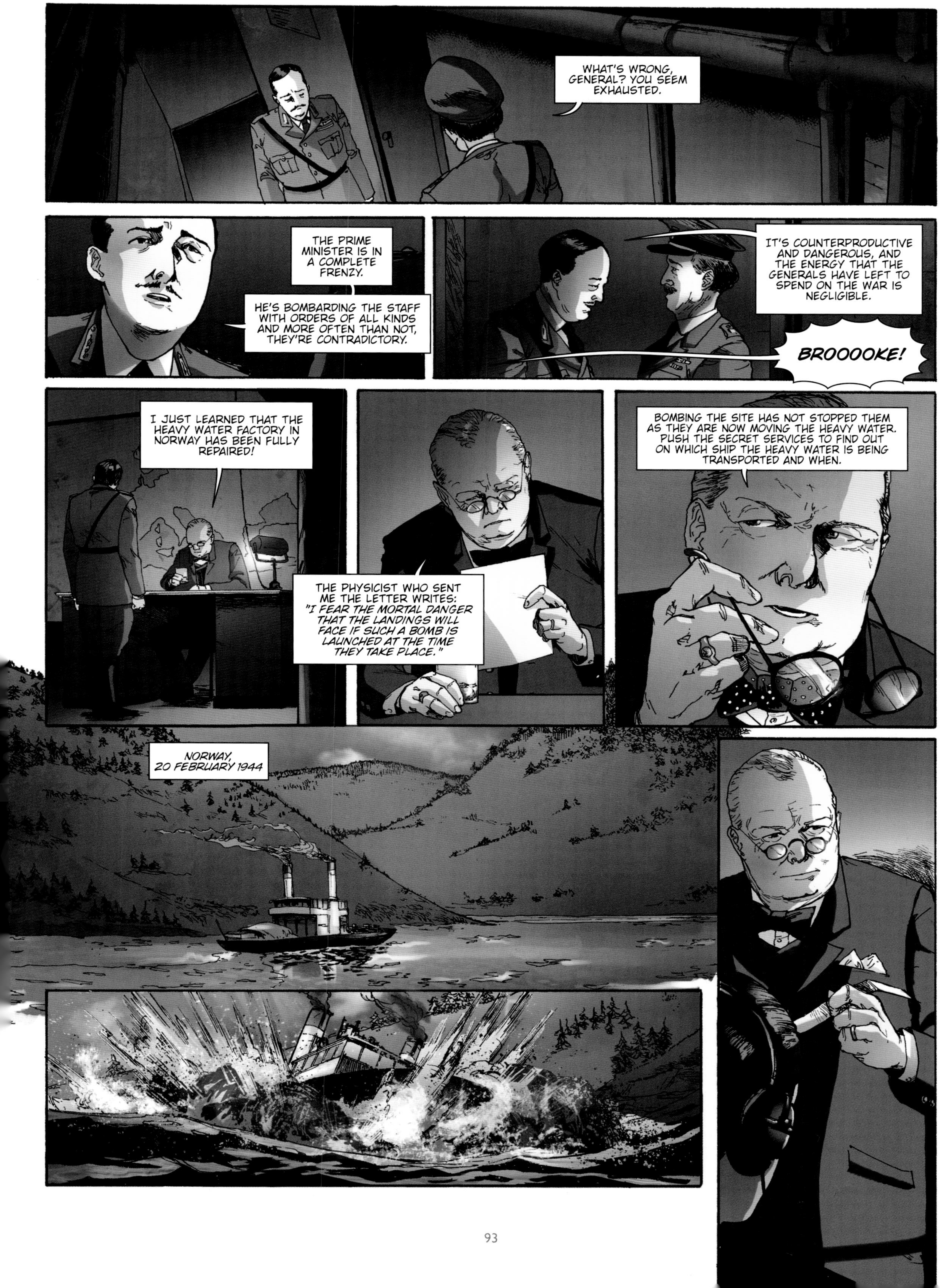
WHAT'S WRONG, GENERAL? YOU SEEM EXHAUSTED.
THE PRIME MINISTER IS IN A COMPLETE FRENZY.
HE'S BOMBARDING THE STAFF WITH ORDERS OF ALL KINDS AND MORE OFTEN THAN NOT, THEY'RE CONTRADICTORY.
IT'S COUNTERPRODUCTIVE AND DANGEROUS, AND THE ENERGY THAT THE GENERALS HAVE LEFT TO SPEND ON THE WAR IS NEGLIGIBLE.
BROOOOKE!
I JUST LEARNED THAT THE HEAVY WATER FACTORY IN NORWAY HAS BEEN FULLY REPAIRED!
THE PHYSICIST WHO SENT ME THE LETTER WRITES: "I FEAR THE MORTAL DANGER THAT THE LANDINGS WILL FACE IF SUCH A BOMB IS LAUNCHED AT THE TIME THEY TAKE PLACE."
BOMBING THE SITE HAS NOT STOPPED THEM AS THEY ARE NOW MOVING THE HEAVY WATER. PUSH THE SECRET SERVICES TO FIND OUT ON WHICH SHIP THE HEAVY WATER IS BEING TRANSPORTED AND WHEN.
NORWAY, 20 FEBRUARY 1944

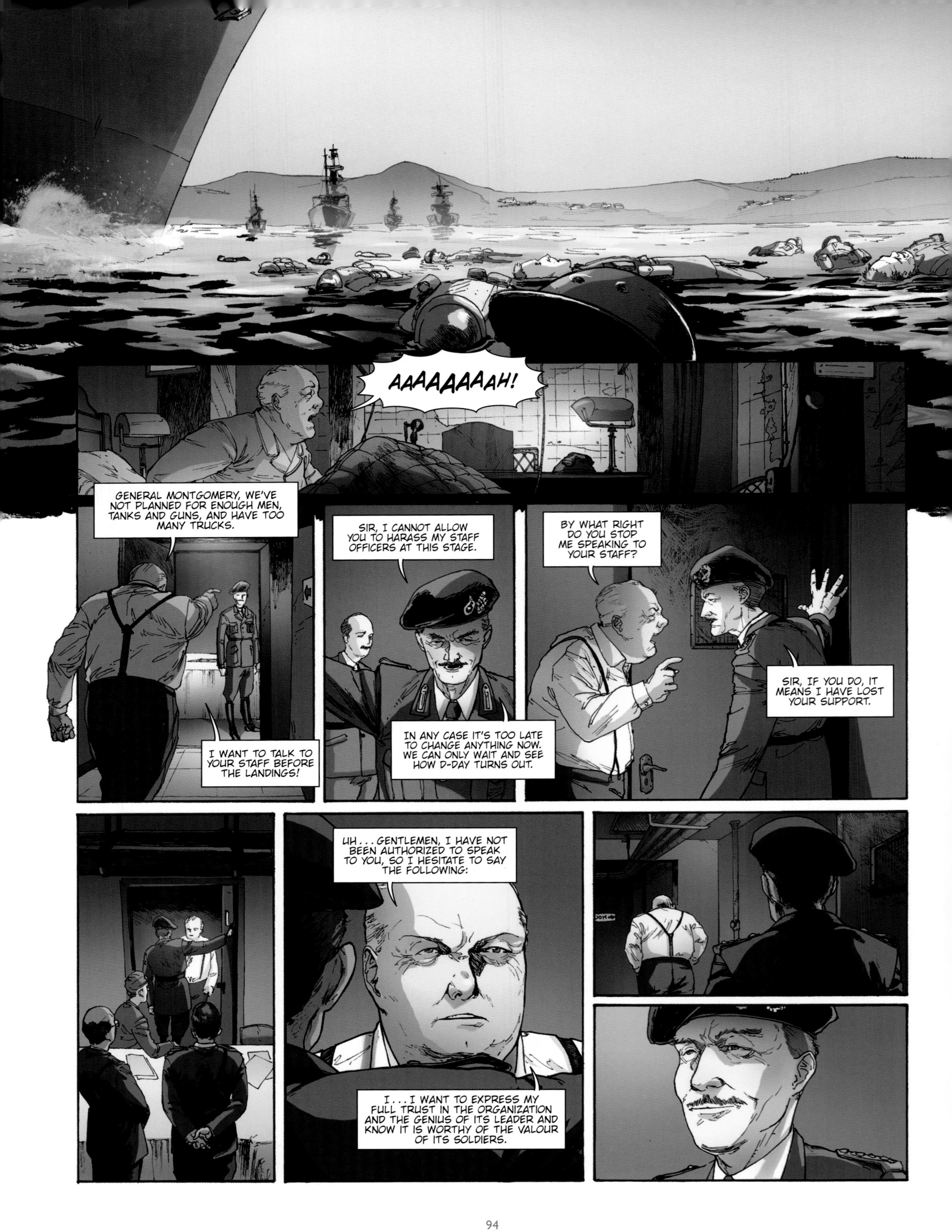

AAAAAAAAH!
GENERAL MONTGOMERY, WE'VE NOT PLANNED FOR ENOUGH MEN, TANKS AND GUNS, AND HAVE TOO MANY TRUCKS.
I WANT TO TALK TO YOUR STAFF BEFORE THE LANDINGS!
SIR, I CANNOT ALLOW YOU TO HARASS MY STAFF OFFICERS AT THIS STAGE.
IN ANY CASE IT'S TOO LATE TO CHANGE ANYTHING NOW. WE CAN ONLY WAIT AND SEE HOW D-DAY TURNS OUT.
BY WHAT RIGHT DO YOU STOP ME SPEAKING TO YOUR STAFF?
SIR, IF YOU DO, IT MEANS I HAVE LOST YOUR SUPPORT.
UH . . . GENTLEMEN, I HAVE NOT BEEN AUTHORIZED TO SPEAK TO YOU, SO I HESITATE TO SAY THE FOLLOWING:
I . . . I WANT TO EXPRESS MY FULL TRUST IN THE ORGANIZATION AND THE GENIUS OF ITS LEADER AND KNOW IT IS WORTHY OF THE VALOUR OF ITS SOLDIERS.

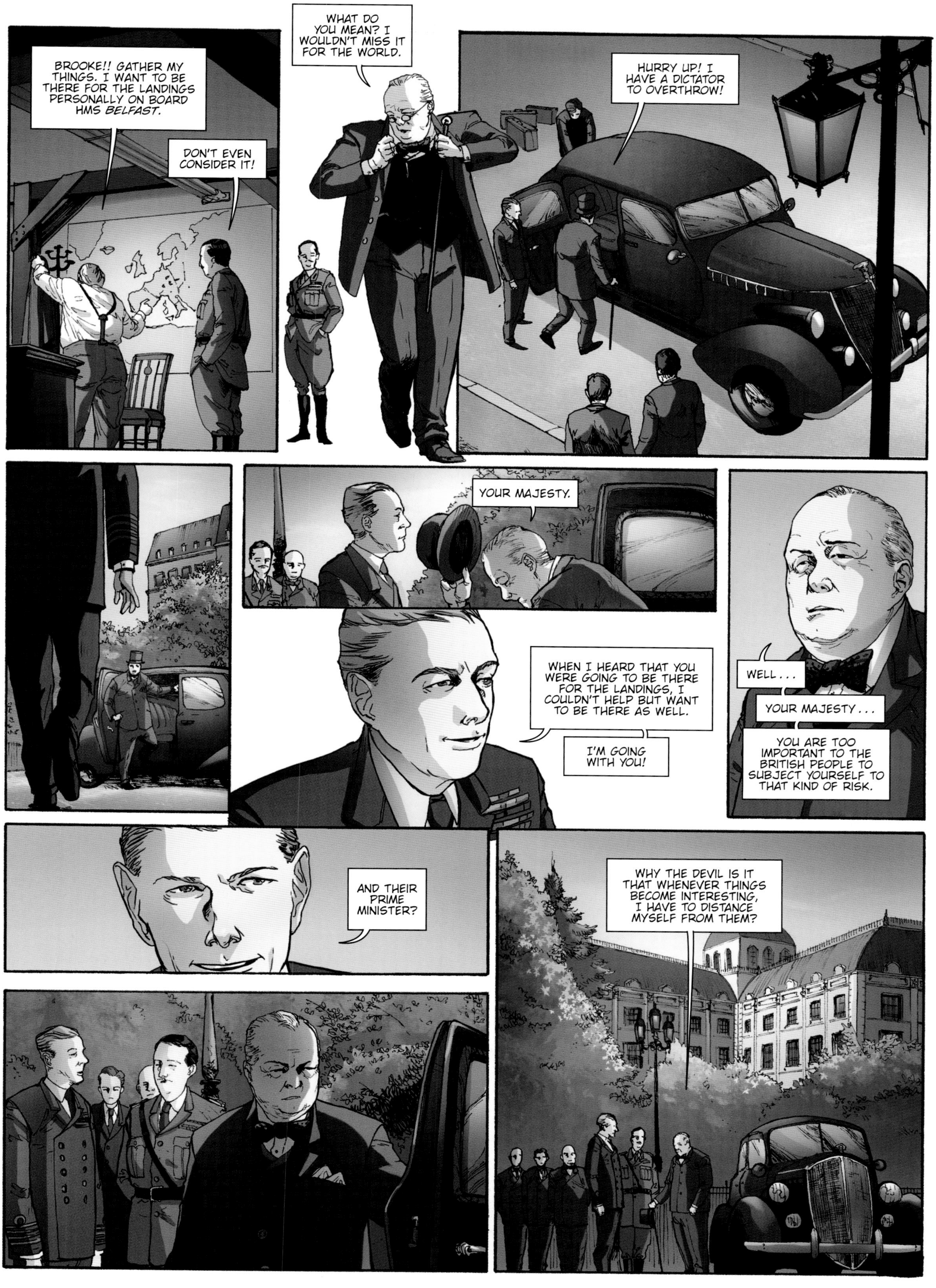
BROOKE!! GATHER MY THINGS. I WANT TO BE THERE FOR THE LANDINGS PERSONALLY ON BOARD HMS *BELFAST*.
DON'T EVEN CONSIDER IT!
WHAT DO YOU MEAN? I WOULDN'T MISS IT FOR THE WORLD.
HURRY UP! I HAVE A DICTATOR TO OVERTHROW!
YOUR MAJESTY.
WHEN I HEARD THAT YOU WERE GOING TO BE THERE FOR THE LANDINGS, I COULDN'T HELP BUT WANT TO BE THERE AS WELL.
I'M GOING WITH YOU!
WELL . . .
YOUR MAJESTY . . .
YOU ARE TOO IMPORTANT TO THE BRITISH PEOPLE TO SUBJECT YOURSELF TO THAT KIND OF RISK.
AND THEIR PRIME MINISTER?
WHY THE DEVIL IS IT THAT WHENEVER THINGS BECOME INTERESTING, I HAVE TO DISTANCE MYSELF FROM THEM?

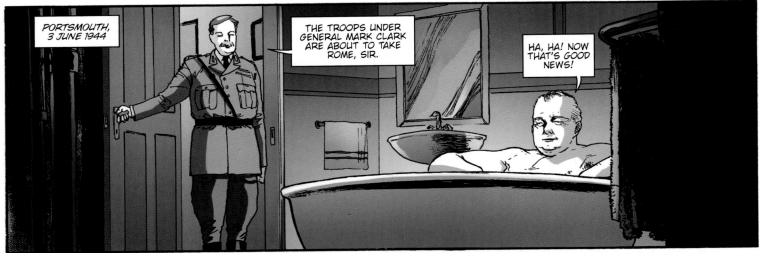

PORTSMOUTH, 3 JUNE 1944

THE TROOPS UNDER GENERAL MARK CLARK ARE ABOUT TO TAKE ROME, SIR.

HA, HA! NOW THAT'S GOOD NEWS!

PFFF! WHY HAVE YOU NOT CONTINUED?

DON'T YOU KNOW THAT SOUND TRAVELS THROUGH WATER AS WELL AS AIR?

4 JUNE

PRIME MINISTER, GENERAL DE GAULLE.

I'VE HEARD THAT THE GOVERNMENTS IN WASHINGTON AND LONDON ARE TRYING TO KEEP US OUT OF THE PICTURE.

MAY I REMIND YOU THAT IN 1940 GREAT BRITAIN AGREED TO PROTECT ALL FRENCH POSSESSIONS AND TO RESTORE FRANCE'S INDEPENDENCE AND GRANDEUR.

I DIDN'T EXPECT GENERAL EISENHOWER TO PROCLAIM THAT FROM NOW ON FRANCE WAS UNDER HIS AUTHORITY. AND HE NOW SAYS THAT THE ALLIES ARE GOING TO ISSUE THEIR OWN CURRENCY THERE . . .

YOU'RE TRYING TO LIBERATE FRANCE WITHOUT THE FREE FRENCH!

UNDERSTAND THIS, GREAT BRITAIN AND THE UNITED STATES WILL NOT QUARREL OVER FRANCE!

AND IT IS ON THIS BASIS THAT YOU WANT US TO WORK TOGETHER?

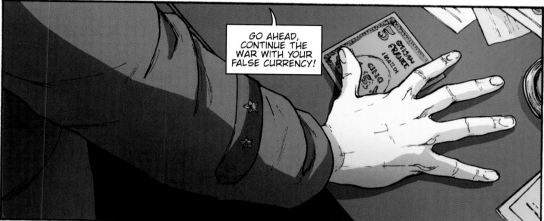

GO AHEAD, CONTINUE THE WAR WITH YOUR FALSE CURRENCY!

ANY TIME THAT I MUST CHOOSE BETWEEN YOU OR ROOSEVELT, I WILL CHOOSE ROOSEVELT EVERY TIME!

THE PRIME MINISTER DID NOT SPEAK IN THE NAME OF THE BRITISH CABINET...

MAJOR! PUT DE GAULLE IN AN AIRCRAFT AND SEND HIM BACK TO ALGERIA. IN CHAINS IF NEED BE.

HE MUST NOT BE ALLOWED TO RETURN TO FRANCE!

SHOULD WE TAKE HIM LITERALLY?

WRITE UP THE ORDER BUT WAIT BEFORE SENDING IT.

HIS MOOD WILL CHANGE BY TOMORROW...

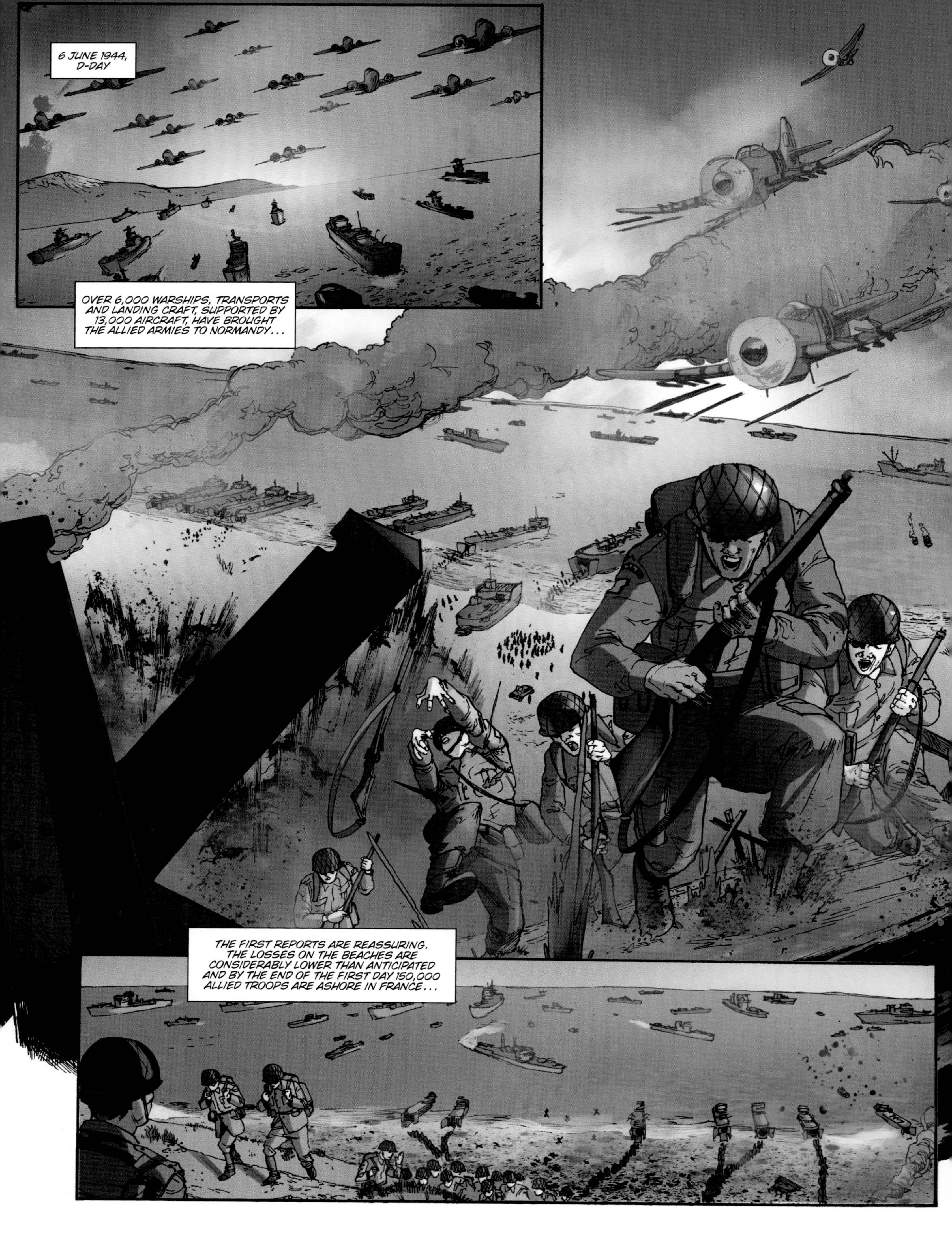
6 JUNE 1944, D-DAY
OVER 6,000 WARSHIPS, TRANSPORTS AND LANDING CRAFT, SUPPORTED BY 13,000 AIRCRAFT, HAVE BROUGHT THE ALLIED ARMIES TO NORMANDY...
THE FIRST REPORTS ARE REASSURING. THE LOSSES ON THE BEACHES ARE CONSIDERABLY LOWER THAN ANTICIPATED AND BY THE END OF THE FIRST DAY 150,000 ALLIED TROOPS ARE ASHORE IN FRANCE...

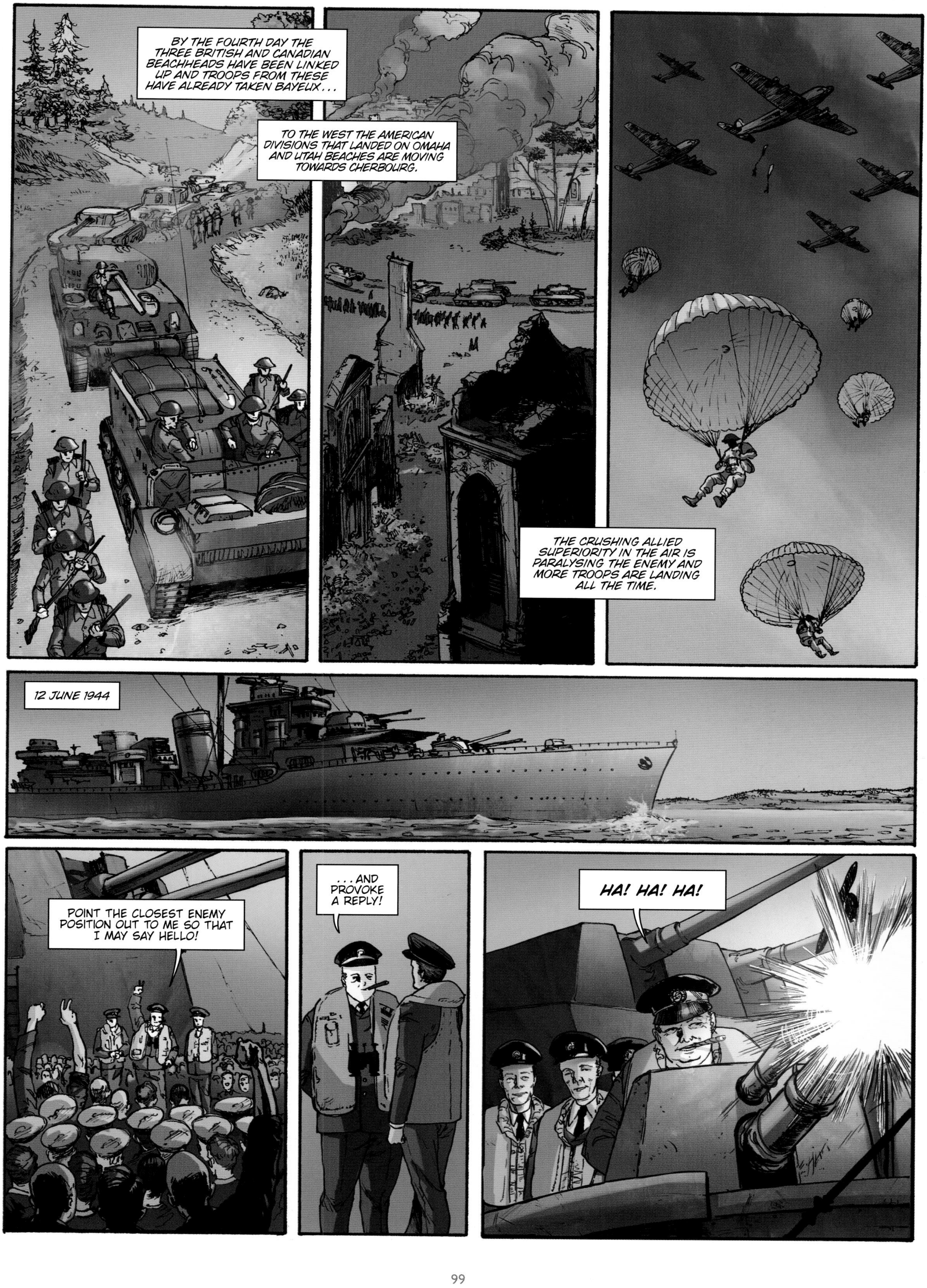
BY THE FOURTH DAY THE THREE BRITISH AND CANADIAN BEACHHEADS HAVE BEEN LINKED UP AND TROOPS FROM THESE HAVE ALREADY TAKEN BAYEUX . . .
TO THE WEST THE AMERICAN DIVISIONS THAT LANDED ON OMAHA AND UTAH BEACHES ARE MOVING TOWARDS CHERBOURG.
THE CRUSHING ALLIED SUPERIORITY IN THE AIR IS PARALYSING THE ENEMY AND MORE TROOPS ARE LANDING ALL THE TIME.
12 JUNE 1944
POINT THE CLOSEST ENEMY POSITION OUT TO ME SO THAT I MAY SAY HELLO!
. . . AND PROVOKE A REPLY!
HA! HA! HA!

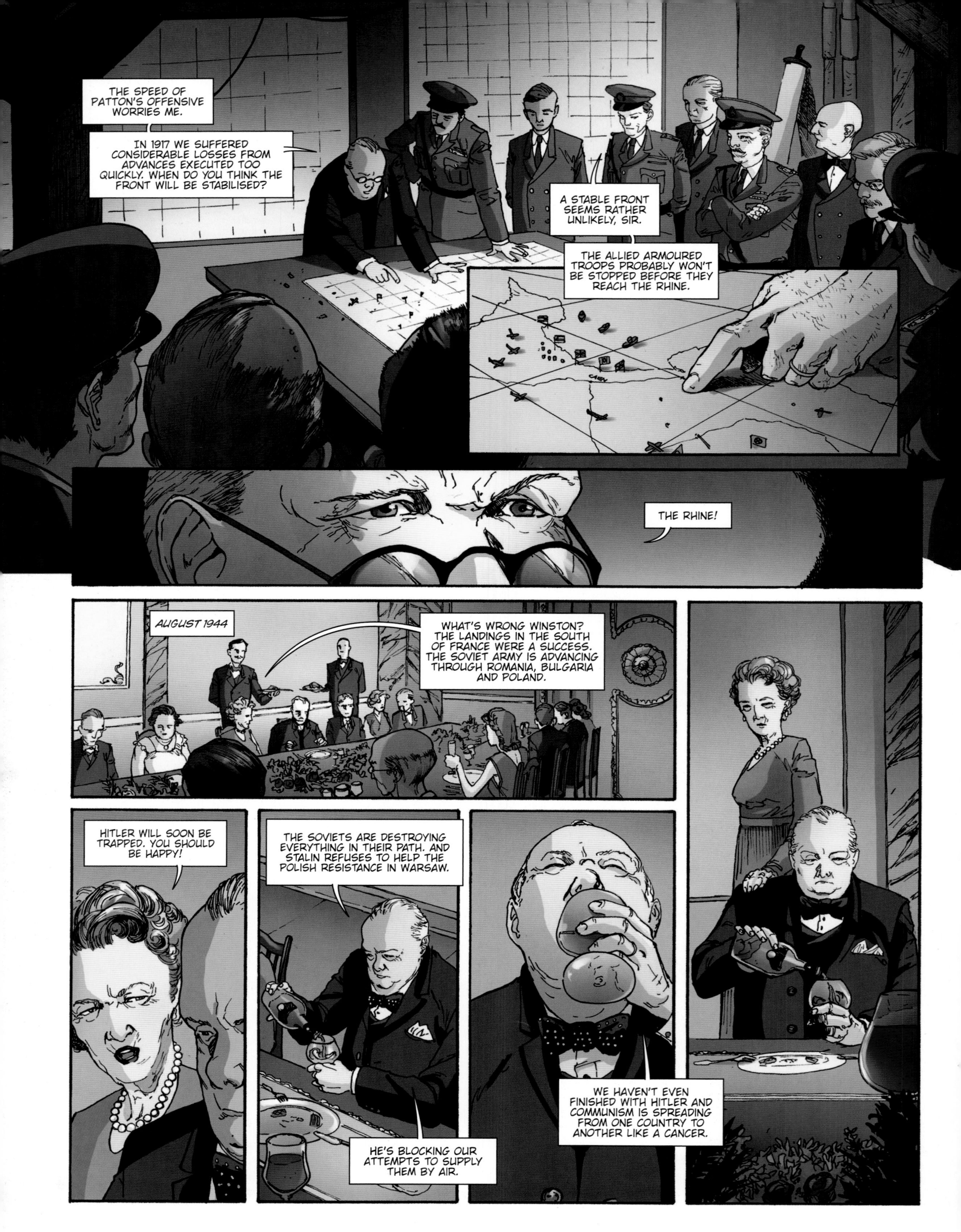
THE SPEED OF PATTON'S OFFENSIVE WORRIES ME.
IN 1917 WE SUFFERED CONSIDERABLE LOSSES FROM ADVANCES EXECUTED TOO QUICKLY. WHEN DO YOU THINK THE FRONT WILL BE STABILISED?
A STABLE FRONT SEEMS RATHER UNLIKELY, SIR.
THE ALLIED ARMOURED TROOPS PROBABLY WON'T BE STOPPED BEFORE THEY REACH THE RHINE.
THE RHINE!
AUGUST 1944
WHAT'S WRONG WINSTON? THE LANDINGS IN THE SOUTH OF FRANCE WERE A SUCCESS. THE SOVIET ARMY IS ADVANCING THROUGH ROMANIA, BULGARIA AND POLAND.
HITLER WILL SOON BE TRAPPED. YOU SHOULD BE HAPPY!
THE SOVIETS ARE DESTROYING EVERYTHING IN THEIR PATH. AND STALIN REFUSES TO HELP THE POLISH RESISTANCE IN WARSAW.
HE'S BLOCKING OUR ATTEMPTS TO SUPPLY THEM BY AIR.
WE HAVEN'T EVEN FINISHED WITH HITLER AND COMMUNISM IS SPREADING FROM ONE COUNTRY TO ANOTHER LIKE A CANCER.

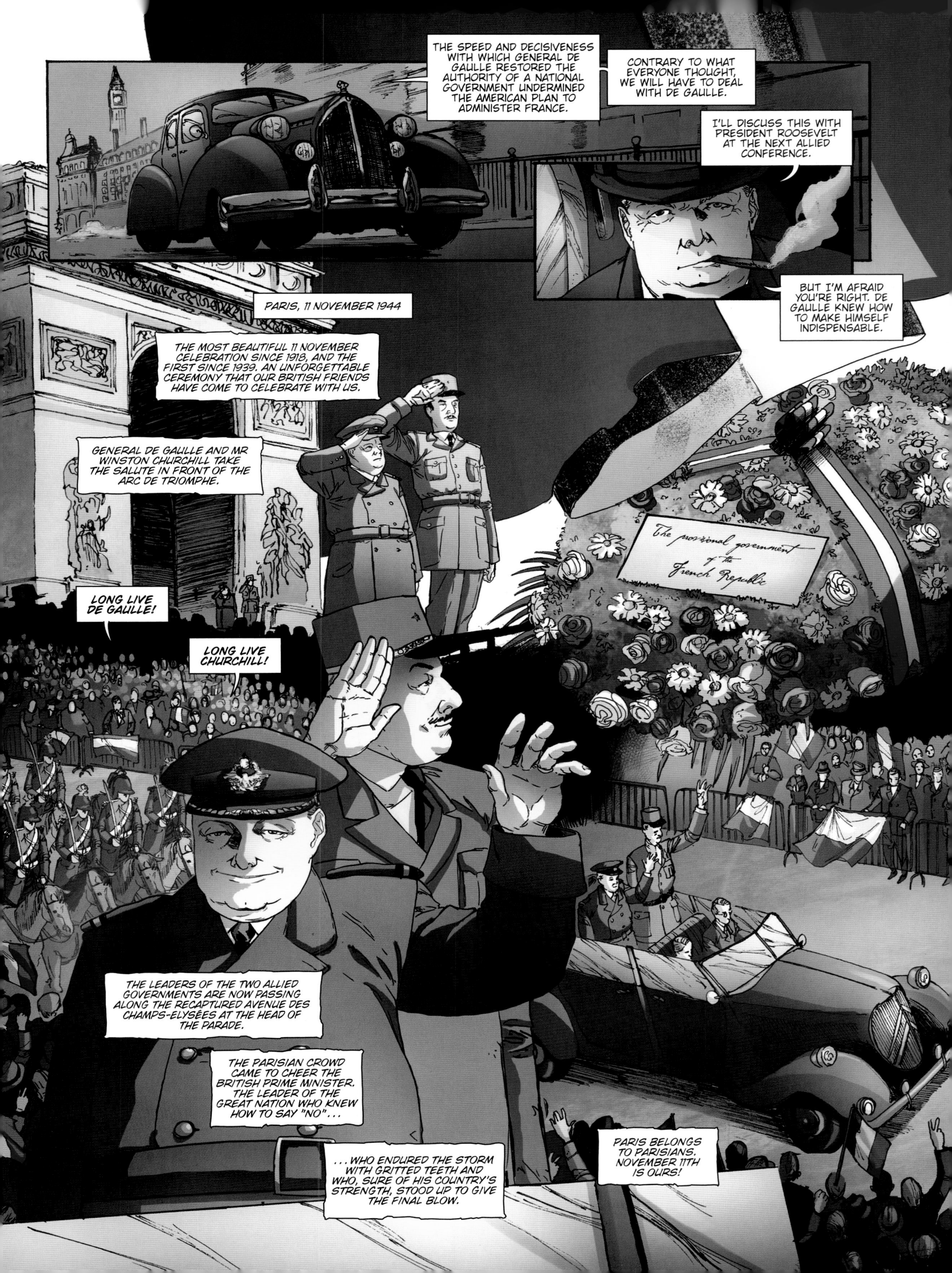

THE SPEED AND DECISIVENESS WITH WHICH GENERAL DE GAULLE RESTORED THE AUTHORITY OF A NATIONAL GOVERNMENT UNDERMINED THE AMERICAN PLAN TO ADMINISTER FRANCE.
CONTRARY TO WHAT EVERYONE THOUGHT, WE WILL HAVE TO DEAL WITH DE GAULLE.
I'LL DISCUSS THIS WITH PRESIDENT ROOSEVELT AT THE NEXT ALLIED CONFERENCE.
BUT I'M AFRAID YOU'RE RIGHT. DE GAULLE KNEW HOW TO MAKE HIMSELF INDISPENSABLE.
PARIS, 11 NOVEMBER 1944
THE MOST BEAUTIFUL 11 NOVEMBER CELEBRATION SINCE 1918, AND THE FIRST SINCE 1939. AN UNFORGETTABLE CEREMONY THAT OUR BRITISH FRIENDS HAVE COME TO CELEBRATE WITH US.
GENERAL DE GAULLE AND MR WINSTON CHURCHILL TAKE THE SALUTE IN FRONT OF THE ARC DE TRIOMPHE.
The provisional government of the French Republic
LONG LIVE DE GAULLE!
LONG LIVE CHURCHILL!
THE LEADERS OF THE TWO ALLIED GOVERNMENTS ARE NOW PASSING ALONG THE RECAPTURED AVENUE DES CHAMPS-ELYSÉES AT THE HEAD OF THE PARADE.
THE PARISIAN CROWD CAME TO CHEER THE BRITISH PRIME MINISTER. THE LEADER OF THE GREAT NATION WHO KNEW HOW TO SAY "NO"...
...WHO ENDURED THE STORM WITH GRITTED TEETH AND WHO, SURE OF HIS COUNTRY'S STRENGTH, STOOD UP TO GIVE THE FINAL BLOW.
PARIS BELONGS TO PARISIANS. NOVEMBER 11TH IS OURS!

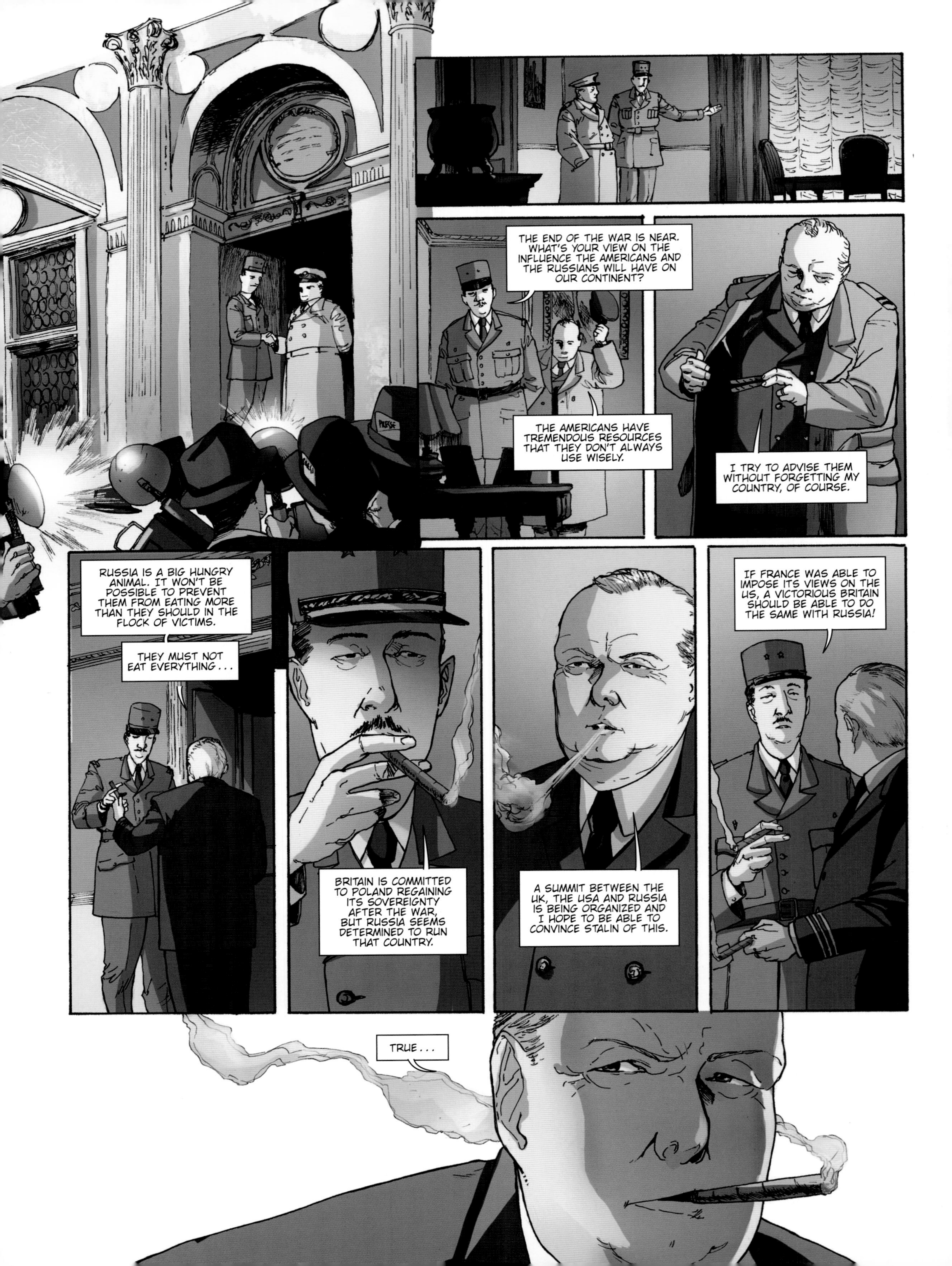
PRESSE
THE END OF THE WAR IS NEAR. WHAT'S YOUR VIEW ON THE INFLUENCE THE AMERICANS AND THE RUSSIANS WILL HAVE ON OUR CONTINENT?
THE AMERICANS HAVE TREMENDOUS RESOURCES THAT THEY DON'T ALWAYS USE WISELY.
I TRY TO ADVISE THEM WITHOUT FORGETTING MY COUNTRY, OF COURSE.
RUSSIA IS A BIG HUNGRY ANIMAL. IT WON'T BE POSSIBLE TO PREVENT THEM FROM EATING MORE THAN THEY SHOULD IN THE FLOCK OF VICTIMS.
THEY MUST NOT EAT EVERYTHING . . .
BRITAIN IS COMMITTED TO POLAND REGAINING ITS SOVEREIGNTY AFTER THE WAR, BUT RUSSIA SEEMS DETERMINED TO RUN THAT COUNTRY.
A SUMMIT BETWEEN THE UK, THE USA AND RUSSIA IS BEING ORGANIZED AND I HOPE TO BE ABLE TO CONVINCE STALIN OF THIS.
IF FRANCE WAS ABLE TO IMPOSE ITS VIEWS ON THE US, A VICTORIOUS BRITAIN SHOULD BE ABLE TO DO THE SAME WITH RUSSIA!
TRUE . . .

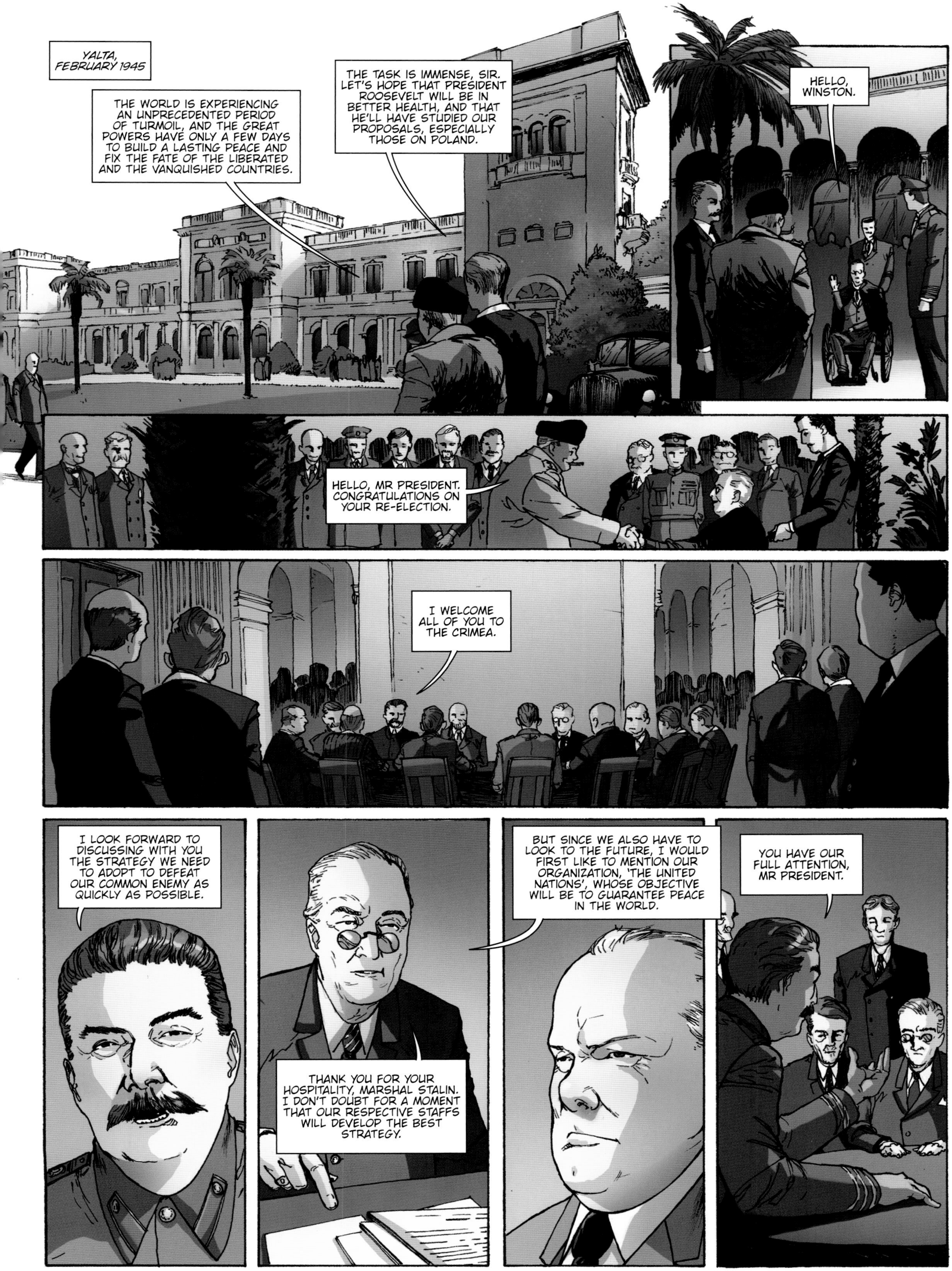

YALTA, FEBRUARY 1945
THE WORLD IS EXPERIENCING AN UNPRECEDENTED PERIOD OF TURMOIL, AND THE GREAT POWERS HAVE ONLY A FEW DAYS TO BUILD A LASTING PEACE AND FIX THE FATE OF THE LIBERATED AND THE VANQUISHED COUNTRIES.
THE TASK IS IMMENSE, SIR. LET'S HOPE THAT PRESIDENT ROOSEVELT WILL BE IN BETTER HEALTH, AND THAT HE'LL HAVE STUDIED OUR PROPOSALS, ESPECIALLY THOSE ON POLAND.
HELLO, WINSTON.
HELLO, MR PRESIDENT. CONGRATULATIONS ON YOUR RE-ELECTION.
I WELCOME ALL OF YOU TO THE CRIMEA.
I LOOK FORWARD TO DISCUSSING WITH YOU THE STRATEGY WE NEED TO ADOPT TO DEFEAT OUR COMMON ENEMY AS QUICKLY AS POSSIBLE.
THANK YOU FOR YOUR HOSPITALITY, MARSHAL STALIN. I DON'T DOUBT FOR A MOMENT THAT OUR RESPECTIVE STAFFS WILL DEVELOP THE BEST STRATEGY.
BUT SINCE WE ALSO HAVE TO LOOK TO THE FUTURE, I WOULD FIRST LIKE TO MENTION OUR ORGANIZATION, 'THE UNITED NATIONS', WHOSE OBJECTIVE WILL BE TO GUARANTEE PEACE IN THE WORLD.
YOU HAVE OUR FULL ATTENTION, MR PRESIDENT.

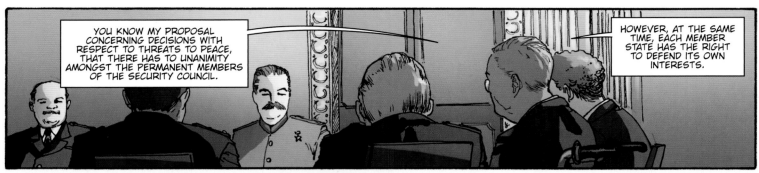

YOU KNOW MY PROPOSAL CONCERNING DECISIONS WITH RESPECT TO THREATS TO PEACE, THAT THERE HAS TO UNANIMITY AMONGST THE PERMANENT MEMBERS OF THE SECURITY COUNCIL.

HOWEVER, AT THE SAME TIME, EACH MEMBER STATE HAS THE RIGHT TO DEFEND ITS OWN INTERESTS.

I AGREE WITH THESE POINTS. OUR GOAL IS TO PREVENT ANY NEW WARS, BUT THE RISK IS THAT WE MAY GIVE THE IMPRESSION THAT THE THREE GREAT POWERS WANT TO RUN THE WORLD.

PRIME MINISTER, ARE YOU IMPLYING THAT SOVIETS HAVE THE INTENTION OF RUNNING THE WORLD?

NO, WHAT I AM SAYING IS THAT OUR DECISIONS WILL BE INTERPRETED AND COMMENTED ON AROUND THE WORLD. THAT'S WHY I THINK IT'S ESSENTIAL TO DEFINE OUR ORGANIZATION ALSO WITH RESPECT TO THE RIGHTS OF SMALL NATIONS.

MR PRESIDENT, DO YOU INTEND TO GIVE THE VOICES OF SMALL NATIONS THE SAME WEIGHT AS OURS?

NO, WE THREE MUST ASSUME THE MOST RESPONSIBILITY. BUT THE PLACE OF SMALLER NATIONS MUST BE ADDRESSED. TAKE THE CASE OF POLAND AND THE LUBLIN COMMITTEE, THE PROVISIONAL GOVERNMENT YOU HAVE SET UP THERE, MARSHAL . . .

THE POLISH-AMERICAN COMMUNITY REFUSE TO RECOGNIZE IT BECAUSE IT REPRESENTS ONLY A TINY PART OF THE POLISH PEOPLE.

MY POSITION IS THAT A NATIONAL UNITY GOVERNMENT SHOULD BE FORMED, BRINGING TOGETHER ALL THE PARTIES WHILE WAITING FOR DEMOCRATIC ELECTIONS.

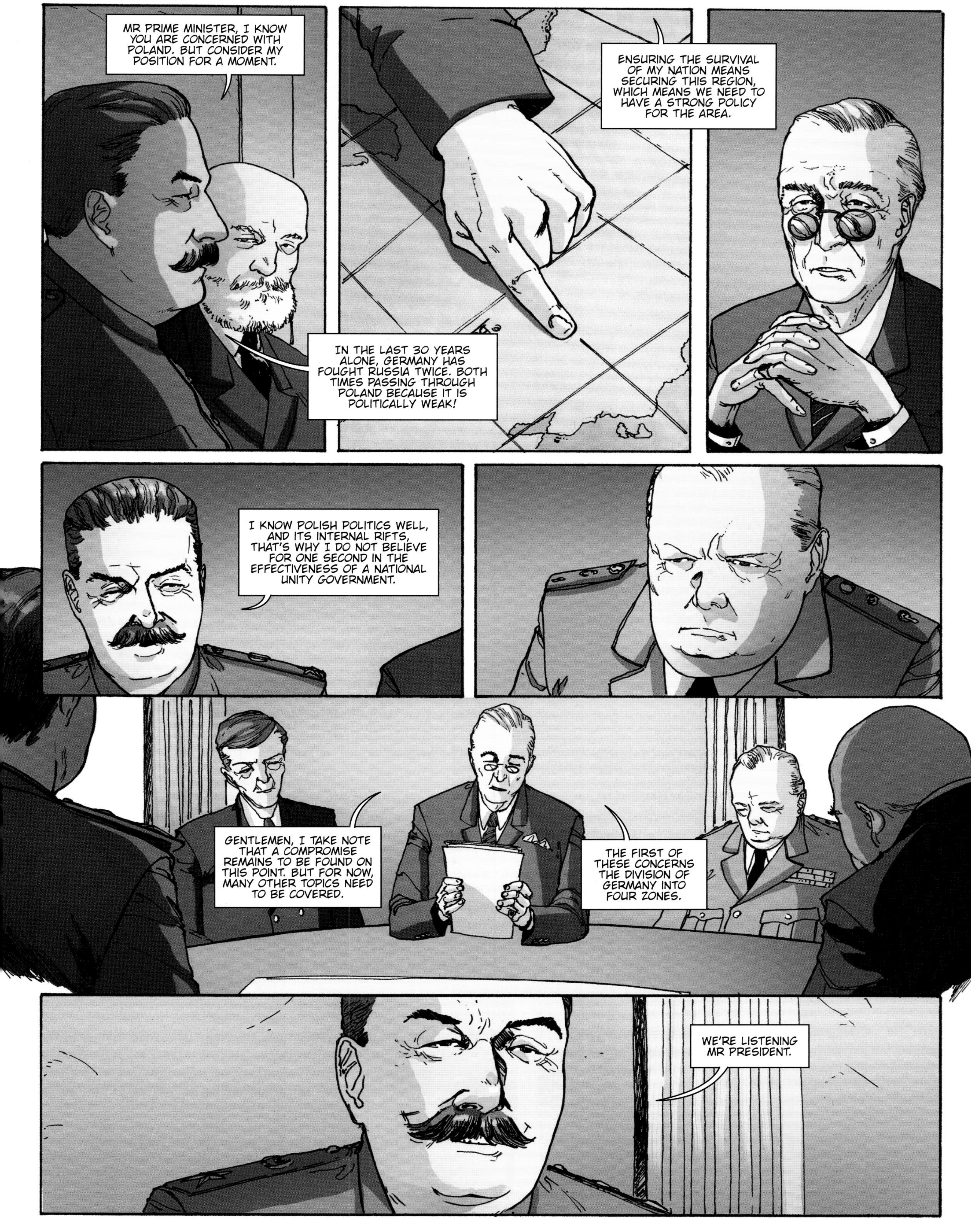
MR PRIME MINISTER, I KNOW YOU ARE CONCERNED WITH POLAND. BUT CONSIDER MY POSITION FOR A MOMENT.
IN THE LAST 30 YEARS ALONE, GERMANY HAS FOUGHT RUSSIA TWICE. BOTH TIMES PASSING THROUGH POLAND BECAUSE IT IS POLITICALLY WEAK!
ENSURING THE SURVIVAL OF MY NATION MEANS SECURING THIS REGION, WHICH MEANS WE NEED TO HAVE A STRONG POLICY FOR THE AREA.
I KNOW POLISH POLITICS WELL, AND ITS INTERNAL RIFTS, THAT'S WHY I DO NOT BELIEVE FOR ONE SECOND IN THE EFFECTIVENESS OF A NATIONAL UNITY GOVERNMENT.
GENTLEMEN, I TAKE NOTE THAT A COMPROMISE REMAINS TO BE FOUND ON THIS POINT. BUT FOR NOW, MANY OTHER TOPICS NEED TO BE COVERED.
THE FIRST OF THESE CONCERNS THE DIVISION OF GERMANY INTO FOUR ZONES.
WE'RE LISTENING MR PRESIDENT.

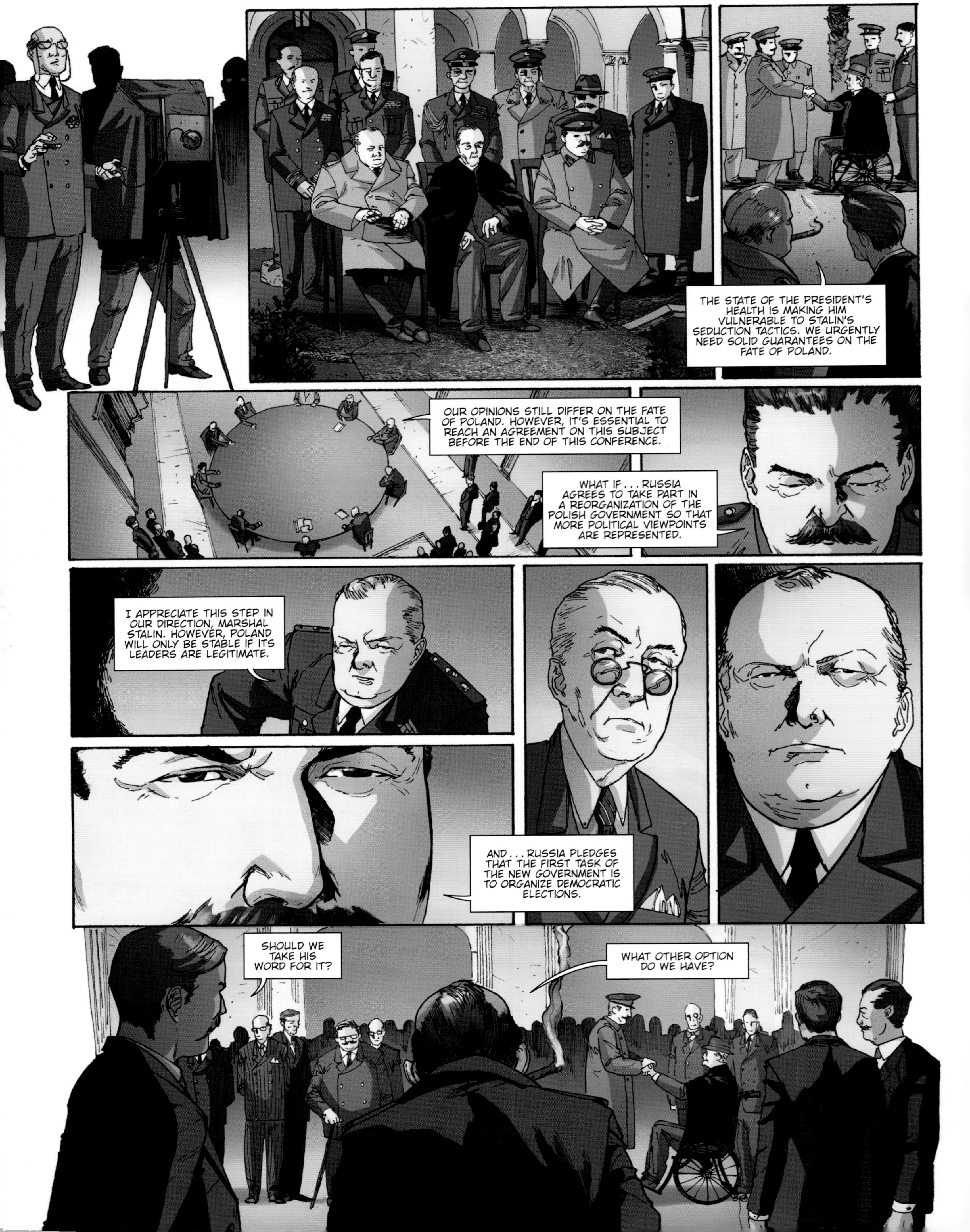
THE STATE OF THE PRESIDENT'S HEALTH IS MAKING HIM VULNERABLE TO STALIN'S SEDUCTION TACTICS. WE URGENTLY NEED SOLID GUARANTEES ON THE FATE OF POLAND.
OUR OPINIONS STILL DIFFER ON THE FATE OF POLAND. HOWEVER, IT'S ESSENTIAL TO REACH AN AGREEMENT ON THIS SUBJECT BEFORE THE END OF THIS CONFERENCE.
WHAT IF . . . RUSSIA AGREES TO TAKE PART IN A REORGANIZATION OF THE POLISH GOVERNMENT SO THAT MORE POLITICAL VIEWPOINTS ARE REPRESENTED.
I APPRECIATE THIS STEP IN OUR DIRECTION, MARSHAL STALIN. HOWEVER, POLAND WILL ONLY BE STABLE IF ITS LEADERS ARE LEGITIMATE.
AND . . . RUSSIA PLEDGES THAT THE FIRST TASK OF THE NEW GOVERNMENT IS TO ORGANIZE DEMOCRATIC ELECTIONS.
SHOULD WE TAKE HIS WORD FOR IT?
WHAT OTHER OPTION DO WE HAVE?

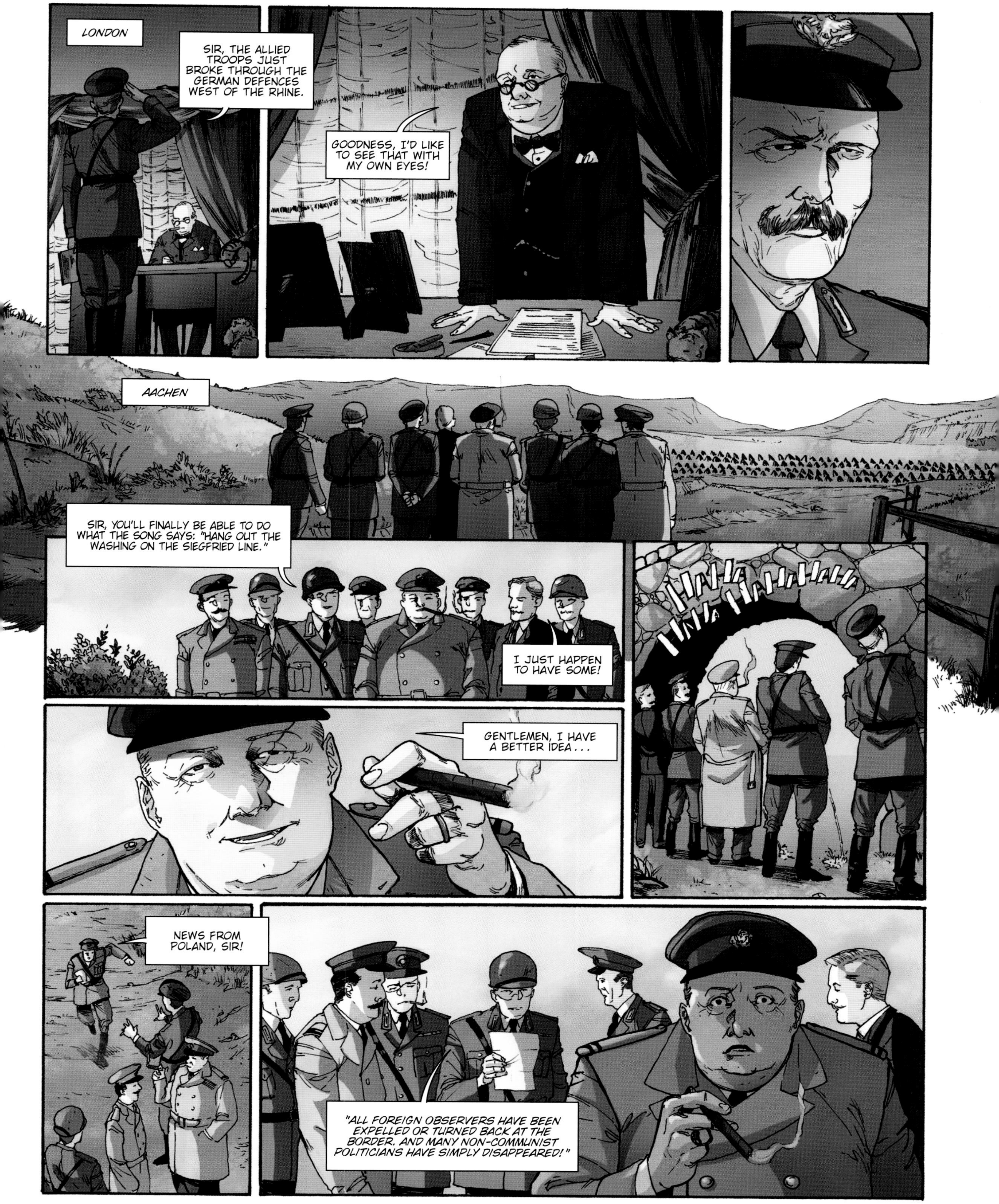
LONDON
SIR, THE ALLIED TROOPS JUST BROKE THROUGH THE GERMAN DEFENCES WEST OF THE RHINE.
GOODNESS, I'D LIKE TO SEE THAT WITH MY OWN EYES!
AACHEN
SIR, YOU'LL FINALLY BE ABLE TO DO WHAT THE SONG SAYS: "HANG OUT THE WASHING ON THE SIEGFRIED LINE."
I JUST HAPPEN TO HAVE SOME!
GENTLEMEN, I HAVE A BETTER IDEA . . .
NEWS FROM POLAND, SIR!
"ALL FOREIGN OBSERVERS HAVE BEEN EXPELLED OR TURNED BACK AT THE BORDER. AND MANY NON-COMMUNIST POLITICIANS HAVE SIMPLY DISAPPEARED!"

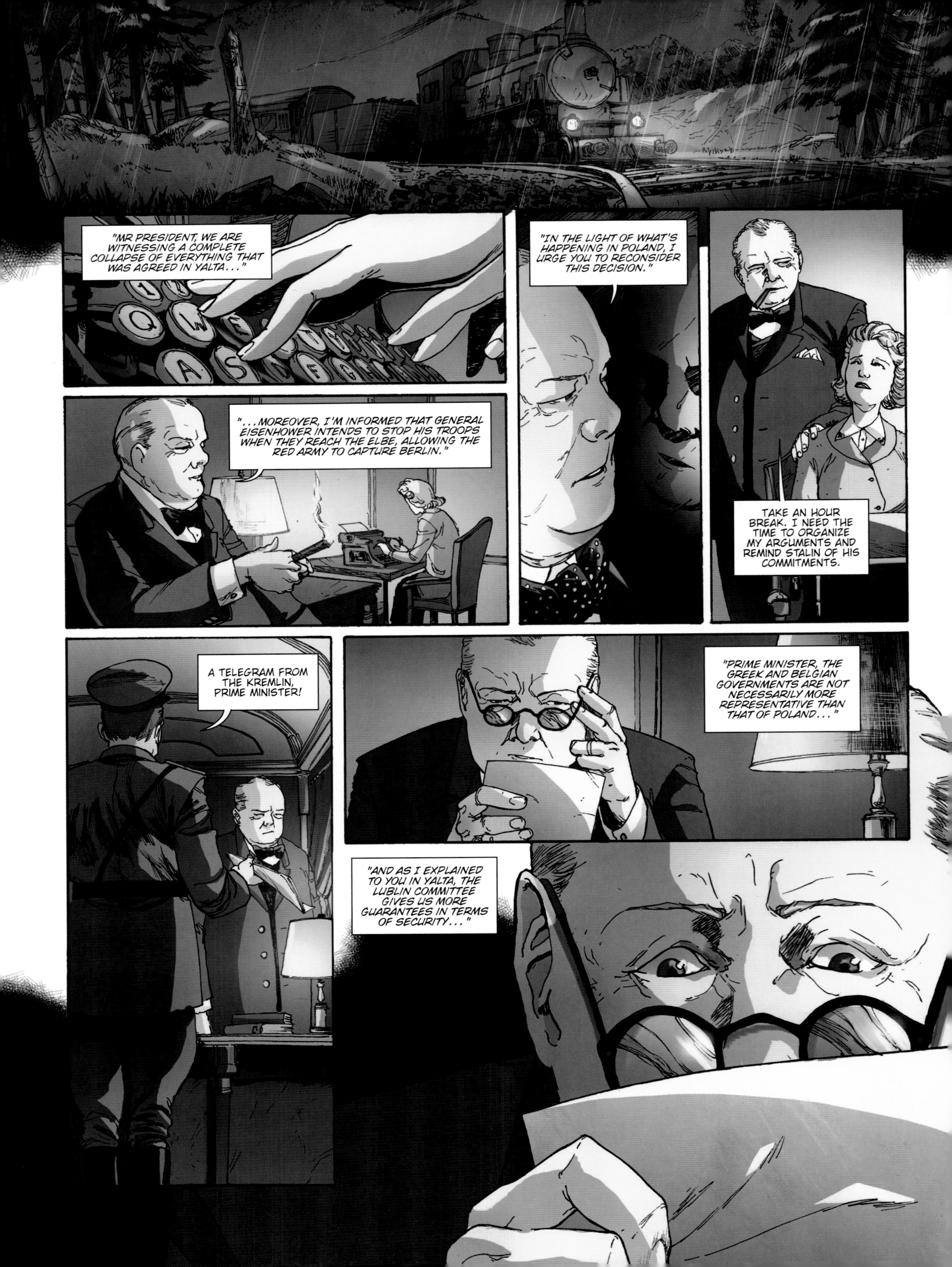
"MR PRESIDENT, WE ARE WITNESSING A COMPLETE COLLAPSE OF EVERYTHING THAT WAS AGREED IN YALTA . . ."
"IN THE LIGHT OF WHAT'S HAPPENING IN POLAND, I URGE YOU TO RECONSIDER THIS DECISION."
". . . MOREOVER, I'M INFORMED THAT GENERAL EISENHOWER INTENDS TO STOP HIS TROOPS WHEN THEY REACH THE ELBE, ALLOWING THE RED ARMY TO CAPTURE BERLIN."
TAKE AN HOUR BREAK. I NEED THE TIME TO ORGANIZE MY ARGUMENTS AND REMIND STALIN OF HIS COMMITMENTS.
A TELEGRAM FROM THE KREMLIN, PRIME MINISTER!
"PRIME MINISTER, THE GREEK AND BELGIAN GOVERNMENTS ARE NOT NECESSARILY MORE REPRESENTATIVE THAN THAT OF POLAND . . ."
"AND AS I EXPLAINED TO YOU IN YALTA, THE LUBLIN COMMITTEE GIVES US MORE GUARANTEES IN TERMS OF SECURITY . . ."

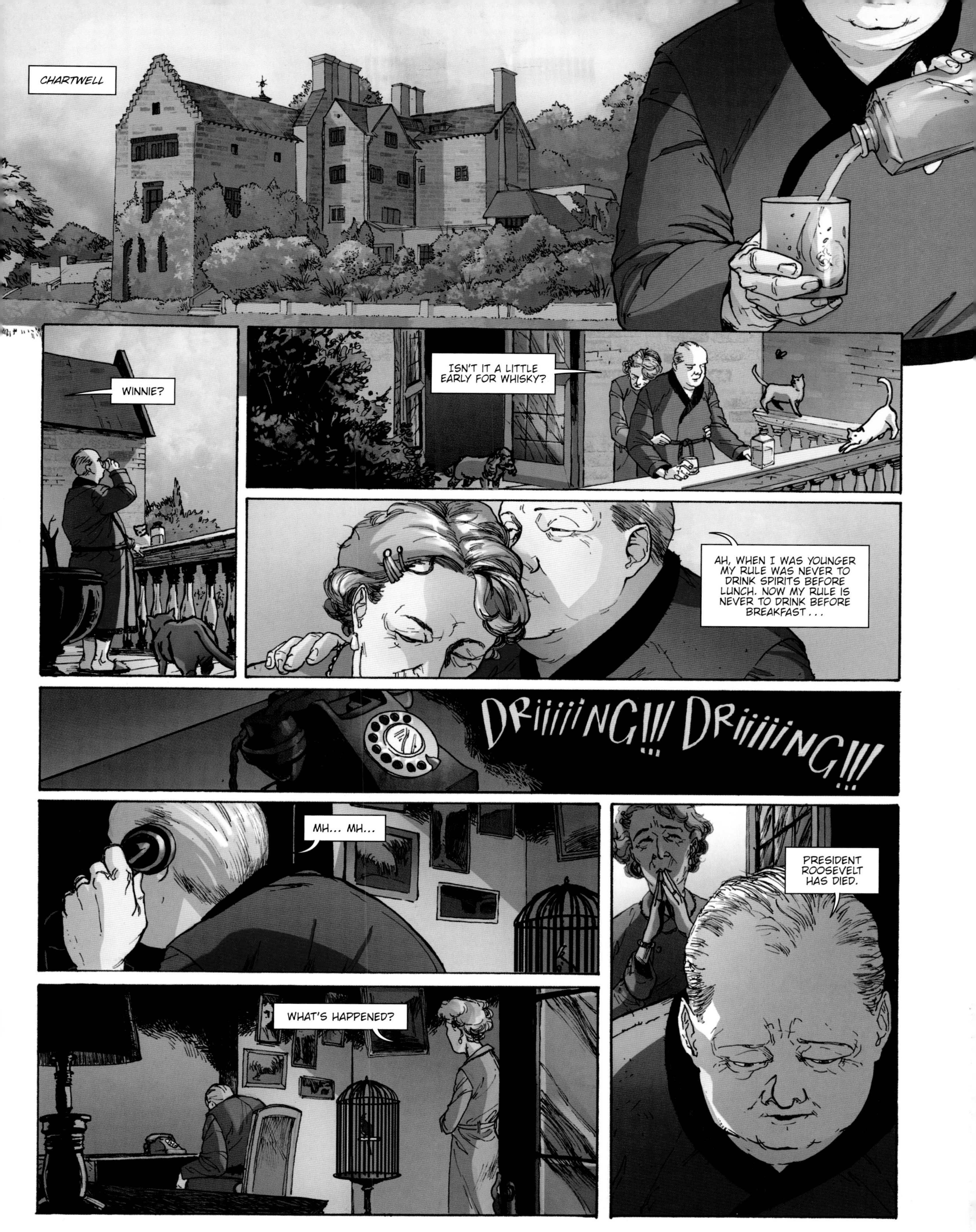
CHARTWELL
WINNIE?
ISN'T IT A LITTLE EARLY FOR WHISKY?
AH, WHEN I WAS YOUNGER MY RULE WAS NEVER TO DRINK SPIRITS BEFORE LUNCH. NOW MY RULE IS NEVER TO DRINK BEFORE BREAKFAST . . .
DRiiiiiNG!!! DRiiiiiNG!!!
MH... MH...
WHAT'S HAPPENED?
PRESIDENT ROOSEVELT HAS DIED.

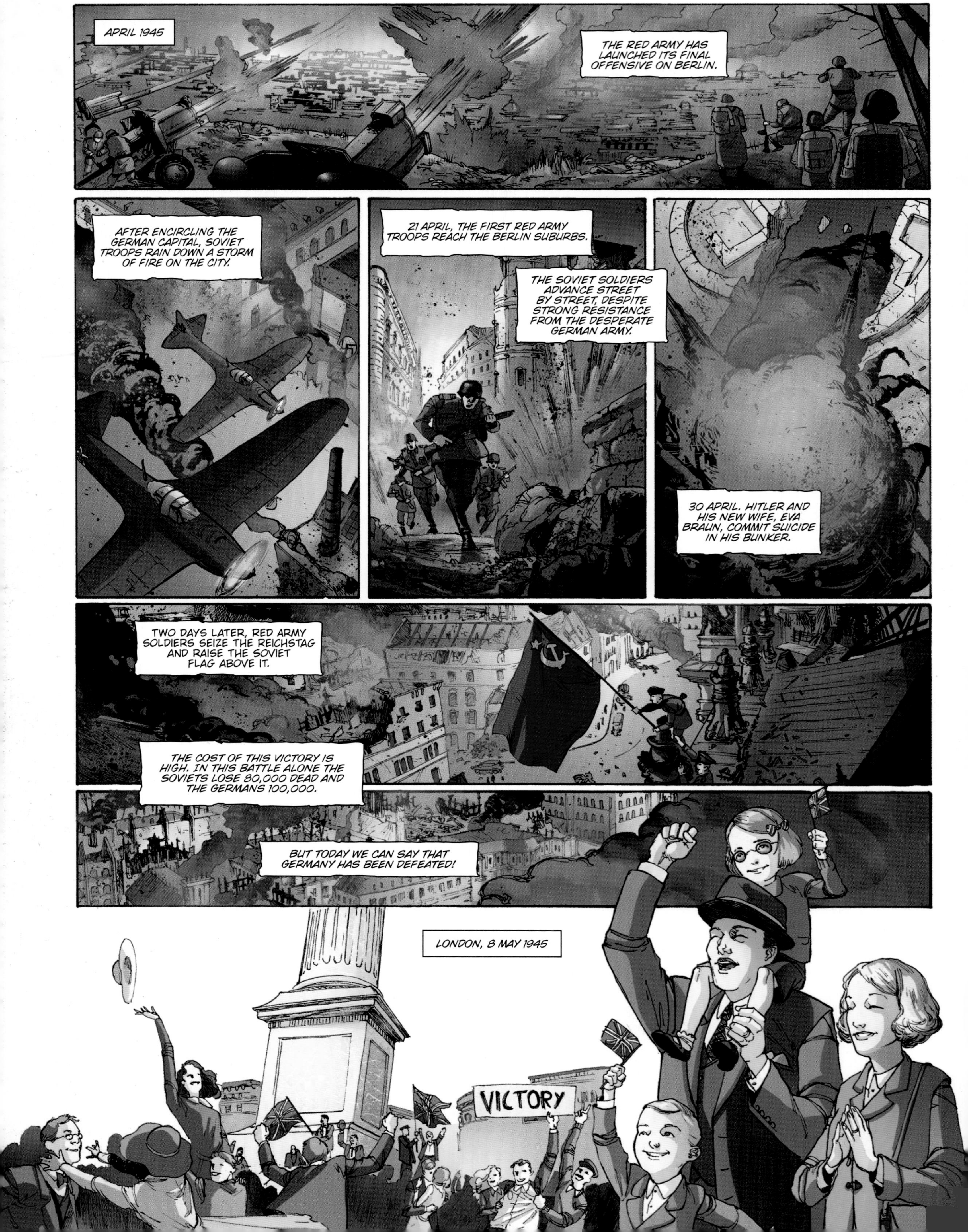

APRIL 1945
THE RED ARMY HAS LAUNCHED ITS FINAL OFFENSIVE ON BERLIN.
AFTER ENCIRCLING THE GERMAN CAPITAL, SOVIET TROOPS RAIN DOWN A STORM OF FIRE ON THE CITY.
21 APRIL, THE FIRST RED ARMY TROOPS REACH THE BERLIN SUBURBS.
THE SOVIET SOLDIERS ADVANCE STREET BY STREET, DESPITE STRONG RESISTANCE FROM THE DESPERATE GERMAN ARMY.
30 APRIL. HITLER AND HIS NEW WIFE, EVA BRAUN, COMMIT SUICIDE IN HIS BUNKER.
TWO DAYS LATER, RED ARMY SOLDIERS SEIZE THE REICHSTAG AND RAISE THE SOVIET FLAG ABOVE IT.
THE COST OF THIS VICTORY IS HIGH. IN THIS BATTLE ALONE THE SOVIETS LOSE 80,000 DEAD AND THE GERMANS 100,000.
BUT TODAY WE CAN SAY THAT GERMANY HAS BEEN DEFEATED!
LONDON, 8 MAY 1945
VICTORY

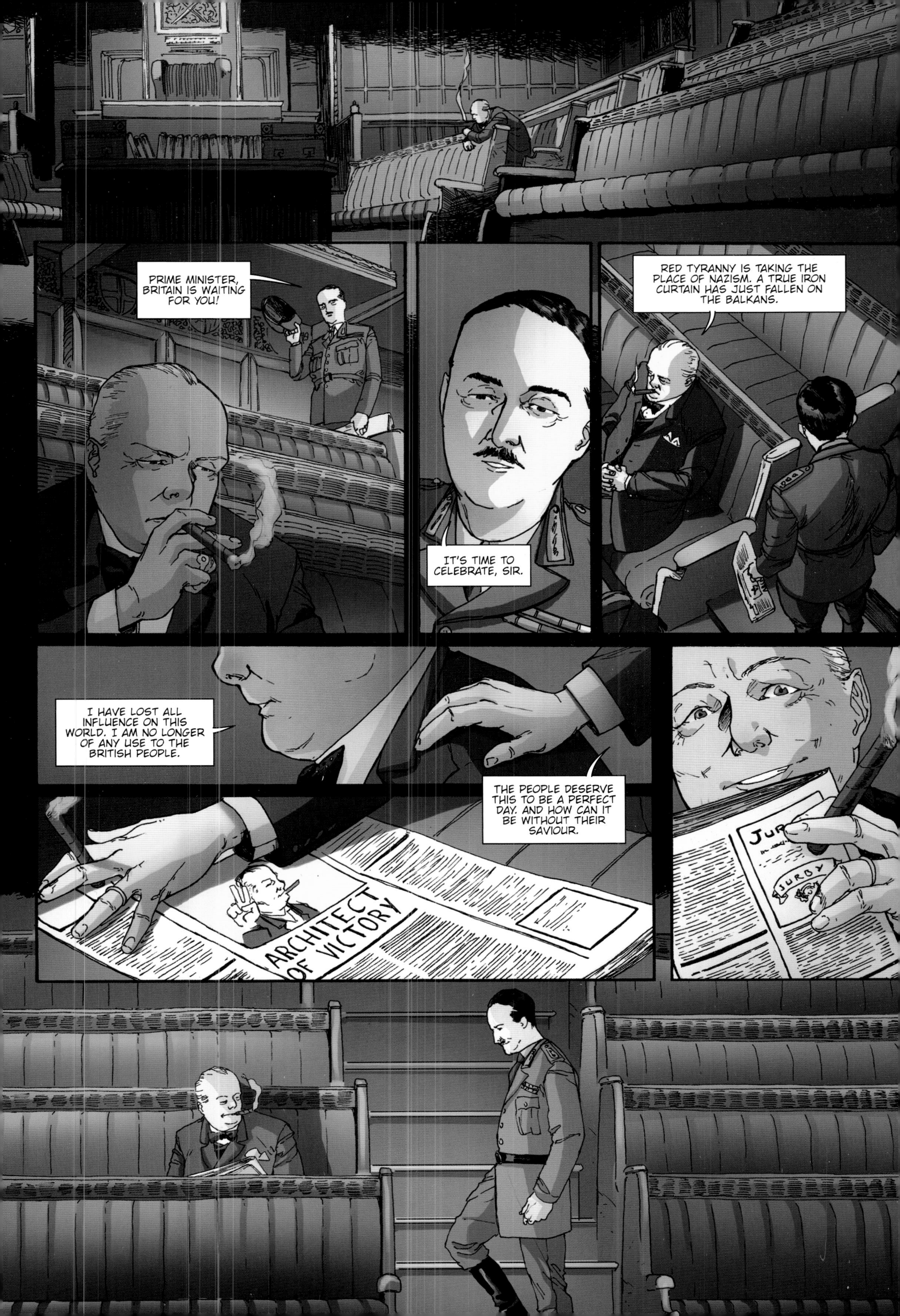
PRIME MINISTER, BRITAIN IS WAITING FOR YOU!
IT'S TIME TO CELEBRATE, SIR.
RED TYRANNY IS TAKING THE PLACE OF NAZISM. A TRUE IRON CURTAIN HAS JUST FALLEN ON THE BALKANS.
I HAVE LOST ALL INFLUENCE ON THIS WORLD. I AM NO LONGER OF ANY USE TO THE BRITISH PEOPLE.
THE PEOPLE DESERVE THIS TO BE A PERFECT DAY. AND HOW CAN IT BE WITHOUT THEIR SAVIOUR.
ARCHITECT OF VICTORY
JURBY

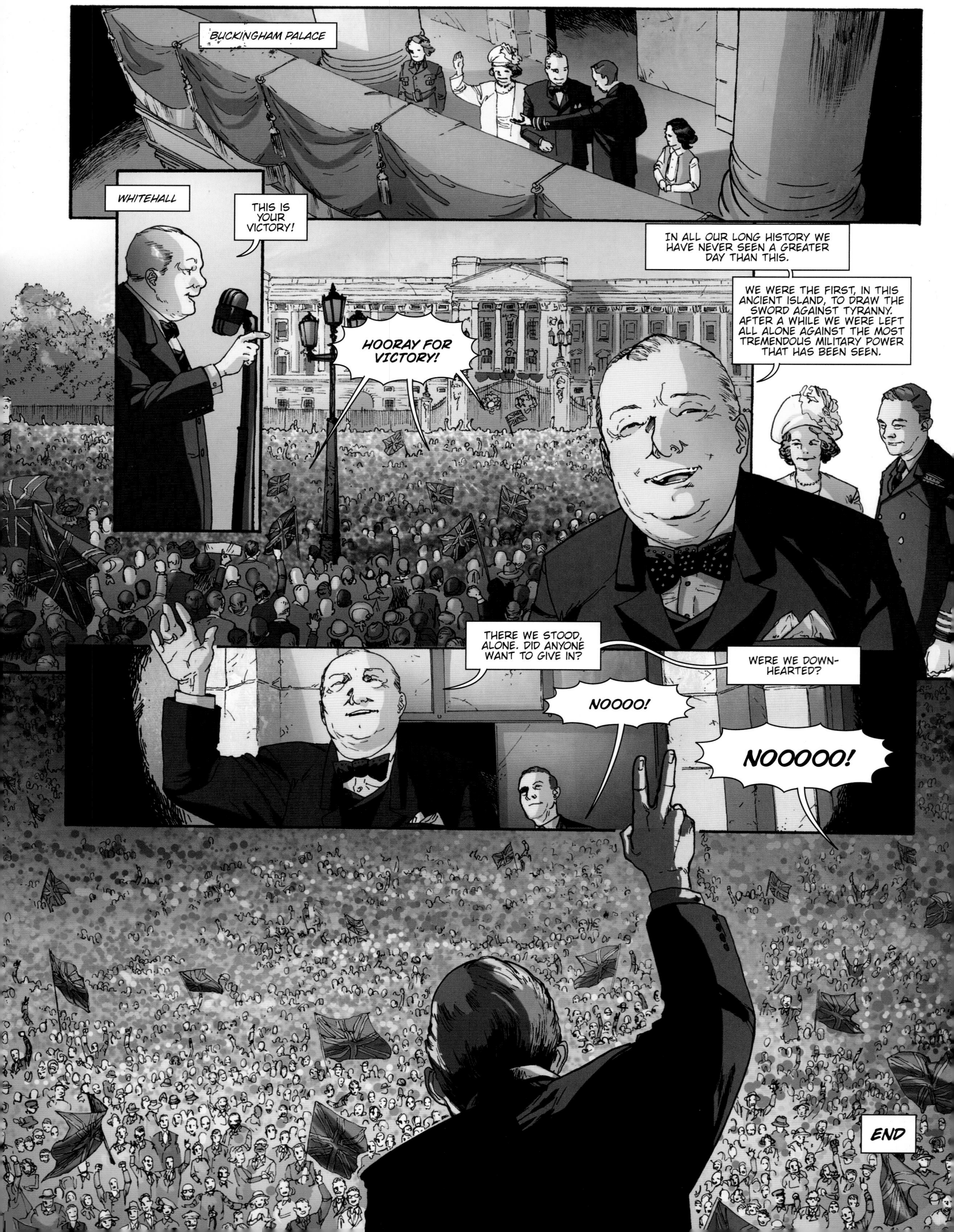
BUCKINGHAM PALACE
WHITEHALL
THIS IS YOUR VICTORY!
HOORAY FOR VICTORY!
IN ALL OUR LONG HISTORY WE HAVE NEVER SEEN A GREATER DAY THAN THIS.
WE WERE THE FIRST, IN THIS ANCIENT ISLAND, TO DRAW THE SWORD AGAINST TYRANNY. AFTER A WHILE WE WERE LEFT ALL ALONE AGAINST THE MOST TREMENDOUS MILITARY POWER THAT HAS BEEN SEEN.
THERE WE STOOD, ALONE. DID ANYONE WANT TO GIVE IN?
NOOOO!
WERE WE DOWN-HEARTED?
NOOOOO!
END